YOUR GLORY REFLECTED

SHEILAH WARD LING

YOUR GLORY
REFLECTED

Twenty outstanding Christians
of the twentieth century

ST PAULS

Cover photos: Mother Teresa by A. Del Canale; Archbishop Tutu by R. Giacomelli; D. Bonhoeffer reproduction by A. Del Canale; E. Stein painted by S. & N. Gregori: all © Edizioni San Paolo; L. Cheshire by Don Honeyman.

ST PAULS
Middlegreen, Slough SL3 6BT, United Kingdom
Moyglare Road, Maynooth, Co. Kildare, Ireland

© ST PAULS 1993
ISBN 085439 457 5
Printed by The Guernsey Press Co. Ltd, Guernsey, C.I.

ST PAULS is an activity of the priests and brothers of the Society of St Paul who proclaim the Gospel through the media of social communication

For Arthur Schmidt,
for his invaluable help –
For Peter,
without whom …

Contents

INTRODUCTION

Who are the outstanding Christians of the twentieth century?

The question haunted the gestation of this book. Should it exclude all those born in the nineteenth century? Time is a seamless garment, with no neat cut-off points. All the great threats to twentieth century christianity – atheistic Communism, aggressive nationalism, militant fundamentalism and unrestrained capitalism – had their seeds in the past, as did their antidotes.

Charles de Foucauld's worker priests have had an influence out of all proportion to their numbers, and ensure the presence of their holy founder, although he was killed before the century had completed its second decade. The youngest, Jackie Pullinger, born in 1944, gains a place among her elders, as she uses her charismatic Christianity to combat one of the scourges of the age – drug abuse.

Two world wars darkened the first half of the century. After 1918, there was hardly a family amongst the combatants that did not mourn a well-loved member, as a whole generation of potential leaders was lost. Those who came back from the hell of the battlefields were broken men, prey to cynicism. What the war had begun, a world slump completed. The Churches suffered an eclipse that looked like death, but there were those who kept the flag of faith flying by service, like Dorothy Day, setting up her Houses of Hospitality and using journalism to defy the prevailing gloom. And Teilhard de Chardin had begun to use his scientific work as a geologist to prove the existence of God, in his own unorthodox fashion.

Between the wars, Russia and Germany forged themselves into godless States, bent on empire-building; lone voices within, like that of the martyred Dietrich Bonnhoeffer, were almost drowned in the sea of propaganda poured forth by their respective governments, holding sway over communication by newspapers and radio. In Germany the tide of hate made the holocaust in which Edith Stein perished possible. By 1945, those on both sides had become sickened by the diet of lies and evasions, and sought truth in Christianity. Religious Orders flourished, and Thomas Merton made the monastic life attractive to his contemporaries. Others, like Leonard Cheshire, sought fulfilment in service to the sick and destitute.

The Catholic Church was radically changed by the Second Vatican Council, called into being by the beloved Pope John XXIII. It was welcomed with joy as the hope of the century, but one effect was to deplete the presbyteries and religious congregations, as freedom went to the heads of those who had been kept on too tight a rein in the past. Only the most dedicated remained, with new roles that took them into the community, leading it to celebrate new liturgies and take part as it had never done before. The sight of lay-women in the sanctuary became commonplace.

Germany had been dismembered in defeat, but Russia and China remained, with an iron grip on dissent. Yet in the Nineties this was broken by the thousands upon thousands of ordinary people, taking to the streets to protest against their imprisonment behind the Iron and Bamboo Curtains. Civil disobedience, which had been first tried against the British in India by Mohandas Gandhi became their weapon. Martin Luther King and Desmond Tutu, both great orators who could provide a voice for the black populations, preached non-violent claims to civil rights in America and Africa. The South American under-classes shared their aspirations, and acclaimed their own martyrs, like Archbishop Oscar Romero, gunned down in his cathedral while saying Mass.

Billy Graham was the first evangelist to use modern techniques to amass vast audiences; radio made the voices of religious leaders familiar throughout the world, but television brought their every gesture into the home, and beamed the travels of Pope John Paul II to every corner of the globe. It popularised the work of religious writers like C.S. Lewis, through adaptations of their books; it made mystics of the calibre of Simone Weil accessible through documentaries about their lives, and Albert Schweitzer's Lambarene became as familiar to viewers as the hospitals of Western Europe. Padre Pio's hands, bearing the stigmata, could be seen as he prayed the Eucharist, and the English journalist Malcolm Muggeridge brought the work of Mother Teresa of Calcutta to the screen; the sight of her face, glowing with joy and faith, has made her almost a saint in her lifetime.

But instant communication, through which events all over the world can be seen as they happen, has created tensions unknown to previous generations. Sometimes the tragedies it reveals lose their impact. A kind of dreadful inertia of the spirit sets in, and ordinary people despair of ever being able to act in the face of calamity, natural or man-made. In contemplating the lives of these outstanding Christians, perhaps we can recover the Christian virtue of hope, renew our faith, and reactivate our charity. May you come to love them as I have done.

My thanks are due to the Abbot of the Carmelite Friary at Aylesford in Kent; Brother Ian Latham of the Little Brothers of Jesus; Westminster's Father Norman Brown; in Hastings Father Kevin Ward SCA and Margaret Handel, co-worker of the Missionaries of Charity, Bridget Wilson of the Hastings Padre Pio Group – and to all those friends who have supplied videos, books and information without end, and those who suggested names of outstanding Christians, from which the final list was – with great difficulty – compiled.

DOROTHY DAY

The first time Dorothy Day collided with a major news event was at the age of nine when she was a survivor of the San Francisco earthquake of 1906. Her family – two older brothers and a younger sister, Della – had come to live on the west coast when her journalist father John Day was offered a job on one of the city newspapers.

One evening, after a visit to see his horse at a nearby race-track, he reported that all the occupants of the stables were unusually restless. The cause of their disturbance became clear; in the middle of the night there was an ominous rumbling and the earth shook. John Day snatched his sons from their beds, and Della was rescued by her mother, but Dorothy was left, sliding to and fro in her brass bedstead, listening to the water-tank in the backyard slopping its contents on to the roof.

Oakland, the suburb where they lived, was overrun by refugees pouring across the Golden Gate Bridge to escape the devastating fires in the city. Dorothy never forgot how the community, ignoring the lesser tremors that followed the main shock, turned out with food and clothing to succour those who had lost everything. Not long afterwards, her un-employed father took his family to Chicago.

He filled his enforced leisure by trying to write a novel and some short stories. The children had to keep out of his way so he could concentrate, but he did not like them roaming the streets. Naturally exuberant, they were dreadfully bored by this repressive regime; but Dorothy, who had learned to read at the age of four, revelled in the classical authors her father approved: Dickens, Stevenson, Scott and Hugo among the Europeans, and native writers like Cooper and Poe.

When she was six, she had discovered a Bible in an attic,

and read it avidly, despite a lack of any parental guidance in religious matters. Her father and mother never attended church, and if a visiting vicar, shocked by the children's deprivation, had not enrolled them in the Episcopalian Church, they would not have had any religious experience. Dorothy admired the robes her brothers wore as members of the choir – and took a less sisterly interest in the blond solo chorister.

At fourteen, her life was transformed when after many miscarriages her mother had a successful pregnancy. The baby, a boy called John like his father, became the centre of Dorothy's existence. Requests to "Keep the baby quiet" meant that she could lavish on him all the passionate interest of her dawning womanhood. About this time she began a lifelong habit of committing to paper all the events of her life; her diary was frequently stolen by her brothers and its contents mocked, until she found a safe hiding-place for it.

She was now reading extensively, and devoured Dostoevski, Upton Sinclair and Jack London. She found Herbert Spencer indigestible, but made sense of Huxley and Darwin, though the heady diet had a negative effect on her faith in God. One of her elder brothers started work on a paper supporting the trade union movement, which was gaining momentum in spite of rigorous opposition by captains of industry; his writings gave Dorothy an interest in politics that would never leave her.

At school she studied Latin and Greek, with an ability to translate that eventually won her a scholarship to the University of Illinois, sponsored by a newspaper. It did not pay for much of her board and tuition, and she had to work her way through college. She took a mischievous delight in shocking the managers of the local YMCA, although as they organised jobs for students she found herself landed with the most menial tasks, for the poorer members of the Faculty who needed help with their children. She consoled herself through her hardships with the thought that she was lucky to receive higher education, unlike those girls who slaved away in shops and factories with no hope of advancement.

She soon had a chance to show her solidarity with them. Leaving college early, she sought work in New York on a left-wing paper called *The Call*. To interest its young editor, she proposed to live on five dollars a week and write a series of articles about the experience, exposing the difficulties of workers who tried to exist on a similar sum. Her enthusiasm secured her the job, with the prospect of a permanent position and a twelve-dollar rise.

Renting a room near the newspaper office on the Lower East Side, she became acquainted with real poverty; the smells, the vermin in the walls, the constant search for cheap food from stalls and cafes – a habit which continued for a long time. She reported on the picket-lines from the strikers' point of view, and wrote a major feature about a woman prisoner who was on hunger-strike for the right to birth control, later discovering that the stories about her were untrue. It shocked her to realise that bias was not restricted to the capitalist press.

The City Editor, Mike Gold, became a firm friend and together they interviewed Trotsky on the eve of the Russian Revolution in 1917, but their resulting article was heavily cut. When news of the successful uprising came from Moscow, they marched to Madison Square Garden with other young socialists to celebrate. War fever was rife, but her sympathy was with the conscientious objectors; she would always be on the side of the under-dog.

She was persuaded to join a Suffragette demonstration in Washington, which resulted in her first jail sentence of thirty days. Desperately bored, she asked for a Bible, and to her surprise was greatly comforted by the Psalms.

On her release she went back to New York and, looking up old friends, discovered Mike Gold was having a play produced at the Provincetown Playhouse, the theatre which had given the first performances of Eugene O'Neill's work. O'Neill held court in the back room of a seedy restaurant called 'The Golden Swan'; Dorothy took on the task of getting him home to bed whenever he succumbed to alcohol, sometimes creeping in after him to cradle his head. Her admiration for him made her an interested spectator of his battle with God, and she was often to be found seated at the back of a neighbourhood Catholic Church. A tragic incident caused her to reassess her own life, when a young friend took an overdose of heroin and died in her arms.

In 1918 there was a rush to don uniform, and although her principles kept her from directly aiding the war effort, she saw no objection to becoming a nurse, and so went from the licentiousness of Greenwich Village to the rigid discipline of caring for the sick. She fell hopelessly in love with one of her patients, a journalist called Lionel Moise, who had once been a colleague of the writer Ernest Hemingway and was his ideal of a 'man's man' – hard-drinking and sometimes violent, using women with rough contempt.

Together they faced death, which became a daily commonplace during the influenza epidemic of 1919, and Dorothy's love of life drove her into Lionel's arms. Unable to flirt, she declared her passion, then went home and told her mother that she was going to live with him. Grace Day did not attempt the impossible task of dissuading her; she knew the extent of Dorothy's willpower, and merely warned her not to become pregnant. Dorothy had no intention of doing so, as she knew Lionel would leave her if she did. But nature decided differently, and in May 1919 her pregnancy was confirmed.

She tried to resolve her dilemma by throwing herself on Lionel's mercy, hoping he would be changed by the news that she was having his child, but he arranged for an abortion, and while she was undergoing the operation he moved out of the apartment they had shared.

Alone, she spent some time in Europe where she wrote her only novel, *The Eleventh Virgin*. It drew heavily on her own life, and was considered too rambling and crudely realistic by the reviewers, but her publishers sold the film rights for a substantial sum.

After her abortion, she had a strong desire for motherhood, and she looked for a man who would father her child. She found him in Forster Batterham, the son of English parents, who had a hunting-shooting-and-fishing lifestyle and a manly reticence. He agreed to spend weekends with her in a property she had bought on the west end of Staten Island: a fisherman's shack, within sight and sound of the Atlantic.

She was still writing articles and getting them published, but her diary was more important as a means of expression and in June 1925 she confided to its pages that the longed-for baby was on its way. Forster did not feel ready for the responsibility of being a parent, and as a determined atheist he was furious when in gratitude she turned to God. Sometimes he escaped to the city, or to his boat on the bay, but these rifts could not depress Dorothy.

The baby – a little girl she named Tamar, the Hebrew for 'little palm tree' and Teresa for the great Saint of Avila - was born in March 1926.

Dorothy wrote a glowing account of the birth for a socialist paper, *The New Masses*, and it was reprinted in similar papers worldwide. Dorothy was determined that Tamar would be baptised and that the Catholic Church – the church of the poor and needy – should be the one to receive her.

When she approached the nuns at a nearby convent, they told her that if Tamar should be accepted for baptism, Dorothy would have to take instruction. She began to hope for baptism herself, but hesitated when she was told that it would mean living as a single parent. Neither she nor the priest she consulted were sure if this would really be in Tamar's interests. But she wrote later, in *The Long Loneliness*:

"One of the disconcerting facts about the spiritual life is that God takes you at your word. Sooner or later one is given a chance to prove his love... No human creature could receive or contain so vast a flood of love and joy as I often felt after the birth of my child. With this came the need to worship, to adore... My very experience as a radical, my whole make-up led me to want to associate myself with others, with the masses, in loving and praising God."

The obstacle to Dorothy's baptism was removed after a final break-up with Forster in December 1927. He remained devoted to his daughter, and never lost touch with Dorothy.

The Depression made little difference to her, as she was living near the poverty line anyway. In November 1932 a liberal Catholic paper called *Commonweal* commissioned her to write an article about a Hunger March on Washington. Dorothy was very moved, as rank on rank of workers, tired and dirty after their journeys from all parts of the Union, filed past. On the feast of the Immaculate Conception she went to the National Shrine dedicated to Our Lady and prayed for a vocation. If possible she wished to find some way of helping the Church – opposed to Communism and under obligations to capitalist benefactors – to become once more the protector of the poor.

When she returned to New York, the answer was waiting for her in the form of a stocky French immigrant of fifty-nine called Peter Maurin. He looked like a tramp who had slept in his clothes, and she soon found out that was more or less how he lived. For several days he followed her about as she did her household chores, and even when she tried to work at her typewriter. When she begged him to go, he always came back; eventually, it seemed easier to listen to him.

He was anxious that the poor should be taught to take responsibility for their own lives, and work in self-governing co-operatives. He was determined that communal farms should be set up, far away from the inhuman atmosphere of large cities. As for the unemployed, he proposed that they should be offered basic help in Houses of Hospitality by people who shared voluntarily in their poverty. He was against any kind of Government intervention, saying that the State should only be a last resort when private and parish charity was exhausted.

As Peter Maurin strove to complete her Catholic education, badgering her into thinking and reading and praying, Dorothy's mind took fire from his burning idealism. They became as close as father and daughter, teacher and pupil, but did not suffocate one another. Often Dorothy would race ahead of him; when he suggested founding a paper to popularise his ideas, she came up with the concept of the *Catholic Worker*, and proceeded to bring it to reality with her intuitive grasp of practical essentials.

The first issue appeared on the streets of New York on May Day 1933. There was a great rally of radicals in Union Square, with hope in their hearts as Franklin Roosevelt implemented his proposals to end the Depression. In Germany the Nazis were celebrating their early triumphs, and the Communists made a show of strength in Moscow. The revolution of Catholic workers was slower; Dorothy and Peter sought to change hearts by the technique of water dripping on a stone.

Helpers began to live 'over the shop' at the makeshift office

Dorothy had found for the newspaper. It became a haven for the dispossessed. The movement grew, not as an organisation but as an organism, gradually taking over empty shops in the area. Dorothy never became accustomed to the noise and dirt that seemed an integral part of succouring the poor and outcast, but the young helpers who flocked to her discounted hardship. They worked at the humblest tasks, talked all night, fell in love, and left to set up Houses of Hospitality elsewhere.

By 1935 the *Catholic Worker* had a run of 110,000 copies. Most went on sale in parishes and schools, but Dorothy still maintained the tradition of street-selling in New York. The sales staff were her shock troops. One enjoyed having a pitch near the Daily Worker vendor, countering his cry of "Read the *Daily Worker*!" with "Read the Catholic Worker – daily!" Another rallied passers-by during a downpour with "Read the *Catholic Worker* – the only thing that isn't wet." Such incidents raised the profile of the Catholic Worker Movement in the city streets.

Dorothy's own contribution was a weekly column that sometimes changed its name, but never its content. She used the events of her everyday life to encourage the faithful, including the latest news from the picket lines where she was an enthusiastic demonstrator. Dorothy was often arrested – the last time when she was seventy-three, supporting the Mexican Itinerant Workers Union, which was being threatened by the powerful Teamsters.

But the most immediate and tiring work was in the Houses of Hospitality. The people who came there – of all religions, or none – received a complete welcome that embraced all their needs, and became part of a family that included everyone, from the mad or alcoholic to the merely bad-tempered. In 1936, to earn a little money, to publicise the work and encourage donations, Dorothy joined the lecture circuit. By this time there were thirty Houses in all parts of America and one in England. Dorothy found public speaking arduous; she was nervous, and delivered her message without any frills, but audiences appreciated her forthright personality and she was asked back again and again. She travelled the country on speaking engagements for forty years, until old age forced her to retire.

She proclaimed the need to help the poor, and her pugnacious stance shocked the stuffier women's clubs. She met the dispossessed farmers of the Mid-West, and the casual labourers in the fruit groves of California; she was able to describe their hardships vividly and made others feel for them. The *Catholic Worker* appealed to many, both inside and outside the Faith, bringing home not only to the laity but to Princes of the Church the Jesus of the Gospels and his compassion for the poor.

In the mid-Thirties the breadlines snaked their way round the Houses of Hospitality – sometimes as many as a thousand waited for meals, provided by donations from all sides. Often the contributions came in the form of surplus goods, of food or clothes. The organisation was always in debt, and when the coffers were empty a delegation would go to church and 'picket' St Joseph's statue. Miracles happened so frequently, they almost ceased to marvel at them.

Dorothy joined in the controversy that grew up round the Spanish Civil War, when many felt called on to choose between the Government forces and Franco, who insisted he was defending the Church against the socialists. Dorothy, a liberal to her roots, could not stomach his claims. Rather than oppose conservative Catholic opinion directly, she declared herself neutral, and this evolved into a pacifist opposition to all wars. There was a reaction against this, and many institutions cancelled their orders for the *Catholic Worker*.

She afterwards wrote: "It is a matter of grief to me that most of those who are Catholic Workers are not pacifists, but I can see too how good it is that we always have this attitude represented among us. We are not living in an ivory tower."

At this time too, anti-semitism, spreading from Germany, was adopted by some clerics, but Dorothy found common cause with the Jews, whom she had always chosen as friends and neighbours.

When war was declared again in Europe, she was facing a small war of her own. Several of the inmates of her New York Houses of Hospitality had been referred from mental hospitals and were very disruptive. She would never turn them out, however violent they became; although she was often in danger, she tried to heal their wounds with the perfect love that casts out fear. All too human, she was aware that she sometimes fell short of compassion. At such times she would meditate on Jesus's agony in Gethsemane, under the weight of sin he carried for the whole world. Compared with that, the trials of the Catholic Worker Movement seemed manageable. She felt the war was adding to those sins every day, and schooled herself to blot out the radio and ignore the newspapers, concentrating on the beauty of the created world and the daily round; so she preserved her sanity.

In June 1940 she went into print, explaining that if America ever faced invasion by the Nazis she would opt for non-violent resistance on the Ghandian model, quoting the Sermon on the Mount as her justification. A personal letter was despatched to all the Houses of Hospitality, asking that any helpers who disagreed with her pacifism should dissociate themselves from the movement. The reaction was not by any means one of unanimous support.

By now she was approaching middle age, conscious of her own mortality, and her spiritual life was enriched by retreats. To those who accused her of escaping from reality, she pointed to the hardships of her life. The military build-up as America prepared for war absorbed surplus labour, but there would always be the unemployable. The work of nursing the incontinent, those with diseased limbs, the faces with cavities instead of eyes and noses, the smells and noise, the vermin - these were her realities; for her, 'blood, sweat and tears' were part of everyday life.

By the end of the war there were only eleven Houses in operation; Peter Maurin's bright inspiration was dimmed as he succumbed to the infirmity of old age, and Tamar was married. People began to talk of Dorothy's influence in the past tense. Yet the *Catholic Worker*, thanks to the women who had run it while the men were away, went from strength to strength. Dorothy's column was as direct and compelling as ever, and through shoals of correspondence she kept in touch with her readers. Answering their letters was an important part of her apostolate.

In 1952 Harpers published the considered autobiography of her later years: *The Long Loneliness*. In it she reviewed her life in the light of her own death, and it is a moving apologia. She received the best notices of her career, which led the *New Yorker* to run a two-part profile of her, and this encouraged her to write a biography of St Therese of Lisieux, whose 'Little Way' had inspired her throughout her Catholic life.

In 1955, compulsory clearing of the streets during practice air-raids was introduced. Failure to comply involved imprisonment, and for the next five years, every time the sirens sounded Dorothy was arrested. She welcomed each prison sentence as a chance to show solidarity with her beloved poor, but she felt her impotence:

"One of the greatest evils of the day among those outside of prison is their sense of futility. Young people say: 'What good can one person do?'... They cannot see that we must lay one brick at a time; we can be responsible only for the one action of the present moment. But we can beg for an increase of love in our hearts that will vitalize and transform all our individual actions, and know that God will take them and multiply them, as Jesus multiplied the loaves and fishes..." Such was her philosophy.

May Day 1958 marked the twenty-fifth anniversary of the *Catholic Worker*. It had become almost a venerable institution in a land where novelty could dictate public taste. The secret of the paper's success was that it kept its original freshness, always taking a stance in the vanguard of opinion. Although of retirement age, Dorothy worked harder than ever, travelling constantly. In 1962 she paid a visit to Cuba: her view of the Castro regime was misunderstood because she never had a chance to question anyone in authority about censorship or the repression of religion, and – typically – she gave the official 'Bad Guy' the benefit of the doubt.

This year saw the foundation of the Pax Christi Movement in America, which strove to influence the hierarchy in the cause of peace. One of the Houses of Hospitality was host to its meetings, attracting Catholic intellectuals, members of the entertainment profession, and some trendy priests in secular dress. Dorothy did not approve of these, but in 1965 she travelled to Rome with a group from the Movement, hunger-striking on the Pope's doorstep to provoke the Vatican

Council to a commitment to non-violence and the banning of nuclear weapons; she did not live to see the cause succeed.

In New York, a young student set fire to himself in front of the United Nations Building; when he was taken to hospital he claimed to be a Catholic Worker. He had done some table-laying at a House of Hospitality in New York, and although Dorothy had never consciously met him, she was blamed for his death. The news shocked and divided the peace movement. She addressed an audience of students and tried to disclaim any involvement with the tragedy, but they would not listen to her. She did not understand the youth of the permissive age; reacting against her own promiscuous youth, she struggled to prevent others from following her example.

She was taken ill while on a speaking engagement in Florida, and a string of infirmities were diagnosed; her response was to undertake strenuous tours of India, Africa and Australia. She reached Russia in 1971 and addressed a meeting of writers, praising Solzhenitsyn who was in disgrace with the authorities.

After Vatican II she welcomed the new innovations, especially the use of the vernacular in the Mass, but deplored the effect on those who seemed to her too lax in their attitude to abortion, birth control and divorce. 1973 saw the foundation of a house for elderly women who were homeless when discharged from hospital, and in 1976 she gave a simple and moving account of her conversion and the love of God in her life to the Eucharistic Congress in Pittsburgh. It was her last public appearance. Soon afterwards she had a heart attack, and although she wrote almost to the end of her life, she became less and less mobile. Her eightieth birthday brought greetings from Pope Paul VI and visits from her grandchildren. She died on 29 November 1980; her beloved daughter was with her, and it was the quiet death she had prayed for.

Her funeral was attended by people of all ages and colours, from every State in the Union, united in the loss of their friend and champion. As a Cardinal stepped forward to pronounce a blessing, an intruder, obviously unbalanced, broke through the crowd, gazing down at her coffin with unnerving intensity. No-one stopped him; perhaps he stood for all those strangers in whom Dorothy had seen the face of Jesus Christ.

THOMAS MERTON

Christmas 1914 – the date by which the first World War was supposed to finish – had come and gone, and there was no end in sight. Owen Merton, an artist from New Zealand, and his American wife Ruth were in France, far from the battlefields, at a small town called Prades in the Pyrenees. They were Francophiles, and it was the fulfilment of a dream for Owen to work, like the Impressionists, in the magic light of the South.

The Mertons were not over-pious. Owen had something of a religious sense, but Ruth was clear-cut and cerebral; the kind of liberal who would leave her children to search for their own faith. Their elder son Tom was born on 31 January 1915, and was baptised at his father's instigation. Ruth's parents were uneasy about their grandson being brought up in a country at war, and pressed them to bring him to America, which they did when he was about a year old.

The grandparents figured largely in Tom's life: 'Pop', flamboyant and extrovert, and 'Bonnemaman', more cautious and reserved – qualities also to be found in her daughter. Ruth educated Tom at home, determined he should learn to think for himself. Her expectations were too high for him to achieve, and he was conscious of being a disappointment to her.

His brother John Paul was born in November 1918, and immediately showed a pleasant and equable temperament, in strong contrast to Tom's rebellious stance. But when Tom was six years old, Ruth developed cancer of the stomach and entered hospital, leaving her young sons to be cared for by their grandparents.

Owen Merton paid the hospital bills by acting as organist at an Episcopalian church and at a local cinema, but his principal income came from gardening; fully occupied, he had little time to spend with his sons. Ruth insisted that all news of her illness should be kept from the boys, so Tom was quite unprepared when his father gave him a letter from his mother in which she said that she was going to die, and he would never see her again. When he spelled out this message, he was shocked beyond tears. The end came, and the grown-ups were too taken up by their own grief to comfort him.

Without the necessity to earn so much money, Owen was able to paint again. John Paul, the accommodating child, was left with his grandparents, but for a time Tom shared a vaga-bond life with his father. When he returned to his grandparents' home in Douglaston, he found John Paul firmly ensconced in their affections, and to assert himself he was inclined to snub and humiliate his younger brother. This did not prevent John Paul from hero-worshipping Tom.

When Owen travelled to Europe, John Paul was considered too young to go with him, but Tom was old enough to cope. They settled in the little southern town of St Antonin, where they were surrounded by the landscapes his father loved to paint, and his paintings found ready buyers. There seems no particular reason why the French dislike some aliens and take others to their hearts, but Owen Merton found a warm place in the life of the town. In later years Tom retained memories of the flamboyant characters who staged enormous feasts after weddings and funerals; the women cooked and served vast quantities of food, while the men ate and danced and sang and indulged in rough horseplay.

Tom shared his grandfather's dislike of Catholicism, but his father exerted an influence on his spirituality, following no method at all but merely passing on his perceptions spontaneously as they occurred to him. His son remembered an occasion when, standing in the hallway of their apartment, Owen told him of St Peter's betrayal of Christ, and his remorse when the cock crew at dawn; weeping bitterly, the artist shared the saint's grief.

Yet he was quite capable of leaving his son in the charge of friends he made during his travels. None of them seem to have been unkind, though Tom sometimes found himself confused by their very different approaches to life and culture. He seemed doomed to be an alien wherever he went. After a visit to England, to exhibit and sell his paintings, his father turned up and announced that he had discovered some English relatives who had recommended a prep school for Tom.

The headmistress accepted him, but made it clear that she disapproved of Owen Merton's life-style, asking Tom if he was going to be a dilettante like his father. She had some pity for his motherless state, and made an effort to cushion the blow when his father was admitted to the Middlesex Hospital with a malignant tumour on the brain. When Tom visited him, he could see the swelling on his forehead, and his father explained that surgery would be attempted, but that the prognosis was not hopeful. He asked his son to pray for him, but when Tom tried to comply with his request, he found he had no faith or comfort, which added to his distress.

The operation was not completely successful, and Owen remained in hospital, while Tom tried to carry on with his life.

By this time he was at a public school, where the headmaster encouraged him to study modern languages and literature, and after a promotion to the sixth form he acquitted himself well at rugby and boxing, acted in school plays, and debated politics from the socialist point of view. He would always be happiest in a predominantly masculine atmosphere.

In 1930 Pop, Bonnemaman and eleven-year-old John Paul came over to Europe. Although Pop's business was hit by the depression, he made a generous gift of an annuity to the two boys, to cover their education and immediate needs. He could do nothing about their impending bereavement. On a hospital visit they discovered that their father's condition had deteriorated; his face was a swollen mass, the tumour greatly enlarged, and he could no longer speak. Tom felt he was in the presence of helpless animal suffering. On a subsequent visit he was encouraged to find sheets of blue notepaper on the bed, covered with tiny pictures of saints, whose bearded faces, each surrounded by a halo, had the look of Byzantine icons. Through Tom's cloud of grief filtered a hope that his father had retained not only his ability to draw, but his humour and his faith. Just before his sixteenth birthday in January 1931 the headmaster sent for Tom and broke the news that his father was dead.

For two months the pain of his loss left him numb. His adolescence made him very vulnerable. His father had wished him to complete his education in England, and selected as Tom's guardian an old New Zealand friend, Thomas Bennett, who was a consultant at the Middlesex, while John Paul remained in the care of his grandparents.

The Bennetts were very smart; their house in Harley Street was furnished with valuable antiques and Tom lived in an agony of apprehension that he would break something. They held advanced views and read deeply in the atheistic and liberal literature of the day.

Tom was successful in the three subjects – French, German and Latin – which he took for his Higher School Certificate, and obtained a scholarship at Clare College, Cambridge, that would eke out Pop's gift. His guardian gave him a celebratory dinner, but advised him against studying philosophy, as he wished, and counselled using his languages to enter the Diplomatic Service. But when Tom followed this advice, and crossed the Channel to study the languages at source, Mr Bennett answered an SOS for money with a long letter that enlarged on Tom's cavalier attitude to his finances, his drinking and smoking, and the dangers he could incur by his irrepressible practical joking. Like most people of his age, Tom was very thin-skinned, and thoroughly cast down by criticism.

In due course he reached Rome, where his first task was to find a dentist; he would always be plagued by toothache. Rid of a diseased molar, he started to explore the city. He intended to find the Imperial Rome of his Latin studies, but quite by chance he looked into a ruined church at the foot of the Palatine hill, where he was brought up short by the frescoes it contained. He became a pilgrim almost by accident, bought himself a Vulgate, and read in the New Testament the story behind the artists' visions.

He was still tied to a love of life's luxuries, indulging in them with a greedy appetite. Then, alone in his room one night, he had a sense of his father's presence and underwent a kind of conversion. He felt his being penetrated as if by a flash of lightning, bringing tears to his eyes for his past sins and a consciousness of God. He used the memory of his father as a stairway to the Almighty, and mounted it with rapid steps.

Next morning he made his first Catholic act, taking holy water from the stoup in a Catholic church and crossing himself. He made his way to the altar rail and, kneeling, said the 'Our Father' taught him by his New Zealand grandmother. This seemed to him complete, and he left; a dream of happiness carried him along. He visited a Trappist monastery, but was afraid to enter and stayed outside, wishing he could share the monks' silence by joining their number.

He spent the summer in New York, where his spirituality vanished, enjoying to the full the seedy glamour of the burlesque shows and the giant fun-fair of Coney Island. When he returned to take up residence at Cambridge after the excitements of Manhattan, he brought the values of the underworld with him.

For someone from his background, with neither mother nor sisters, and the product of single-sex education, the question of women presented a problem. He could neither treat them as friends, nor love them with respect. The current works on psycho-analysis regarded sex repression as an unimaginable evil, so he chose as partners girls from the town, to whom he could feel superior, and dazzled them by his intelligence and charm into sharing his bed. One of them became pregnant with his child.

Owing to his reticence about the episode, it is not clear whether he told his guardian, or whether he found out when legal proceedings were threatened. Either way, Mr Bennett was unsympathetic to Tom's dilemma. He had not told his ward that attempts to live by the ethics of modern literature could have dire consequences. The girl was bought off for a sum that would make it worth her while not to contact him again.

Later, he heard that the child was a boy, and that both he and the mother were killed in the London blitz, but he never met her again, or saw his son.

When he returned to America, he received a final letter from his guardian – to all intents and purposes washing his hands of Tom. Shocked and grieved, Tom turned against England, blaming it for the corruption he had found there. He decided to take a degree at Columbia University and commute from his grandparents' house at Douglaston. New York was an exciting environment, where rich and poor rubbed shoulders, and Tom saturated himself in the communism that was currently fashionable among the intellectuals, and also became a committed pacifist. For the first time he reached out to his brother, discovering that they had a mutual interest in jazz and the cinema; they claimed to have seen every movie that appeared between 1934 and 1937.

Tom became known as a jazz piano-player with such a heavy touch, he rendered the instrument unplayable by anyone else. He contributed to college magazines – notably *The Jester*, which published his cartoons and humorous pieces, and whose editor Bob Lax became a lifelong friend. Although never a great success on the running-track, he characteristically persevered with it until one day – just after his beloved grandfather had died without any warning – he collapsed on crossing the finishing-line.

This was followed by a classic panic attack, in a train on his way to college. The doctors gave conflicting diagnoses; none of them seem to have suggested that his illness was in fact a nervous breakdown, compounded by Pop's death and an unhappy love affair. This was the lowest point in his life; afterwards he was to see it as the will of God, breaking him down in order to build him up in his own image.

In the fall semester of 1937 he elected for a course in French Medieval Literature that brought him in touch with Catholic culture again, and he found himself seeking some place where he could worship God.

He graduated in the summer of 1938 and decided to become an academic, hoping to write books during his vacations from teaching, and he enrolled in the Graduate School of English. A new edition of Blake's poetry was just off the presses; when he was ten, Tom had been introduced to the 'Songs of Innocence' by his father. Looking back, he thought that he had been either too old or too young for them at that age, but now they held the emotional impact of being his father's favourites, and he decided on 'Nature and Art in William Blake' as his Master's thesis.

Also at this time he was introduced to Bramachari, a small, genial Hindu monk who had been in America for seven years, having been invited to the Chicago World Fair, but from the tiny sums he received for speaking to social and academic groups, he was never able to make up the fare home. Bramachari had a profound effect on Tom and his friends, who were taking an interest in Eastern religion, although his advice to Tom was to read St Augustine. He was not the only person who would see something Augustinian about Tom Merton.

His study of Blake saved him from communism, since Blake insisted that salvation could not be obtained by working for the economic equality of the poor unless it was applied with the 'charity' of St Paul.

Tom made a painfully self-conscious visit to a Catholic church where Mass was being celebrated, but still felt like a bystander rather than a possible convert. Then he took what he thought of as a minor step, though it put paid to his chances of staying outside the Church: he added the 'Hail Mary' to his prayers.

He was studying the poems and notebooks of Gerard Manley Hopkins, and read his account of his conversion by Newman. At the point where Hopkins wrote of his doubts, and Newman's dismissal of them, Tom felt stirred to action himself, urged on by an inner voice. It seemed to be the only stable point in a world wracked by crises – the Second World War was on the horizon, and he was of military age.

He found himself in the presbytery of Corpus Christi, a local church, telling a priest he wanted to become a Catholic. He was given instruction and received into the Church in November 1938. He described his first confession as "like teeth being pulled", as he dragged out his sins, and was afraid that nervousness would dry up his mouth so he could not swallow the Host. When these fears proved groundless, he went through the day in a blissful dream. He described his intense closeness to the Father in his first communion:

30

"In the Temple of God that I had just become, the One Eternal and Pure Sacrifice was offered up to the God dwelling in me: the sacrifice of God to God, and me sacrificed together with God, incorporated in His Incarnation."

Afterwards he came down to earth. He did not ask for, and was not offered, any form of follow-up to his reception. Essentially he remained the same – perhaps rightly, because it was his unique personality that God had loved and called – but he considered all was not well with him, and that he might have to make a more generous gift of himself. It was his first call to the priesthood, though he did not recognise it at the time. He thought he wanted to become a great writer; yet going down the street one day, Bob Lax asked him what he wanted to be, and Tom answered: "A good Catholic."

That was not enough for Lax, who said he was called on to be a saint. Realising that his friend had more insight into his religion than he had, Tom set his sights higher.

At the same time he and his friends were unsettled by the events in Europe, which culminated in Hitler's invasion of Poland and the declaration of war on Germany by the Western powers – though the young men still went on dating girls, getting drunk and staying up till dawn.

After one of these misspent nights, Tom declared he wanted to become a priest. His friends ignored him, and he went out into the morning, wandering about the city until he found himself in a church where Benediction was being said. When the Host was raised for adoration, he felt the invitation being repeated, and answered it with a resounding: "Yes – make me a priest."

In spite of his study of Hopkins for the Ph.D., Tom was not attracted to the Jesuit order – the shock troops of the Pope. It was the Franciscans he approached, feeling they had the joy and informality of their founder. He was advised to take up a teaching post he had been offered at Columbia and finish his thesis, aiming to join the novitiate in the summer of 1940. He visited his brother, who was at Cornell, and discovered that John Paul had been in touch with the Catholic chaplain there, who shared his interest in flying.

Within weeks of joining the Franciscans, remorse about

the girl who had borne his child began to weigh him down. He reflected that the Franciscan brothers he had talked to did not really know him, so he went to them and told them about his past. After a day or two of reflection he was told to write to the Provincial and say that he was reconsidering his application. This was not what he had expected, and he was plunged into the depths of despair.

Outside a recruiting office, he met John Paul by chance, who was all for his walking in and joining the flying arm of the U.S. Navy as he had done, but Tom explained that he was going to teach English in a Catholic University. It was there he finally gave up smoking and drinking, reading books that were on the *Index*, and going to the movies. He followed a routine closely modelled on the monastic life, and resigned himself to the idea that he had no vocation.

During the Holy Week of 1941 he decided to make a retreat, and when a friend recommended the Trappist monastery of Gethsemani in Kentucky, he spent the great commemoration of Jesus's last days on earth there. The hours in choir, the absolute silence, and the physical toil in garden and forest were deeply attractive to the side of him wanting to give generously and completely to God.

Meanwhile he continued to teach and write, acquiring an agent, Naomi Burton, who looked after his literary output for the rest of his life. He had already determined to enter Gethsemani if he could, and the trial of his vocation was hurried on by the Japanese attack on Pearl Harbour in November. The physical requirement for Forces personnel were stretched to include lower categories, and Tom received a notice to attend a Draft Board. Hurriedly he gave away all his possessions that would not fit into one suitcase, and destroyed his writings, except for a few poems and a journal. He took those to Kentucky, where he prepared himself to live according to the Cistercian Order. He was given the name of Father Louis, and received the habit on the feast of St Lucy, 13 December 1941.

Without a vocation the austere life, for which his temperament and physical health seemed entirely unfitted, would have been like perpetual imprisonment. But the deep joy it gave him spilled over into poetry which he composed during the few odd moments not governed by the Rule.

He was followed into the Catholic faith by his brother, who visited him in 1942. The last of Tom's immediate relations, John Paul died the following year, when his plane was shot down. Henceforth, Thomas Merton would have no family but the Community of Gethsemani.

Bob Lax, who also became a Catholic, visited him in 1944 and Tom showed him his poems. Bob took them to a publisher and they appeared, with the permission of his superiors, as *Thirty Poems*.

He was ordained priest in 1949, but the effort of training for it taxed his always precarious health, and he was given lighter work to do, writing hagiography, poems, religious pamphlets and translations. He wrote of his vocation:

"In the last seven years I have found out somewhat of what God wants to do with people, and what his love means. When I say that this life is wonderful it doesn't mean that every other vocation isn't wonderful, too: but to be in the sort of place where God wants one – that certainly is a marvellous thing. As soon as you get set in your groove – boy, do things happen."

His attempt to tell the story of his conversion was called *The Seven Storey Mountain* in America (*Elected Silence* in England) and brought him worldwide recognition. It caused many young men who left the Service, wanting a more meaningful life, to try their vocations. The novitiate swelled to many times its pre-war numbers, and Father Louis was made Master of the Novices, turning this new material into good monks; he was firm, but treated them with care and tact, revealing himself to be a born teacher.

He had left the world, but the world followed him to his obscure corner. His correspondents were both eminent and obscure; he took an intense interest in politics and economics, supporting the peace movements of the fifties, though this involvement caused friction with his superiors. The conflict told on his physical and mental health; Father Louis and Thomas Merton were uneasy companions in an enclosed order, and he underwent treatment by a psychiatrist.

In the sixties his desire for a solitary life was satisfied in a cabin within the grounds of the monastery; he acted as a forester, and wrote, prayed and offered Mass by himself. All the invitations he received to lecture and visit were turned down; spells in hospital were his only excursions outside the enclosure. During one of these in 1967 he had an emotional relationship with a woman. Once he had confessed this to his Father Abbot, it ceased to trouble either of them; the clashes that arose between them were on a different plane. The winds of change generated by the Second Vatican Council blew many religious from their course, and there were wholesale defections from monasteries and presbyteries. Father Louis remained faithful, thinking for himself as he had always done, without disturbing the existing order.

Near the end of his life, he questioned his own credentials to speak to the outside world:

"And we must not arrogate to ourselves the right to talk down to modern man, to dictate to him from a position of supposed eminence, when perhaps he suspects that our cloister walls have not done anything except confirm us in unreality."

1968 saw the election of a new superior, and under his direction Father Louis was allowed some relaxation. Permission was given for him to undertake a journey to Bangkok for a meeting with Asian religious leaders, arranged by a Benedictine group. He planned an ambitious tour, including many Eastern cities and a stop-over in the Himalayas to discuss with the Dalai Lama the role of contemplative prayer in Hinduism and Buddhism. He reached his goal on 9 December and gave a paper on 'Marxism and the Monastic Perspective', pleading for greater ecumenism and openness to new ideas.

This attracted the attentions of the TV cameras; hiding his face behind his paper, he begged leave to disappear - "So we can all have a coke or something." After lunch he retired to his room to rest. Subsequently it was established that a cry had been heard but not investigated until the end of the rest period, when his body was discovered with an electric fan across it, which had inflicted several wounds. It was never confirmed whether he had died from an electric shock or from a heart attack. A week later his remains were received by the Community at Gethsemani, who performed the last rites of the Church he loved so well.

Although his political writings have lost some of their impact in the light of recent events, his explorations of the spiritual life still appeal to people of all faiths and none. He was among the first to speak for Christianity in the terms of twentieth-century man, and he re-introduced mysticism into a materialistic age.

LEONARD CHESHIRE

When Leonard Cheshire was born on 7 September 1917 his father was in the basket of a balloon above the front line, observing enemy troop movements – the most vulnerable position in the Royal Flying Corps. The life of a Flying Officer, who could at least dodge and weave his way out of trouble, was estimated at six weeks, but the lone observer was a tethered sacrifice to the war. However, he survived, and after his demobilisation returned to Exeter College, Oxford, where he held a chair in Jurisprudence.

Young Leonard was neither dull nor precocious; for years he would bear the label 'Good average'. The circumstances in which his brilliance would shine had not yet come about. As a small child he sought privacy from prying adults by escaping into a world of his own. When his mother told him Bible stories, he was moved to tears by the sad parts, and by the sight – frequent in those days – of derelicts from the war begging in the streets. His compassion did not extend to his younger brother Christopher, who contracted polio, and whose cries of pain disturbed Leonard's sleep. When the illness was diagnosed, he suffered remorse for his insensitivity, and henceforward sought to smooth Christopher's path in life, as elder brothers can.

He attended day schools until he was thirteen and did well enough at his public school, Stowe, to get a scholarship to Merton, at his father's university, in 1935. He spent the vacation before he went up in Germany, where he found the inhabitants businesslike, disciplined and efficient; he was as little capable of appreciating the trend toward territorial expansion as his elders and betters. In Leonard's case it was understandable, as he spent most of his time watching the victorious German racing-drivers flash round the Berlin circuits at speeds previously thought impossible.

He lost no time in purchasing an old Alfa-Romeo and crept out of college after dark to drive it to London and sample the nightclubs – though caution, always one of his traits, made him do a nominal amount of work. But as his distinguished predecessor at Merton, Max Beerbohm, said: "All the nonsense that was knocked out at public school was gently put back at Oxford." Leonard showed this when a distinguished regular officer in the RAF, hearing that he had bought a light single-engined aircraft, offered to teach him to fly, provoking the arrogant reply that he would agree – provided the instructor knew his job properly.

In spite of the implied criticism, he was soon on good terms with his instructor, and by June 1937 he was flying solo, the most deft and fearless pilot in the university squadron. His first action on obtaining his pilot's licence was to join the RAF Volunteer Reserve, possibly in order to avoid being called up for the Army in the event of war; the horrors of the trenches had penetrated the consciousness of his generation. He was a typical undergraduate, enjoying a hectic social life and generally behaving as if he were indestructible.

When the anticipated war came in 1939 Cheshire and his contemporaries welcomed it; whatever happened now, they would not be bored. The Thirties had been drab, with overtones of the Depression; the Forties were bright with the promise of honours to be won on their own special battlefield. At first sight it seems surprising that Cheshire, with his mercurial temperament, should have been chosen to train as a bomber-pilot. It was the fighter-pilots, engaged in one-to-one combat with the enemy, who were the darlings of the nation, and Cheshire was ambitious for recognition. But his superiors soon realised his qualities of leadership, and bomber-pilots flew with a crew.

He developed his own technique for familiarising himself with the lay-out of new aircraft, putting on a blindfold and testing himself by touch, and he was held in almost superstitious regard by his crews. His luck was famous, but it went with a meticulous attention to detail. When he came back after hours of flying through enemy air-defences, in freezing temperatures and with the fuselage riddled with holes, he did not immediately follow his peers in search of a bath, a meal, copious alcohol and feminine company. After de-briefing, he would seek out the men who serviced the aircraft and talk to them knowledgeably about the work in hand.

He was later to write and lecture about his experiences, and said a number of conflicting things about courage – most notably, that he was usually too busy to be afraid. Only once, when his aircraft was plunging earthwards over Magdeburg, did he give the order to abandon her, until the wireless operator reminded him that the crew expected better leadership. He was humble enough to admit to a temporary panic, and it never occurred again. He became the veteran of more than a hundred trips over enemy territory, and received the DSO with four bars, the DFC, and later the Victoria Cross. He was quick to point out that these honours belonged not to him, but to all his colleagues, including every member of the squadron.

And he was always learning. After a mission which he considered less than successful, he commented:

"I'll remember that an opportunity missed is missed for ever; and come what may I'll never hesitate again – at least, not once I've caught sight of the target. So help me God."

His ability to form conclusions about aerial warfare was invaluable to his superiors; he formulated ideas about precision bombing, the marking of targets, and a new way of approaching them below the range of anti-aircraft guns. Technology was still being developed by which these skills could be safely used, and he was always taking risks, though they were carefully calculated.

After his first tour he was sent to Canada to ferry a new machine back to the war-zone. He shared the popular view of America as exciting and glamorous, and when he made a trip to New York, his be-ribboned uniform was the passport to lavish hospitality. He was accompanied to many parties by a forty-two-year-old divorcee, with whom he contracted a more than usually hasty wartime marriage.

They returned to England in a blaze of publicity, and when

he was promoted to an administrative post, he filled his increased leisure by writing a book called *Bomber Pilot*, which was a runaway success.

Always impatient of the rules and regulations he was now supposed to uphold, he longed to get back into the air, and after the strategy changed and precision bombing gave way to mass attacks on German cities, he took part in these operations. When in due time precision bombing came back in vogue, he was its most skilled exponent. Then in 1942 his wife became seriously ill with a nervous breakdown, brought on by the difficulties of marriage to a much younger man; and he saw it was impossible for them to remain together.

However, he took compassionate leave to join her in New York, and was on the spot when the Americans invited two British observers to join a project which they believed would bring the war against Japan to an end. A successful test of an atomic bomb had been made in the New Mexican desert on 26 July 1945, which meant that the High Command could go ahead with a plan to use it on Japanese cities.

An airfield had been built on the island of Tinian, from which the bombers were to fly. Wing-Commander Cheshire arrived eight days after the New Mexico test and his admiration for the application of mass-production techniques was overwhelming. His fellow-observer was a distinguished physicist, William Penney, and they got on well together; among the American pilots, he found many who had shared his experiences in the skies over Europe. As they waited for the bombs to arrive, speculation was rife: would the Japanese surrender before the raid could be carried out? In the tense emotional climate, Cheshire shared the prevailing view that this – the most destructive weapon ever made – must be put into action; there was dark talk of ignoring any move toward peace with the enemy.

He was prevented from going on the Hiroshima raid by a shortage of space on board, but received clearance to go on the follow-up mission, and found himself over Nagasaki – the most Christian city in Japan – as the mushroom-shaped cloud formed above it. They circled for an hour, making observations, and Cheshire sketched his impressions. Time was when his crews had sung all the way home, to relieve their tensions, but this return was in uneasy silence; even the naturally exuberant Americans were reduced to muttered technicalities. Cheshire accepted that he would not fit into the peacetime RAF and was invalided out on grounds of psycho-neurosis; the anxiety state he had incurred on his country's behalf had become semi-permanent. He was ordered to rest for a year but found it impossible to obey, and after considering several projects he settled down to write fortnightly articles in the *Sunday Graphic*. Soon he began to receive letters from ex-servicemen like himself, looking back to the comradeship they had found in war-time, the reduction of class distinction in the face of a common need, the pooling of talent in serving a cause.

It was in Cheshire's nature to lead, and he felt his correspondents were looking to him to devise a scheme that would use their skills. His first idea was to run a disused airfield as a commune, but after a public meeting had considered the plan it was decided to take over a large country house, and he set about finding one. His aunt offered him Le Court, her estate in Hampshire, and a loan from his father got the scheme off the ground.

Although he had not done so during his wartime dangers, he now found himself increasingly turning to God. He had taken this direction after an incident that occurred at the end of a mammoth party given for his brother Christopher, when he was released from a German prisoner-of-war camp. The last guests were sitting in a Mayfair pub, all more or less inebriated, and someone introduced the subject of religion. Cheshire began to laugh at this incongruity, when a pretty girl turned to him and said: "How much do you know about God?"

He trotted out his sketchy thoughts about individual conscience being the only guide, and religion being irrelevant. When he had finished the girl retorted that God was a person, and told him he knew that perfectly well. Nothing he had heard from the pulpit in his schooldays had prepared him for this simple statement, and he found he could not shrug it off.

He worked hard at Le Court, organising a professional

administration and making the proviso that when finances permitted, six disabled servicemen should be housed there in a dormitory of their own. The *Daily Graphic* gave some publicity to the enterprise, and the Editor encouraged him to go to Europe and arouse interest there.

For the first time he saw from the ground the devastation caused by the raids in which he had taken part, and he was also disturbed by the poverty of the vanquished, in contrast with the high living among the occupying forces.

It was Christmastime, and he was acutely aware of the appearance of God-made-man, poor amongst the poor.

He needed all his mental and physical strength to return to England; he also had to face the fact that his marriage was ending in divorce. Le Court had staggered from crisis to crisis, reaching its nadir during the exceptionally hard winter of 1947. When Spring came, he was feeling no better, so he made the best arrangements he could for the future of the project, and took a holiday in Canada with a family friend, a retired Anglican Bishop. Bishop Embling was wise enough to leave his spiritual conflicts to settle themselves, and introduced him to the mysteries of logging instead. On a visit to a bookshop he picked up a prayer-book which contained the 'Hail Mary', and he found that its recital made an accompaniment to his solitary walks.

In his absence the Le Court project had collapsed, and he returned, as he thought, to wind it up – but, as he wrote later:

"Everything works out for the best... Even failure."

He was met by his secretary who told him that their pig-man, Arthur, was in hospital. With the utmost reluctance and only after an interval of several days, Cheshire visited the hospital and was told that Arthur's case was incurable – and that they needed the bed.

Arthur himself had not been informed that he was terminally ill, and was making plans to live independently. With great courage, Cheshire took it upon himself to tell Arthur the truth, and later, when all enquiries for a refuge proved in vain, offered to nurse him at Le Court; he could not turn away a comrade in arms. Arthur accepted, explaining that he had lost touch with his family, who had shunned him when he became

41

a Catholic; Le Court was the only place where he had ever felt at home. It seemed that Arthur was the one success of the entire episode.

Cheshire entered on the task of nursing him with all his genius for improvisation and characteristic zeal. Eventually he tried out his next scheme on him, suggesting they should accept other people in a similar situation; wisely, Arthur advised him to leave God to send those in most need of help.

Arthur insisted on being as independent as possible, and Cheshire learned a great deal about the care of the sick; as the end drew near, he got advice from the hospital about laying out the body. When Arthur became unconscious, a chance visitor suggested that a Catholic priest should be called. He arrived that night and performed the last rites, telling Cheshire that this was the greatest comfort he received from being ordained.

It was about midnight when Arthur gave a sigh and died. While Cheshire was waiting to attend to the body, alone in the empty house, he chanced on Vernon Johnson's account of his conversion to Catholicism, and he completed the laying-out by twining Arthur's rosary beads round his fingers. In due course he asked the visiting priest to give him instruction, and was received into the Church at the Midnight Mass of Christmas.

He weathered many trials in establishing the Cheshire Homes as a national and international institution; not the least was when he suffered 'burn-out' and had to leave the administration to others.

As he said: "Life was becoming a struggle. It was a struggle to work, a struggle to decide the future, a struggle to know how to accept all those who were calling out for help."

An X-ray revealed the reason: he had contracted tuberculosis and was confined to bed, having four lung operations before he was finally discharged.

In 1955 he decided that he would like to meet Sue Ryder.

During the war, she had volunteered for service with the S.O.E. (Special Operations Executive) and was attached to the Polish Section, becoming devoted to Poland and its people. When she was nineteen she looked after agents while they trained to be dropped into enemy territory, and was inspired by their courage. Many of them were captured, tortured and killed, and she wanted them to have a living memorial.

After the war she saw the pitiful state of the victims who had suffered in German concentration camps, especially those whose homes and families had disappeared into the chaos that prevailed. When the international agencies pulled out, she stayed on, driving thousands of miles and visiting the prisons where so many finished up, having got involved in crime in order to survive. Her dream of founding a home to rehabilitate her 'boys' as she called them, was fulfilled when she established one at St. Christopher's, near Celle in Germany.

The first home in England was founded when her mother gave up her house at Cavendish in Suffolk, and Sue was able to purchase it. Mrs Ryder came from a family who regarded their privileged background as an opportunity to serve those less well off, and passed the tradition to her daughter; Sue had begun to visit the poor and needy with her mother at the age of nine. She learned, as Leonard Cheshire had done, to do good without patronising the recipient.

Six years her senior, he discovered when they met that the young woman who drove enormous trucks all over Europe was diminutive, just five feet tall. Because of her absences abroad, she had never heard of him; for a man whose exploits had kept him in the full spotlight of publicity, it was a refreshing experience. But they had so much in common, they quickly filled the gaps in their knowledge. They had both had early experiences of the building trade: Sue learned carpentry in the workshop on her father's estate – Cheshire's father had waited until the builders of his house knocked off for the day, then mounted the ladders to add more roof-tiles, followed by his sons. And of course their projects, designed to help the disabled and the homeless, were complementary. They had the same faith, the same trust that Providence would provide funds, and it set a seal on their compatability that she too was a convert to Catholicism.

Much of this emerged as Leonard showed Sue round the house and grounds at Ampthill, his newest Cheshire Home for the physically disabled. At the time of his illness there had been only four, but by now the movement had grown into a worldwide network. The Sue Ryder Foundation included houses in which cancer patients could be nursed – Holiday Homes so that carers of the sick could have a rest from their arduous duties – a scheme offering hospitality to nationals from Poland and the Eastern bloc – and staff who did social and relief work and prison visiting. One source of income was the chain of Sue Ryder Shops, a familiar sight in many High Streets, with their stock of bric-a-brac, small items of furniture and immaculate second-hand clothing donated by well-wishers and sold to an appreciative public.

There was an immediate affinity between them, but they were both busy people. Sue had to go to Moscow to discuss the repatriation of Russians still held in German prisons. This parting of the Iron Curtain was something she had earned; even the Soviet Empire acknowledged her integrity. As they were due to be in India at the same time in 1957, Cheshire arranged his schedule so that he could meet her at the airport in Delhi. Together they toured the country by public transport, contacting as many people as possible in an attempt to find out what they could do to alleviate the appalling poverty they saw on every side. Courageous and generous Indians undertook the maintenance of the homes as they were set up; the Indian Army, which kept the structure created by the Raj after Independence, renovated and serviced an old ambulance for them. They christened it 'Ezekiel', and took turns to drive it on long journeys, crisscrossing the country.

Near Dehra Dun, in Uttar Pradesh, the government had offered Cheshire a thirty-acre site which they earmarked as a centre for handicapped and under-privileged children in great need. They named it 'Raphael', and it led to other joint ventures. A year later they decided to embark upon the adventure of marriage.

Before they became formally engaged, in February 1959, they sent a declaration to all their members of staff, volunteers and friends, giving them notice of their intention. They outlined their hope that with mutual support they would be able to continue the work with greater zeal, and asked for their approval. Mother Teresa, a good friend to them both, also gave them her blessing.

They were married in Bombay by Cardinal Gracias on 5th April 1959 in his private chapel. The bride arrived after a hectic trip to Poland and Czechoslovakia, grateful for a quiet, simple ceremony. The Cheshire Home on the outskirts of the city gave them a reception, and there was another at their beloved Raphael. They allowed themselves a three-day honeymoon, camping out in a hut by the Jamna River until they were dispossessed by a family of six Indians. Then they plunged into a tour of Australia and New Zealand, where they lectured in order to raise funds. Many times in the years that followed they would undertake such tours, impressing everyone with their simple accounts of their work, and tapping a deep vein of charity without claiming any credit for themselves.

They made their home at the headquarters of the Sue Ryder Foundation at Cavendish in Suffolk, at first in a modest bed-sitter. In this room they worked long hours and relaxed occasionally, listening to tapes or – even more rarely – watching television. Neither of them drank or smoked, and they enjoyed simple, nursery-type food.

Their children – Jeremy born in 1960, and Elizabeth (Gigi) born in 1962 – were delivered by local midwives at home, Sue working until a few hours before they were born. As the children grew up, their parents were inevitably absent a great deal, but their welfare was looked after by a resident nanny, and they were practically adopted by the resident patients – nicknamed 'the Bods' by their mother, in memory of the wartime resistance fighters.

Living at first in one room, and later in two, called for tidiness on the part of the occupants, and both members of the partnership kept their papers in order. Sue favoured ring-binders, in which she wrote and planned everything. The sending of Christmas cards kept their friendships in repair, but they had to begin writing them in August, as there were over three thousand recipients, all listed on a computer.

There was one real difference between Sue Ryder and Leonard Cheshire: she was an early riser – between 4.30 and

5.00 am – and would feel lost if she did not use the quiet of the morning for prayer and work; while he worked on, late into the night. Against all the odds their marriage worked, and they celebrated their Silver Wedding with a nuptial Mass at St Peter's in Rome, concelebrated by eleven priests. Their party, made up of an international group from all parts of the Foundations, including non-Christians, had an audience with Pope John Paul II. It must have been a special joy to the first Polish Pope that when Sue was made a Life Peeress in 1978, she took the title of Lady Ryder of Warsaw, with the permission of the city authorities. It was an honour she was reluctant to accept, and only did so because it might be of some help to the Foundation. She took her seat in the Lords, and with her sense of history enjoyed the experience; it gave her the opportunity to promote the understanding of her work, and the work of charities in general.

Leonard Cheshire received the Order of Merit in 1981, many honorary degrees, and was ennobled in the Birthday Honours of 1991. The pressure of visiting their far-flung families at home and abroad often kept them away from each other. They tried as far as possible to arrange their itineraries so that they could meet occasionally, and this threw into relief their fondness for one another. Their marriage was unique in that they came and went frequently and freely, yet had a complete understanding of each others needs.

Leonard Cheshire gave credit for the success of their work to: "The self-sacrifice and fundamental goodness of many men and women of every denomination, religion and class... All of whom have been touched by the needs of the sick and the homeless."

Even in later years he was capable of coming up with imaginative schemes which had an element of symbolism. He conceived a plan for turning redundant nuclear weapons into fountain-pens – a neat variation on swords into ploughshares – and suggested one of these should be used to sign the treaty between Russia and America for the curtailment of nuclear weapons.

He enjoyed good health, and played tennis as a relaxation after long hours of travelling or desk-work, until – in his seventies – he developed motor-neurone disease, and died on 31 July 1992. The world paid tribute to the fighting man who had become a knight errant for peace; he never threw up his arms in horror at the world's suffering, but rolled up his sleeves and did his best to alleviate it.

The Mass of thanksgiving for his life was held the following September. He had given some thought to it, asking the celebrant, Cardinal Basil Hume, not to give a eulogy, but a homily on prayer and meditation. His wife read a prayer they had composed together when they became engaged, promising service to the poor until death. The recessional hymn was one that is often sung in Anglican churches at the annual service for the commemoration of those who died in the country's wars.

'O, valiant hearts, who to your glory came
Through dust of conflict and through battle flame;
Tranquil you lie, your knightly virtue proved.
Your memory hallowed in the land you loved.'

(Sir John S. Arkwright; 1872-1954)

It could well stand as his epitaph.

SIMONE WEIL

At the turn of the century the people of France were, as a nation, riddled with self-doubt about their defeat in the Franco-Prussian war of 1870. The territory of Alsace, where Simone Weil's father Bernard was born, was one of their losses. As soon as he could, Bernard became a French national and qualified to practise medicine in his adopted country. He married a young woman called Selma Reinherz, who, like his own family, was Jewish, but neither of them was devout.

In 1905, the year after their marriage, their son André was born, and great things were expected of him. He was precociously intelligent, and every sign of talent was fostered by his loving parents. They encouraged him with gentleness rather than coercion, and the values in the family were those of enlightened liberalism.

Cleanliness came emphatically before godliness: Bernard enjoyed telling anti-Semitic jokes, but hygiene was taken very seriously. Both André and his sister Simone, who was just two years and nine months younger, had an almost morbid fear of microbes. Even close relatives were discouraged from kissing the children, and André would push open doors with his elbows to avoid contaminating his hands. In Simone, who had very intense emotions, this resulted in a lifetime avoidance of physical contact.

After the 1914-18 war, in which France recovered self-respect through victory – though at an appalling cost in casualties – the Weils moved to Paris. André was the apple of his mother's eye; he excelled in mathematics and was handsome and well co-ordinated – from Simone's viewpoint, across that yawning gap of nearly three years, it was impossible to follow in his footsteps. Of course, she never stopped trying.

Her mother claimed that Simone was extremely obstinate, for she was one of those children who know what is best for them, and could fight her corner, taking on both parents if necessary. Bernard was amused, but Selma, equally stubborn herself, was worried by this trait, though she may well have helped to develop it by insisting that her daughter should have a masculine directness instead of what she described as "the simpering graces of a little girl".

Until Simone was twelve she received very informal education at home, and when she was eventually sent to school, she had some difficulty in settling down. She felt no-one understood her, and dreamed of a friend who would be her ideal companion, and share her inmost secrets. She did find some congenial elements among her peers, and did well enough to head her class in French literature and composition – and, unexpectedly, in mathematics, which her parents considered André's especial province. Her success was the more remarkable as she was two years younger than her classmates.

This was not enough to cure her feeling of inferiority, as she compared herself exclusively with André. She had no contact with religion at this time, either Christian or Jewish – indeed, she had only recently become aware that there was any difference between them, as her parents were silent on the subject. Her idea of heaven was a place where those possessed of genius could commune with one another in an atmosphere of goodness, truth, beauty and perfect wisdom. She considered herself doomed to be excluded from this paradise.

However, she evolved a way of qualifying for it by sheer persistence and concentration; her expression for this was "deep attention". It was near to religious meditation, as she emptied herself and tried to contain the object contemplated, as an artist does.

As she wrote: "Attention consists of suspending our thought, leaving it detached, empty, and ready to be penetrated by the object; it means holding in our minds, within reach of this thought but on a lower level and not in contact with it, the diverse knowledge we have acquired, which we are forced to make use of... Above all our thought should be empty, waiting, not seeking anything but ready to receive in its naked truth the object which is to penetrate it."

After months of deep despair, she came to believe that this technique was not only open to her, but that she could teach the disadvantaged to attain it. She was becoming politically aware, and all her sympathies were with the poor and needy, but she believed that the most important part of life was the moment of death, when there would be an accounting for one's actions and a revelation of truth.

Staying in a hotel on a family holiday, she demonstrated her awakening interest in sociology by talking to the staff about their conditions of work, and advising them to join a union. Her own destiny, she felt, lay with Greek Stoic philosophy. She had studied the subject at the Lycée, her teacher describing her as "Among the six most brilliant students he ever taught"; lessons often turned into a dialogue between them.

In October 1925, when she was sixteen years old, she followed her brother to the Lycée Henri IV, hoping to study for the entrance examination to the Ecole Normale Superieure. This was the gateway to the leading positions in the French Establishment; her brother had succeeded brilliantly at the Ecole, and girls had only recently been accepted.

There she met her great friend and later biographer, Simone Petrement, who gives a vivid account of her three years at Henri IV. Simone's subjects were French, English and History, but she neglected them in favour of the famous Professor Alain's philosophy lectures. He had enormous influence on his pupils, amongst whom were numbered a whole generation of French writers, politicians and sociologists.

Simone was indebted to Alain for giving a direction to her brilliant and unusual intellect. She shared with him a passionate interest in mathematics – geometry in particular giving her an almost religious perception of the shape of the external world – and myth and legend as an insight into the nature of goodness.

Alain was anti-clerical, a stance she herself adopted. From

the first, he praised her lucidity and distinction in analysis, but he called her 'The Martian' and felt she passed judgment on everyone she met. Her fellow-pupils found her almost inhuman, only later appreciating the qualities of tenderness and sympathy in her writings.

Already she had made a resolution to forego physical fulfilment in order to dedicate her life to helping the under-privilleged. In spite of this she seems to have had a warm attachment to at least one of the young men with whom she conversed all night in the Paris cafés. Along with other students of Alain she also taught railway workers, anxious to improve their job prospects.

In 1927 she headed the list in the B.A. philosophy passes at the Sorbonne, but her failure in history meant that she could not enter the Ecole Normale Superieure. With characteristic energy she tackled the subject, and a year later was the only girl accepted. She spent her time in political agitation – her friends grew to dread her approach with yet another request for their signatures to petitions – more classes for the railway-men, and writing a dissertation for her Diploma in Higher Studies, on the subject of 'Science and Perception in Descartes'.

In her second year, Simone had a sinus infection which became chronic and caused her to have debilitating head-aches; it also gave her a high nasal voice – but those who listened were aware that she had something to say. She had spent one of her holidays helping with the harvest in Normandy, insisting on separating thistles with her bare hands. This, and her conversations with the railwaymen, made her feel an affinity with those who earned their livelihood from manual labour. Aware that poverty drained the human spirit of its creativity, she was anxious to improve their conditions, and she hoped to change the system that made their lives so hard.

In her third and final year she had great success in the examinations. Only eleven candidates were given passes out of a hundred and seven, and she was placed seventh. She hoped to find a job as a manual worker so that she could put her theories of work to practical use. Her idea of training for this was to dig potatoes for ten hours a day on a farm near one

51

of her relatives. But the crumbling markets on Wall Street in 1929 resulted in world-wide unemployment, and she would not dispossess someone who depended on manual work for a livelihood.

Like most of the intellectuals of her generation, she believed that the events leading to the Depression could be attributed to the failure of capitalism, yet she hesitated to join the Communist party, as she was not convinced that the Russian experiment was a success. Indeed she considered that the revolution of the proletariat had become the dictatorship of unfeeling bureaucrats, a tyranny as hard as that of the Czars.

There was a third way, more suited to her temperament. She suppported those trade unionists who had been expelled from the Communist party, believing that it was the more independently-minded workers who had the creative energy to change their conditions. A desire to share the lives and experience of the unemployed grew ever stronger. When she eventually secured a teaching post – the only work for which she was qualified – she would not heat her room, because the unemployed could not afford to; she lived on the equivalent of the dole, giving the rest of her salary to union strike funds.

During a visit to a pit, she prevailed on the miners to allow her to wield a pick and try her hand at using a pneumatic drill. The effect of the latter on her frail frame was something she never forgot; the painful vibration led her to conclusions about the subjection of the human body to the tools it used. She decided it was not enough for the workers to overthrow a system of government that legislated against their interests; she urged them to revolt against the technology that turned a human being into an extension of a machine. It seemed to her that the engineers must be involved in creating tools that were in harmony with bodily movement.

An unconventional teacher, her lessons were based on carefully prepared notes which she read aloud, so that she did not make eye-contact with members of her class; rapt in her subject, she paid no attention to her articulation, which made her rather difficult to understand. However, an Inspector gave her credit for thinking deeply and trying to inform and stimulate the minds of her listeners, though he deplored her tendency to use up-to-date news items to illustrate points she wished to make, which he found dangerously close to political propaganda.

Later she would dispense with structure altogether, not giving marks or grades, and was quite arbitrary in choosing whether to teach geometry or hold a conversation in which everyone took part. Naturally enough, her classes were not noted for the number of pupils that passed their examinations, but none of them ever forgot the unique atmosphere created by Simone's dedication and enthusiasm, or the heated excitement her classes generated.

When Hitler came to power in 1933 she did her best to help the refugees who came to France, persuading her parents to give houseroom to a motley collection of dissidents, representing all shades of opinion. She bemoaned the fact that she could not join the beleaguered German opponents of the dictator, and even tried unsuccessfully to take the place of one of them.

At the turn of the year, Trotsky was in Paris to meet representatives of the German and French Workers' parties, and she invited him to stay with her long-suffering parents. She proceeded to disagree with him fundamentally, and their angry voices could be heard all over the apartment. Increasingly aware of the corruption that attended the assumption of power, she gradually withdrew from all political organisations. From now on she would make an independent analysis of the political scene, and speak only for herself.

The summing-up of all she thought and felt so deeply was expressed in the book *Oppression and Liberty*, which she wrote at white heat during the spring and summer of 1934. It did not have an easy passage into the world; she herself referred to it in terms of "a difficult labour". When it was finished, a friend offered to find it a publisher. At the time Simone refused, but the manuscript survived her, and was published in 1955, helping to build up her considerable posthumous reputation.

It was as if she had to write out of herself everything she had formulated so far in her search for truth, to clear the decks for the battle to come when she embarked on her next project – going into the market-place as a manual worker. This bore out her deep feeling that there should be a perfect marriage between intellectual and physical labour; in order that work should have an almost religious aspect in the scheme of things, it had to be thoroughly understood and consented to by the mind.

Of course she knew that the practice in factories at the time fell short of this ideal, but she could not have foreseen the difficulties she would face. To begin with, she was extremely clumsy and inept, and while holding down three jobs more or less briefly, she suffered several industrial injuries. She was also slow, and had great difficulty in keeping up with production targets. In her experience of academic life she had always been successful, but in industry she rated as the lowest of the low – grateful for a kind word, and finally believing she was lucky to be allowed to ride on a bus.

The low esteem in which she was held affected her health, yet she took notes about all aspects of life in the factories where she was employed, and was so scrupulous about living on her earnings, she insisted on paying her parents restaurant prices for the meals she ate with them on Sundays.

It is interesting to find in her notes that she saw a future in which robots would be used for the most soul-destroying tasks, and that workers should be informed about the relevance of their contribution to the final product. Whether she would have approved of the modern Japanese methods of worker management is a moot point, but they are one possible development of the ideas she had about the organization of industry.

Her parents insisted she should take a holiday. It was too late to revive her old light-hearted optimism, but a cruise round the coasts of the Iberian peninsula alleviated her fatigue. She wandered into a village where the feast of Our Lady of Sorrows was being celebrated. The women of the community walked round the fishing-fleet bearing candles, singing what sounded to Simone like the Russian songs sung by the boatmen of the Volga. These revived the old feeling of bondage she had known in the factories; for the first time she

54

was aware that Christianity was the religion of slaves, and that she was marked out for it – this, in spite of the fact that she felt alienated by the dogmas of the Catholic Church, including the proofs of the existence of God, and felt self-conscious about going inside churches.

Although she had a small success in her next teaching post, she made another break with academe when in June 1936 Franco and his Fascists invaded Spain from North Africa in an attempt to overthrow the Republican government. Simone had always taken a pacifist stand on world events, counselling non-intervention when the Germans re-possessed the Rhineland, but in this case her heart ruled her actions. She lost little time in joining the committed workers and intellectuals who thronged the roads across the Pyrenees, determined to fight Fascism.

As always, the elements of anticlimax and black comedy dogged her steps. Her comrades in arms gave her a wide berth when it came to target practice; owing to her clumsiness and poor sight, she was a dangerous companion. In an attempt to keep her from becoming a liability, during one attack on a railway line, she was left behind with the expedition's cook. He became much more agitated than Simone during an air-raid, and left a pan of boiling oil over a fire in a pit. Short-sighted, she stumbled into it, being so badly scalded that she had to be evacuated to a hospital. The severity of her wounds probably saved her life, as the remaining women members of her unit were killed in battle later.

Back in Paris, she became well-known at republican rallies, wearing her uniform and the black-and-red scarf that denoted she was an anarchist, but as incidents of brutality began to accumulate on the government side, her enthusiasm for the cause waned, and she became once more a pacifist. An essay on the subject for a magazine called *Nouveau Cahiers* brought her to the notice of academics, high-ranking civil servants and industrialists, and she joined a group that met at the Café de Flore every Monday evening.

During the spring of 1937 she visited Switzerland and Italy, and spent two days in Assisi, absorbing the Tuscan landscape where St Francis had walked and talked. She entered the Romanesque chapel of St Mary of the Angels, where he had prayed, and an overwhelming tide of feeling flooded through her, bringing her for the first time to her knees. From then on she would count Romanesque architecture as one of the highest achievements of man. In the first instance, it was the artistic heritage of the Church that made her respond to its spiritual message.

When Hitler annexed Austria in March 1938 the map of Europe had to be redrawn, and she foresaw the absorption of Czechoslovakia. While she approved appeasement policies, if a conflagration should break out she advocated guerilla warfare of the kind carried on in Spain, and this form of resistance has been successful in subsequent wars.

In the hope of a respite from the gathering conflict she spent Holy Week in the Abbey of Solesmes in north-western France. This Benedictine community is famous for its performance of the liturgy, but her chronic headaches became intensely painful as she listened to the plainchant. However, she forced herself into such deep concentration on the music and words that she felt the pain, as she said, "heaped up in a corner to suffer".

A young English pilgrim introduced her to the metaphysical poets of his country; one poem in particular – 'Love', by George Herbert – a dialogue between God and a human soul, provided her with a basis for meditation when her headaches were almost unbearable. She felt that it had become a prayer which was answered by Jesus himself taking possession of her. In the course of the next few months this changed her life, overcoming her previous wariness of the supernatural, and making her liken her sense of the presence of Jesus to "the smile on a beloved face".

After Hitler's occupation of Prague, her political views changed profoundly; she became convinced that the time for appeasement had gone by. Increasingly, she argued that Germany should not be allowed to dominate Europe. The outbreak of war found her with her parents in Paris. She spent the 'Phoney War' writing a commentary on the *Iliad*, and tried to reconcile her detestation of the Jehovah of the Old Testament with the love of the Father revealed in the life and death of

Jesus. She had completely rejected her Jewish ancestry, aware of herself only as a French national, influenced by the Christian culture of her country.

After the collapse of France the family made its way south, and Simone wished to organise a nursing corps of women to go to the war zone and assist the Allied forces. To do this, she needed to join De Gaulle's army in exile. While she waited for transport to North Africa, in the unoccupied zone at Marseilles, her paper on the *Iliad* was published in a magazine called *Cahiers du Sud*, and she extended her circle of friends as a result. One of them introduced her to Joseph-Marie Perrin, a member of the Dominican order, who in spite of impaired sight and poor general health counselled a number of people about their spiritual lives.

Sometimes her fierce intellectual honesty clashed with his more orthodox Catholicism, but they became devoted to one another, and he thought she was on the brink of baptism. This was far from true, although she studied the Greek version of the Lord's Prayer with a friend, word by word. She claimed that meditation on it was her first conscious prayer – before that, she had regarded prayer as a form of self-hypnosis. It became a morning offering; typically, she wished to make it perfect, and if she could not give it her special "deep attention", she repeated it until she did.

An amateur philosopher she stayed with echoed the general opinion at this time, saying that his first impression of her was of an ugly eccentric with a monotonous voice, but he came to love her spiritual purity and generosity.

It led her to join the Resistance. She had to make two attempts, but was finally accepted into a cell based on Father Perrin's house, helping refugees and organising the publication of an anti-Fascist and anti-racist magazine. Years later a young assistant in this work paid tribute to her determination to take on the suffering of the whole world.

As she sat with Father Perrin in the parlour of his house – she, racked by headaches and he with red-rimmed, weeping eyes from an infection – he enquired if she was ready to be received, and she felt she could not disappoint him. To this we owe the letters she wrote to him, outlining her views of the

Church. When these were eventually published, many intellectuals were moved to identify with her, since they so accurately mirrored their own position. Not so many could echo the cry of Christ on the cross: "My God, my God, why have you forsaken me?" as Simone did; she admitted that she was envious of his Crucifixion.

Twice she was summoned to interviews with the police, but they did not succeed in making her admit to her illegal activities. At last she and her family set sail for North Africa on their way to New York. In preparation for the journey, she filled several notebooks, summing up all her experiences in the light of the love of God. There were also two reflections: 'The Love of God and Affliction', and 'Forms of the Implicit Love of God', which later appeared as *Waiting on God*, edited by Father Perrin – to whom she gave all her writings to date, for safe-keeping in case the ship should be torpedoed. She also wished him to popularize her thoughts; it was one of the few times she admitted her need to write for posterity.

She did not stay long in New York; once there, she lost no time in contacting a friend from her schooldays – Maurice Schumann, now in London. He passed her on to a member of De Gaulle's cabinet, who found a job for her. Her lack of physical fitness precluded any idea of being sent to France as she wished, and she was set to work, co-ordinating ideas for the post-war reconstruction of her country. But she would not abandon the hope of returning there, and even tried to strengthen her power of resistance against torture, telling anyone who would listen that she would die for the Allied cause.

Her appearance was unkempt, and she would not heat her room or eat more than the rations allowed her countrymen under the German Occupation; she was so thin, she gave an impression of transparency, and her frail body was shaken by a hacking cough. She went to Mass daily at the Jesuit church in Farm Street and longed to take Communion, but her principles would not allow her to accept the Faith.

On 15 April 1941, she collapsed in her room, and remained undiscovered for two days. A friend – Simone Dietz – called to find out why she had not appeared at the office, and saw her into the Middlesex Hospital, where she was diagnosed as having tuberculosis in both lungs. If she had followed the advice she was given, she could have recovered with rest and an adequate diet, but she would not abandon her determination to live as if she were in Occupied France.

A Free French chaplain visited her at her request. Although he found her thought difficult to follow, and a certain obstinacy in her ideas, he had nothing but admiration for her humility and purity, and came to believe that God thought so much of her intellectual honesty, he had witheld from her the gifts of joy and peace.

But she had her own way of dealing with affliction, claiming that: "It is in affliction itself that the splendour of God's mercy shines; from its very depths, in the heart of its inconsolable bitterness." And her background of Stoicism is revealed in her admonition: "We should not speak of the Kingdom of God to those in affliction, for that is foreign to them, but only of the Cross."

According to Miss Dietz, Simone said that if she fell into a coma she wanted to be baptised, and her friend took advantage of this tentative consent to baptise her with water from the hand-basin in her room – only to be told gently that "at least it could do no harm".

In August, to avoid the summer heat in London, she was moved to a sanatorium at Ashford, Kent. Unable to eat, and by now far beyond any desire for recovery, she greeted her room, which had a view of fields, as "A beautiful place in which to die". The faithful Miss Dietz was her last visitor, to whom Simone described herself as "One of the pieces God cut out badly." Only a week after being admitted to the sanatorium, her brave heart ceased to beat.

A coroner pronounced the cause of death as cardiac failure, due to pulmonary tuberculosis and starvation, adding that she had killed herself by her refusal to eat "while the balance of her mind was disturbed." Her mind – disturbed? – the mind that had been the stronghold of reason, drinking always at the fountain of truth! It was an absurd verdict, and a final irony.

Her verdict on herself was: "We owe obedience to the powers that be in all things which do not compromise our conscience; if I were to carry out the ideological and political recommendations of Vichy, I should soil my soul, but in observing its rules about rationing, I only risk at the very most dying of hunger, and that is not a sin."

Only nine close friends were able to attend her funeral, and her parents in New York only learned of it after it was over; she had succeeded in keeping her illness from them. She was buried in the Ashford New Cemetery, in a plot where the Jewish and Catholic sections meet.

Since her death, her legacy has accumulated through the publication of her writings. Her political views have been endorsed by subsequent history, and her sociology has been commended as prophetic. As for her mysticism, she made valiant attempts to express the inexpressible. And the gallantry of her life shines out to encourage all those who would follow her way of fidelity to truth and love.

C.S. LEWIS

Clive Staples Lewis was just a Victorian, being born on 29 November 1898.

Though in many ways he was a thoroughly twentieth century man, history does not have a neat cut-off point, and he shared at least two things with his Victorian antecedents: their anxiety at the apparent failure of orthodox Christianity to survive new discoveries in the scientific field, and a triumphant conviction that in the beginning was the Word.

The introduction of compulsory education in England increased the number of readers as nothing else since Caxton set up his printing press in Westminster four hundred years before. The books the Victorians wrote were penned by giants and avidly read.

We seem to have lost the trick of spawning eccentrics in the way they did. Albert Lewis, father of Clive, could safely be called eccentric. He was a Protestant Ulsterman, a solicitor in the Belfast police courts. His parents' means failed to support him in a career as a barrister, but he was well-educated at Lurgan College, County Armagh. His career was punctuated by flights of oratory, and skill in arguing his cases. He was a great purveyor of humour, and recounted many stories known in the family as 'wheezes'. His youngest son resembled him, yet fought against their similarity every inch of the way.

In 1894 Albert had married Flora Hamilton, the daughter of a Church of Ireland clergyman. During a spell when her father was a chaplain in Rome, Flora strayed into a Catholic church where the body of a local saint was preserved in a glass sarcophagus. She saw the eyelids flutter open, and the young woman, later to graduate in mathematics at Queens, Belfast, was not given to flights of fancy. Her account of the incident was not believed; even she thought it was the result of a Papist manipulating cords from some hidden vantage-point. It was her sole brush with the old religion.

A baby son, Warren (known as Warnie), was born of their union a year later. He and his younger brother Clive – self-styled 'Jack' in infancy – seem to have escaped the worst effects of sibling rivalry, and their friendship lasted all their lives. Their first home was in the centre of Belfast (the ship-yard of Harland and Wolff was only a walk away) and their second, 'Little Lea', was situated in the suburbs. It was ugly and inconvenient, but Jack was to love it for its rambling attics, one of which was the 'Little End Room', into which they retired among the pipes and cisterns, to escape from grown-ups.

They lived surrounded by books, and were lucky enough to read Beatrix Potter's stories hot off the press. A particular favourite was *Squirrel Nutkin*, which gave Jack a great love of autumn, and encouraged him to create his own kingdom, 'Animal Land', which was across the sea from his brother's domain, 'India'; they worked together to combine the two countries into a state called 'Boxon'. The inhabitants were talking animals, with the characteristics of the adults around them. Instead of their interest fading as they grew older, they made it 'the' game of their holidays until well into their teens.

This may have been an escape from the tragedy that oc-curred when Warnie, aged thirteen, was away at school in England and Jack was at home, being educated by a govern-ess. Their mother was diagnosed as having cancer. Their father, whose emotions took extreme forms, was beside him-self with grief, and the household took its tone from him; the boys were largely neglected. Jack remembered a night in August 1908 when he was suffering from headache and tooth-ache and longing for his mother's comfort, while she was in fact dying in another room.

In haste, it was decided that Jack should join Warnie at his prep school in England. The idyll that had been his comfort-able childhood was irrevocably at an end. He retained one memory from it, that shone out like a beacon: his first taste of the bittersweet love and longing he was to mean by the word 'Joy'. When he was very small, his brother had walked into the nursery carrying a biscuit-tin lid, on which he had arranged moss, twigs and flowers to make a miniature garden. Jack's future attempts to imagine Paradise referred back to this first conscious glimpse of beauty.

In contrast, Wynyard House School near Watford must have seemed very like hell. It was run by a sadist who ruled his charges through the fear of floggings which were a daily occurrence. The curriculum consisted mainly of arithmetic, but the attempt to drive it into Jack was an absolute failure. On Sundays the boys were taken to an Anglo-Catholic church. In his letters home, Jack made appeals to be taken away, backing them up with descriptions of the Popish practices they were forced to witness. His appeals fell on deaf ears. Jack remained there, even after Warnie had left to go to his public school, Malvern, until a parent brought a court action for cruelty against the headmaster, and the school collapsed.

Bad health put an end to an Irish school education, and it was decided to send Lewis to a prep school called Cherbourg, overlooking Malvern. As it was a spa town, it appeared from faraway Belfast to have the aura of health, and Warnie was at the college not far away. Jack thrived at Cherbourg, enjoying the work and even playing cricket – though as there were only seventeen boys in the school, he probably represented the scrapings of the barrel of talent. He was hopelessly cackhanded, having inherited a disability from his father – the absence of the first joint in his thumb.

During the holidays, he and Warnie received a gramophone as a present from their father, and Jack discovered the delights of Wagnerian opera. His literary tastes tended toward what he called 'northernness', and he devoured the Norse myths.

It was at Cherbourg that he began to regard Christianity as merely one religion among many; for him, it had lost the impact of truth. He ceased to practise it – with relief, because he had begun the rigorous repetition of any prayer that he had not said with sufficient devotion, which led to long hours on

63

his knees. This childish scrupulousness probably dated back to his trying to placate the savage god who had allowed his mother to die, in spite of his prayers for her recovery.

His brilliance as a scholar obtained him a scholarship at his brother's school, and a holiday for his fellow-pupils – in spite of his taking the examination in the school sanatorium because of yet another illness. Warnie had blotted his copy-book by being discovered smoking, and been asked to leave Malvern; he went to cram for entrance into Sandhurst, as he was destined for the Army, so Jack started at Malvern without his presence and advice.

He hated the fagging system which kept him perpetually tired, resenting the time spent working for older boys, when he would rather be discovering Latin, Greek, English and Celtic literature in the library. He even tried a poem in imitation of a Norse saga, called 'Loki Bound'. But this was the summer term of 1914, and the western world was seeing the sunset of an era. For Jack it meant that his beloved brother would be caught up in the war, and he himself would take his place in the household of his best teacher.

William Kirkpatrick had been his father's headmaster, but now lived in Surrey, and was more of a grandfather than a paternal figure.

Thus Lewis escaped the school system, and Kirkpatrick – known to him and to Warnie as 'The Great Knock' – speedily taught him the elements of logic, and how to argue his corner, whoever was his adversary. By a method peculiarly his own, he turned Jack into a skilled translator of classic authors. It was no doubt in admiration of this excellent teacher that Jack came to share his atheism, going through a Confirmation service entirely to please his father. The Great Knock made some attempt to find him friends of his own age among the neighbours, but he was rather too much of an intellectual to enjoy their company. He was often bored, pouring out his inner life in long letters to a Belfast friend, Arthur Greeves; and also in verse that strikes the outsider as peculiarly inept.

A chance purchase of George MacDonald's book *Phantastes* touched a chord that had been unresponsive since his mother died. In the odyssey of a soul becoming aware of itself in a dream landscape, he was able to recapture the voices of his childhood. Lewis was unaware that MacDonald had been through the same tragic loss as himself; he only knew he had met an author who enriched his life as no other ever had.

By 1917 it almost seemed as if the war was going to last forever, and the Great Knock was anxious that he should begin his career at Oxford before he did his military service. In fact he was not obliged to join the Forces – as an Irishman, he was exempt – but he did not wish to escape the common fate of his generation.

He was accepted by University College, provided he managed to pass a nominal examination called 'Responsions'. It was considered he would have no difficulty in doing this, but the paper included some questions on elementary mathematics, and he failed these, even after being coached by the Great Knock. He was finally accepted on condition that he would become a cadet in the Officers Training Corps. There were only a handful of undergraduates in the college, his rooms were luxurious, and he spent a happy time wandering about and drinking in the atmosphere.

Reality broke in with his Officer Training. He had to share a barrack-like room in Keble College, which had been requisitioned. Fortunately his companion was a fellow Irishman called Paddy Moore, a likeable, rather immature young man with a twelve-year-old sister, Maureen. His mother and father were separated, and Mrs Moore lived in Bristol, making frequent visits to see her son, with whom she had a close relationship. They were living through times when the ever-present danger of death (a subaltern's life-exectancy at the front was reckoned in weeks) forged bonds between unlikely people, and Paddy and Jack made a pact that the survivor would look after the other's family.

Jack was trying to keep on good terms with his father, asking him to visit him, but Albert Lewis was drinking heavily and was reluctant to change his regime for any reason. Jack spent his embarkation leave in Bristol with Mrs Moore and Maureen. With the sketchiest of training – he spent a few days in model trenches in the woods near Oxford – he arrived at the front on his nineteenth birthday. Like many ex-public-schoolboys he found the life in the trenches more bearable than his schooldays. The older officers were kindly disposed towards them, and the men generally cheerful and uncomplaining. He learned not to despise people less academically clever than himself, and to communicate easily on their terms.

A bout of 'trench fever', brought on by appalling living conditions, gave him an opportunity to read G.K. Chesterton's essays in a volume called *The Everlasting Men*. It was the manner rather than the matter that impressed him; he was delighted by the glittering paradoxes and the use of hyperbole. He chose to ignore the religious apologetics, but the time would come when he remembered them – thus proving that "a young man who wishes to remain a sound atheist cannot be too careful of his reading."

But this respite came to an end; he was once more in the front line, now finding the smell of death and destruction familiar. One day he saw to his horror a group of men in German uniforms advancing upon him. Minutes later he realised they had their hands up, to denote surrender, and he was credited with taking sixty prisoners. But the German High Command was determined to stake everything on one last offensive. When the big push came at Arras, Jack was there. He was standing beside Sergeant Ayres, a man who was his mentor in warfare and a devoted friend. A shell burst next to them; Sergeant Ayres was killed instantly, and Jack Lewis was peppered with shrapnel.

One of the pieces went close enough to his lung to take his breath away; he believed he had died, and was surprised to find he was not frightened. Days later he was in a London hospital. He had the prized 'Blighty one' – the wound grave enough to warrant being sent home without being too serious. Still his father would not leave Ireland, although he was anxious about his son.

Mrs Moore became a constant visitor, sharing with him her fears for Paddy's safety – he had been posted missing. In the event it was confirmed that he had been killed, and Lewis was left to carry out the pact they had made. In his account of this time, he warned that he would remain forever silent about one particular matter.

"All I can or need say," he wrote, "is that my earlier hostility to the emotions was very fully and variously avenged."

Janie Moore was middle-aged, but still attractive; a woman suffering great distress – a distress he shared. It would have been natural for them to cling to one another in their grief. Even before his marriage – and he did not marry until after Mrs Moore's death, over thirty years later – Lewis spoke of love, including its physical manifestation, as one who had been through the mill. That Janie Moore was his guide in these matters is a reasonable assumption; in any case, no amount of probing by eager scholars has found another.

When he resumed his undergraduate career in Oxford, Mrs Moore and Maureen took rooms there to be near him. He went up to University College in January 1919 as the published author of a book of poems called 'Spirits in Bondage', which had received a muted welcome in the world of literature. As a returning soldier he was excused Reponsions, claiming afterwards that he would never have got into Oxford if it had been a requirement.

His ambition was a fellowship in an Oxford college, and his father was prepared to back him financially until he achieved this aim. Fellows had to be celibate in those days, to comply with college regulations, and Albert Lewis bitterly resented the complication that Mrs Moore represented. So Jack Lewis embarked on a double life, moving between his old home in Ireland and various lodgings shared with the Moores during the vacations.

He was placed in the First Class of Honour Moderations (Classical Literature) in 1920, and straightaway plunged into study for Greats (Ancient History and Philosophy) which he also passed in the First Class, two years later. On the way he collected the Chancellor's English Essay prize. Everything, including the expansion of the English Faculty, pointed to an early appointment. He was advised to stay on another year and take a degree in English Literature to prepare himself as a candidate; this meant appealing to his father for further funds. "Sharing the living expenses" with the Moores was a euphemism for paying most of them out of his own meagre store; Mrs Moore's absent husband was a very erratic contributor.

In his study of English literature, he began to read authors who were committed Christians; particularly Chaucer, Donne, George Herbert and Milton. Gradually he began to find their outlook occupying more and more of his thoughts. He said it was not so much that the Christians were right, as that the non-Christians were boring. A contributory factor may have been that Christianity offered the hope of assuaging the feeling of guilt at being alive experienced by the survivors of the war. He began to notice amongst the nude bathers at Parsons Pleasure that fewer of them were marked by war wounds. The new generation of undergraduates were lighthearted, extravagant and great poseurs – Evelyn Waugh and his cronies represented their type.

Lewis's friends tended to be Christians, and his materialist philosophy was sorely tried. But they had the whole experience of war in common; like them he had lived a tragedy, and paper logic and speculation about it seemed superficial. But he was checked on his road to belief when Mrs Moore's brother, who shared with him a taste for the occult, lapsed into insanity, shrieking out his fear of hell. He became very violent and Lewis had to hold him down while chloroform was administered. When he was removed to an asylum, after a nightmare fortnight, Lewis was convinced that he would never dabble in the occult again.

He was constantly interrupted in his studies by being called to do domestic chores for Mrs Moore, but when he applied for a fellowship in English at Magdalen College in May 1925, he was successful, and he embarked on a pattern of life that was to continue for most of his career. He became the beloved and stimulating tutor of many students – although there were a small number who could not stand him at any price; the penalty of an expansive personality – and was a skilled administrator of his college, and a spellbinding lecturer.

His father, to whom he wrote immediately about his appointment, was able to enjoy his success, but their relationship was stormy. Lewis had never forgiven his sins of omission as a parent, though he did return to share with him the summer of 1929, when he was dying of cancer.

Lewis was desperately uneasy about the emotions that were aroused when they were together, as he had never lost an early fear of his father. A hazy understanding of the new science of psychology had given him a dread of neurosis. These were the barriers to his acceptance of the spiritual life, which seemed to conflict with the cosy everyday comforts he craved. He did not even have his brother's support; it was was not until the following spring that Warnie returned from a posting in China, and together they literally buried the arte-facts of their youthful fantasies in the garden of their old home.

But that summer was memorable for something else; no less than his complete conversion. This took place during a religious experience in the prosaic setting of the top deck of an Oxford bus. He described it as "the voluntary shedding of a shell or constrictive garments that prevented all movement", and said that after he had chosen freedom he felt as if he were melting like a snowman. Not long after this he made a com-plete surrender by kneeling and praying in his rooms; describ-ing himself as "the most dejected and reluctant convert in England."

He was yet to become a Christian, but he was the friend of a practising Catholic, J.R.R. Tolkien, Professor of Anglo-Saxon, not yet embarked on the work which was to make him famous as the creator of the mythical *Lord of the Rings*. However he had begun to write, and it was the privilege of selected colleagues, including Lewis, to hear him reading his work in progress. Lewis had published a saga called *Dymer*, which gave him status among his peers.

In September 1931 he gave a dinner at Magdalen for Tolkien and another friend, Dyson, also a Christian. After dinner they talked for many hours, Tolkien speaking of the Gospel as "the one true myth". The conversation went on into the small hours of the morning, during a walk under the stars.

Nine days later, Lewis made up a party to visit Whipsnade Zoo. His brother was living with him and the Moores, and Lewis went in the side-car of Warren's motor-cycle combination. It was a pleasant trip, with an unexpected outcome. As Lewis reported: "When we set out I did not believe that Jesus Christ is the Son of God, and when we reached the Zoo, I did."

He gave credit to Tolkien and Dyson for their part in this step forward. On weekdays he began to attend the College chapel, and on Sundays his local church; he also wrote his first book of Apologetics, *The Pilgrim's Regress*, based on Bunyan's masterpiece in a modern setting. His college friends took to dropping in on Thursday evenings; by the mid-Thirties they formed the nucleus of 'The Inklings', a dining club of kindred spirits, united by their friendship with Lewis. He tended to be the star of his circle of friends, and may have been referring to himself when making a point about pride:"Each person's pride is in competition with everyone else's pride. It is because I wanted to be the big noise at the party that I am so annoyed at someone else being the big noise."

His conversion gave him a sudden rush of creative energy. He completed several more books, and began to be spoken of both as a scholar and as the author of a succesful space story, *Out of The Silent Planet*. This led to his being asked to tackle a Christian book on *The Problem of Pain* for a small religious publishing-house. Lewis felt under an obligation to respond to requests of this kind, when he could use his talents in the Christian cause. The book became a best-seller, perhaps because it appeared when the world was gearing itself up to another confrontation with the pagans in the form of Nazi Germany.

World War II made very little difference to his way of life; he continued to lecture and give tutorials. His abrasive brilliance half terrified, half inspired his students, but his heavy drinking, chain-smoking style made him seem human to them. He never lost sight of the fact that they were on their way into the services, as he had been in 1917. The flow of books went on – notably *The Screwtape Letters*, a correspondence from a senior devil to a junior devil about to embark on the damnation of a client. Wickedly observant of the foibles of mankind, it has kept its freshness to the present day.

In the preface he described how his protagonists insinuated themselves into the lives of their clients, adding: "There are two equal and opposite errors into which our race can fall, about the devils. One is to disbelieve in their existence. The other is to believe, and to feel an excessive and unhealthy interest in them."

However colloquial his expression, he was always exact in his definition of the tightrope walk of faith.

One chore he undertook was to lecture on religion in RAF camps. A new simplicity was necessary to meet his motley audience, and he developed it in a series of radio broadcasts for the BBC. Their success was overwhelming, and he became one of the spearheads of a revival in the Church of England. In some ways his popularity brought him into conflict with his colleagues – academics not being noted for their charity.

In his talks he pulled no punches. While speaking of the love of God, he did not hide the consequences of experiencing that love.

"It is not wearied by our sins, or our indifference," he wrote," and therefore it is quite relentless in its determination that we shall be cured of those sins at whatever cost to us, at whatever cost to Him."

He made short work of conventional ideas of conversion: "Fine feelings, new insights, greater interest in 'religion' mean nothing unless they make our actual behaviour better; just as in an illness 'feeling better' is not much good if the thermometer shows that your temperature is still going up."

His space odyssey completed, he began to look for new worlds to conquer. Lewis was now in his forties, far from the haunted small boy who had retreated into fantasy in order to escape the pain of his mother's death; he was able to look at that boy steadily, and in the light of his conversion to create a new environment for him that held the comfort of religion. The result was the series known as the 'Narnia' books, which both as literature and drama have delighted children ever since, on two levels – sheer entertainment, but also as an introduction to religious ideas.

By 1949, in addition to all the demands of his writing and

his academic life, he was nursing Mrs Moore, now completely broken in health. Added to this, Warren was drinking heavily. Mrs Moore was removed to a nursing-home where Lewis visited her every day until her death from influenza in 1951. In every way this was a relief from bondage to her whims, but she had also provided a welcome female influence, and kept his feet on the firm ground of ordinary everyday life; he never forgot her enthusiasm and her belief in him.

After all his years at Oxford, he failed to obtain a professorship, baulked no doubt by jealousy of his success outside the university. Cambridge had no such reservations, and gave him a new Chair of English, specialising in Medieval and Renaissance Literature.

In the audience for his inaugural lecture was Joy Gresham, a divorcee with two young boys. She was an American writer, and one of his regular correspondents; a convert from Judaism and communism. Before she ever met him, she had fallen in love with him by correspondence. She was energetic, with a refreshing American directness that disarmed him. She made the best of first impressions on Lewis – she made him laugh.

She lived happily in Oxford for three years, until in 1956 a blow fell that seemed as if it would ruin her hopes; the Home Office refused to renew her permit to reside in England. Lewis made it possible for her to stay by going through a registry office form of marriage, though he found it difficult to reconcile that with the Christian view of marriage. While he strove to solve his dilemma, they lived in separate establishments.

Then Joy developed a series of painful symptoms that were eventually tracked down to two malignant tumours. Lewis's reply to this was to find a clergyman who would marry them. The ceremony took place on Lady Day 1957, at the hospital where Joy was being treated. It precipitated him into the love of his life. For the first time he had found a woman who satisfied his every need, and although he had come to this taste of heaven late in life, there was nothing autumnal in his reactions. It even seemed that a miracle had been wrought in Joy's condition, for the cancer was arrested.

The respite lasted for two years, and then in the winter of 1959 a check-up revealed that the remission was over.

They had planned to go with another couple on a spring holiday to Greece; it would be Lewis's first journey outside Great Britain. The doctors advised against it, but Joy insisted, saying that she would rather like to expire on the steps of the Parthenon. The trip was greatly enjoyed by the whole party – the Lewises in particular being aware that each day was snatched from the jaws of death. They returned to England to await the end; Joy faced it with courage, and it came on 13 July 1960.

After the funeral Lewis began to write out the full force of his grief. It is a moving account that suppresses nothing of the anger or pain, and when it was published thousands of people similarly bereaved could read of their own unexpressed feelings. He continued to read and write and teach, always against the false in literature and religion, and achieved a certain degree of serenity – if that word can describe such a doughty fighter.

In the vacation of 1963 he had planned to go to Ireland with one of his stepsons, but was prevented by a heart attack on 15 June. After a spell in hospital he came home to die. Warren shared his last days, as they had shared the Little End Room of their childhood. On the day that John F. Kennedy was assassinated, another heart attack finally killed him.

After his death, his papers found their way to America, and devoted scholars have produced studies of his extraordinary talents, not unaccompanied by the kind of academic wrangles that dogged their subject. His books continue to circulate around the world, and the story of his marriage has been told on stage and screen, as *Shadowlands*. The book of his broadcast talks, *Mere Christianity*, was read with enjoyment by Pope John Paul II.

But perhaps the greatest tribute to his work is the close attention of a new generation of children to the dramatisation of the 'Narnia' books on television. Through the square box they have passed, as if through the Magic Wardrobe, into the world of Christian myth, providing for many their first picture of Christian life and death.

DESMOND TUTU

The year 1938, so momentous in Europe for crises and rumours of war, was something else entirely for Afrikanerdom in South Africa.

It was the centenary of the Great Trek, when the Cape Dutch sought to escape British imperialism by going north. On the anniversary, their descendants re-enacted their journey, converging on Pretoria from every part of the Union. Each town on their way welcomed the convoy of ox-wagons; the traditional meals were eaten, and the old songs sung. The English minority and the black majority preserved a discreet silence.

At this time, when there were still some isolated pockets of Africans, coloured people of mixed race, and Indians living in white areas, a small boy of seven was being taught his first lessons in racial discrimination.

His father, the product of a mission school education, was a teacher, the headmaster of a Methodist Primary school. The family was to experiment with worship in several nonconformist churches before settling down to steady participation in the Anglican rites. The boy had been baptised Desmond Mpilo Tutu. He had two sisters, one older and one younger than himself. His mother was kind and caring; she suffered in silence when, due to the constant humiliations non-whites were subjected to, her husband took occasional refuge in bouts of heavy drinking.

This did not prevent him from loving his children, and having ambitions for their continuing beyond education at primary level. Desmond responded to his teachers, who speedily discovered that he was exceptionally intelligent. It was not only in academic subjects that he excelled – he was also adept at finding outlets for various money-making schemes, selling oranges and peanuts at a profit, and in spite of being a rather frail physical specimen, caddying at a local golf-course.

When he was fourteen he attended Western High, a government secondary school situated near Sophiatown. It was the only High School in the West Rand, extremely overcrowded, and short of basic equipment. It was much too expensive to commute from his home every day, so Desmond lived in a hostel run by an Anglican order called the Community of the Resurrection. A friend from his family township was among his companions – Stanley Motjuwadi, future editor of the African magazine *The Drum*. At weekends they whiled away the train journeys to and from their homes by practising card-sharping on their fellow passengers, whom they regarded as fair game.

It would have been easy for Desmond to get on the wrong side of the law, but he inherited his parents' honesty and would not join in the petty thieving that went on in the school. He knew that confrontations with the authorities were to be avoided, though he was not averse to a little gentle teasing of white railway officials, and he was proud of his colour at a time when general black consciousness was still in the future.

As a child, his heroes were outstanding black sportsmen and musicians – Jesse Owens, Paul Robeson, Louis Armstrong among them – but he also began to meet white people who treated him with courtesy and encouraged his talents. He met his principal benefactor through what seemed to be a disaster: one day he was travelling through Sophiatown when he had a devastating attack of breathlessness. Investigations at the Rietfontein Hospital showed that he was suffering from tuberculosis. The treatment was to collapse the lung and take the drug P.A.S. Recovery was slow, and involved complete bed-rest.

For a lively teenager it was a terrible blow. He had been due to sit his Junior Certificate, and without taking this step on the ladder it looked as if he would lose his chance of climbing out of the common rut. But help came in the form of visits from his friend Stanley Motjuwadi, who passed on his school notes – and, even more importantly, from Father Trevor Huddleston of the Community of the Resurrection.

Although he was not their chaplain, he made repeated visits to the hospital where so many of the patients were hopelessly dragging out their lives in the last stages of TB and syphilis. Young Desmond had the buoyancy of youth, even though his progress was not without setbacks. On one occasion, after a bad haemorrhage, he faced the prospect of death and found that his Christian faith sustained him. Knowing that he wished to keep up with his schoolwork as far as possible, the busy priest obtained the books that his classmates were studying and brought them in for him. When he was well, his staple literary diet had been the popular comics of the day, but now he relished English classics, and a whole new world opened up for him.

The friendship with Father Huddleston was not one-sided. Desmond's courage and spiritual resource impressed the older man. For two years he visited him every week, and when Desmond returned to the community he welcomed him to the Church of Christ the King in Sophiatown, where he made his first serious confession.

To his disappointment, Desmond had fallen behind in his work, but he was allowed to move up the school and soon recovered the lost ground. Although he had developed an atrophied right hand he made light of the disability, joining in all the games that went on in the township. He was popular with younger children, as well of those of his own age, and as an altar-server he passed on his experience to others.

At nineteen, he passed the examination of the Joint Matriculation Board of the university of South Africa in six subjects, including the three languages most used in the country – English, Afrikaans and Zulu – together with mathematics, history and zoology.

While he had been totally committed to his studies, commuting from his home to Sophiatown and doing his homework by candlelight as there was no electricity in the township, the much-hated Nationalist Government had passed laws tightening the bonds of apartheid. In addition to those concerning the carrying of passes by every non-white leaving his tribal homeland, which had been in force for many years, there were now harsher penalties for non-observance.

Each individual was categorised by bureaucrats into 'White, African or Coloured'. Some of the tests were absurd; one consisted of putting a pencil in the hair – if it was retained by the tightness of the curls the verdict was 'African' – if it fell through, the designation was 'Coloured'. This arbitrary test sometimes resulted in brothers and sisters receiving different judgments. Once labelled, there was no appeal, and the appropriate restrictions applied. The object of apartheid was to separate the races, keeping the blacks in ghettos, ironically called 'Homelands' although they were often forcibly removed from their homes to populate these reserves, which were always the poorest land available. Sexual contact between the races was forbidden by a law, called the Immorality Act.

The black population existed simply as a pool for labour in the white-run mines, farms and factories, and as servants in white homes. This was the prospect waiting for the overwhelming majority of young blacks leaving school. But with his matriculation certificate, Desmond Tutu had joined an elite, and could hope for a university education. Of course it was segregated, and when he entered the Bantu Normal College, near Pretoria, he discovered that he had to live in a round thatched hut, considered more suitable for Africans than conventional buildings. His old friend Stanley Motjuwadi was a fellow-student, and they were studying for the Teacher's Diploma.

Desmond obtained this in 1954 and was offered a post as a teacher in his old High School. This was a train-ride away from his parents' home, where he was still living, and he used this to keep up with his marking, so that the evenings would be free for him to study for an external BA degree.

It was one of his father's brightest ex-pupils, a girl called Leah Shenxane, who caught Desmond's eye. Although she was a friend of his younger sister, and had been in and out of the Tutu home for years, it was only when he had obtained his degree in 1955 that he felt he could contemplate marriage. He knew that this meant the end of any vocation he might have had to join the Community of the Resurrection.

Something else had come into his life – politics. Although he did not yet take any active part, through Robert Sobukwe who had helped him with his studies for his degree, he was brought into close contact with people who wanted majority rule in South Africa. The great leader, who later became President of the Pan-Africanist Congress, was described by Tutu as being: "...Too great to have a base or mean thought, and so quite amazingly he was untouched by bitterness, despite the unjust and cruel experiences he underwent for what he believed in with all the fibre of his being."

The wedding photographs of Desmond and Leah Tutu show a rather solemn young couple – he, slight in a well-cut suit – she, at once statuesque and vulnerable in a dress and veil of almost Edwardian formality. The best man was his boyhood friend Stanley Motjuwadi, and it was remembered as a joyful occasion, celebrated in a blend of European and African ceremonies.

The young people began their family without delay. The first child was a boy; they named him Trevor for Father Huddleston, and his birth caused his father to remark:"Having a son as a first-born means you have arrived – you have made it." And, more humbly: "You have a kind of religious experience when you see your child for the first time."

Desmond was a remarkably successful teacher. Although his career in teaching was short, he was still remembered by his students thirty years later. Other teachers relied on corporal punishment to keep order; his enthusiasm, even for subjects with which he felt no obvious affinity, kept his pupils spellbound.

But the Bantu Education Act of 1955 had altered the curriculum. It sought to ensure that African children would only be taught 'useful' subjects, cutting to the bone any time spent on academic work, and treating them as the labourers they were intended to be in the future. It was considered that they did not need desks and books, but picks and hoes. This travesty of education was not what Desmomnd Tutu had come into the profession to impart, and he decided to leave –

though not immediately. He stayed for three years to see his youngest students complete their course. By this time he and Leah had added a daughter to their family.

Now Desmond had to decide what to do with his life. For an African, the most prestigious job was that of medical doctor, but he could not afford to go back to student status for the length of time necessary to qualify. Teaching came next, but the conditions imposed were impossible. There remained the office of priest in the Anglican Church. He claimed no great mystical call; he was merely a devout churchman looking for a career. But there are times when God takes over and orders things in his way. So it was to be with Desmond Tutu.

After he had been accepted as a candidate for ordination by the Bishop of Johannesburg, he went to the African College – St Peter's, Rosettenville – which was run by his old friends, the Fathers of the Community of the Resurrection. Desmond followed the course for the Licentiate of Theology, considered equal to that of white ordinands. But apartheid had even crept into the Churches, African priests were less well paid and of lower status than white ones, and black worshippers were confined to benches at the back of the congregation, and were only admitted to Communion after the whites had received.

Desmond was acclaimed as a brilliant student, given private tuition because he was so far ahead of his contemporaries. One of his teachers said he was an assimilator rather than an original mind, and that he surpassed all the white students at their sister-college in Grahamstown. He added: "It is greatly to his credit that he didn't become an intolerable little prig."

However, fathers of young families frequently get cut down to size, and Leah and the children were his sheet-anchor – even though he could only see them during the vacations.

The Fathers did not conduct their spiritual lives in an ivory tower, but brought them out into the market-place. His father-confessor, Father Timothy Stanton, served a prison sentence rather than testify against two of his students in a subversion trial.

As yet Desmond Tutu had not been affected by the great wave of black consciousness that emerged during the fifties.

He followed his father in being content with his position in life, and his contacts with whites were on the whole encouraging; he could even feel superior to many of them. But in the final year of his studies, something happened that even he could not ignore.

On 21 March 1960, a crowd of some ten thousand supporters of the Pan-Africanist Congress – a new militant group who went further than the African National Congress along the road of 'Africa for Africans' – met at Sharpville.

They were waiting for a promised declaration about the relaxation of the pass laws, which had been constantly flouted. There was a heavy presence of armed police, who panicked at the sheer size of the demonstration, and without receiving any orders fired into the crowd. Sixty-nine people were killed, and nearly two hundred wounded. In an attempt to restore order in the riots that followed, the A.N.C. and the P.A.C. were banned, and a state of emergency was declared.

The Bishop of Johannesburg tried to alert the world to the tragedy unfolding in South Africa. He came to St Peter's College and was welcomed rapturously by the students: the government eventually deported him.

In December 1960 Desmond was ordained deacon, and took up a post in an African location. Here his vocation was tried to the uttermost, because the living conditions were appalling. By now the family had a second daughter, and they were housed in a garage which provided space for one room and a kitchen. The rector was a hard taskmaster, and believed in his deacons 'roughing it'. It must have been a great shock for the best student St Peter's had produced, but no complaint from Desmond was ever recorded. Leah too accepted their hardships.

After a year he was ordained priest. The Rector chose to ignore Leah and the children, and they might have missed the ceremony altogether if a friend had not provided transport to Johannesburg. Desmond was appointed to a new church in one of the townships created to house Africans moved out of white areas. The living conditions, though ramshackle, were more spacious, and a four-bedroomed municipal house was their home. Although nominally answerable to a superior,

Desmond actually ran the parish by himself, growing in power as a preacher and delighting in the ministry to his flock.

But he was not destined to live in a backwater for long. His superiors had been looking out for an African ordinand with sufficient scholarship to profit by a degree course in London; the aim was to provide a black member of staff at St Peter's College, and Desmond Tutu had been earmarked for the role. Several bursaries and scholarships enabled him to take up residence in September 1962. After a couple of months a flat was found for him in Golders Green, where his family soon joined him, dispelling his initial feeling of loneliness. He took on some of the Sunday duties in the parish and found that his white congregations were much the same mixture of easy and difficult personalities as the black ones to whom he was accustomed.

He and Leah found it difficult to adjust to the heady freedom of movement in London. They were utterly unused to going about without a pass, and being able to share every facility with the white population; it was like being freed from an enormous weight. Their flat was a haven for all kinds and conditions of people, as they shared their joy in these new surroundings, and Desmond did well in his degree, receiving an Upper Second.

It was decided that he should stay on and take a Master's Degree. He chose Islam for his thesis, as it was a major factor in the religious make-up of Africa. He applied for a curateship in a poorer parish than Golders Green, as he felt it would be a more useful experience in preparation for returning home. But Providence decided otherwise, and he was sent to a typical village in the Home Counties commuter belt – Bletchingley – where he and his family scored a great success with both the people from the council housing estate and the local gentry. Their children were made particularly welcome, another baby being added to the family in 1963.

Desmond had written to the Dean of St Peter's College: "If I go back home as highly qualified as you can make me, the more ridiculous our Government's policy will appear to earnest and intelligent people."

His way of helping his fellow blacks would not be through

militancy but by proving his ability to take the highest office and use the power and influence it gave him for the general good.

His return to South Africa, where the doors of the prison had closed on many activists, was a grim reminder of government domination in every phase of life. It was tempered for him by living on the campus of a seminary shared by four of the South African Churches for the education of African priests. It was run on non-racial lines, and as one of six lecturers, Desmond Tutu managed to capture the love of his students and faculty members alike. He would not countenance any lowering of standards for blacks, determined that they should earn the respect he himself enjoyed.

The college was at Alice in the Eastern Cape, very near the birthplace of the Black Consciousness Movement led by the South African Students Organisation – whose first president was Steve Biko. Tutu was the chaplain of nearby Fort Hare university in 1968 – the year of international student protest. Those at Fort Hare were trying to meet their white Rector, "to persuade him to treat them as responsible human beings, not as a lower form of human life."

Getting no response, five hundred of the five hundred and fifty students sat down on the campus lawns for several days. The Rector called in the police, who arrived in armoured cars, equipped with riot weapons that included tear gas. When they were surrounded, the students sang freedom songs. No-one was allowed through the police cordon until Desmond Tutu came and insisted on joining them. He remained with them until the last one was expelled from the campus at gun-point; his grief at their treatment affected him for ever after.

Although he was due to become Vice-Principal of the seminary in 1970, he decided to move to the university of Botswana, Lesotho and Swaziland, where his children could be educated in an atmosphere free from the poison of apartheid. He was well aware how it could seep into the very fibre of a black's personality and cause a crushing feeling of inferiority. He was his father's son in believing that only education could combat this evil. While he was in his new post, he was hammering out for himself and others the black theology that would liberate his people, comparing them to the Jews in bondage in Egypt, and believing that they too would reach the Promised Land.

He was tempted away by the offer of a post with the Theological Education Fund in London. This had been set up to improve theological education in the Third World, and was administered ecumenically.

Distributions were made on the recommendation of those, like Desmond Tutu, who observed the needs of their area in the field. He saw at first hand the fall of Haile Selassie, experienced the ruthlessness of Amin's soldiery in Uganda, and was saddened by the devastation made by war in Biafra. In spite of incessant travelling, he nourished his spiritual life, and when in England he served as an Honorary Curate at a parish in Bromley, Kent. His knowledge of the situation in all parts of Africa was unrivalled, and he built up a network of contacts throughout the continent.

In 1974 he was in the running for election as bishop of Johannesburg, but was narrowly defeated by the Dean, Timothy Bavin, who immediately invited him to take the post he had vacated. It might have been premature to elect a black Bishop, and Desmond Tutu was not the man to sigh after what might have been. One of his greatest assets as Dean was his contact with the black majority – he took up residence in the township of Soweto, among the least privileged, and did much to make the cathedral a meeting-place for them, giving them a share in its administration.

Living amongst black people made him aware of the explosive temper of the young blacks. He said that he was, "...worried that many whites don't want to know just how deeply hurt and disillusioned blacks are; and change may come too late for it to be significant and peaceful."

He was untiring in his efforts to make the voice of the Church heard in a ministry of reconciliation. Inevitably he was accused of going too far and too fast by those with an interest in preserving the supremacy of the white government, and his enthusiasm and generosity were criticised as extravagance.

Two years later, in June 1976, the disaster he had predicted took place when thousands of children from Soweto made a mass protest against their segregated school system. Police gunfire killed six hundred children and older students within the space of a few weeks.

On the first day of the protest, Tutu was called out of the cathedral, where he was acting as Vicar General in the absence of the Bishop, and strove to dissipate the bitterness of the children and their parents. He was not able to restrain his emotion at this tragedy, which spread to other parts of the country. But he had already accepted the bishopric of Lesotho, and had to leave South Africa to take it up.

During the time he was there, which was only a few months, he spoke out against the non-elected government, and groomed his local successor Philip Mokuko by making him his Dean, arranging to send him on a tour of overseas bishoprics to show him how things were done abroad. He arranged this through the South African Council of Churches, whose General Secretary he was invited to become.

He accepted one engagement to speak in South Africa. This was to give the funeral oration at the graveside of Steve Biko, after his death in the custody of the Security Police. Thirty thousand people gathered on a day in September 1977 to hear him call them to pray for "the white rulers of South Africa" and for the police "that they may realise they are human beings too."

The following March he took up his appointment, finding in the offices of the South African Council of Churches a model of equality between the races, thanks to good leadership in the past. His own contribution was to introduce daily prayer for an hour at the opening of each day's work. Once a month each of the component Churches arranged a Eucharist for the others. He took a world view, not a regional one, of the issues of the day, calling on the Prime Minister of Israel to stop bombing Beirut in 1982, and deploring the United States' backing of the Contra rebels in Nicaragua.

Although some concessions had been made to the black majority – a few parks were desegregated and some artistic events opened to visits by blacks – the Black Consciousness movement had been banned. The vacuum left by this silenc-

84

ing of their leaders meant that the S.A.C.C. was looked to as the voice of freedom. It represented a Church membership of some 12 million souls, and the annual budget was R4 million.

This huge sum, representing contributions from all over the Union, had been maladministered, and the Man of Prayer had to appoint an outside accountant to investigate the damage. As the evidence of financial fraud and simple incompetence emerged, his reputation was tainted by the adverse publicity. Charges of lack of integrity moved him to tears, but the irregularities were shown to date back to his predecessor's regime.

He backed the agencies that looked after uninentional breaches of the Pass Laws – a huge task – and strove to lighten the burden of those forcibly removed from their homes in white areas. Incessant travelling was necessary to raise funds for the work from overseas donors, since most member Churches were predominantly black and poor. Cautiously at first, then with more vigour, the S.A.C.C. accepted that its members would fight the government in a non-violent way – the Ghandian principle of civil disobedience. Desmond Tutu also gave his endorsement to the policy of international sanctions against the South African government as long as the apartheid laws existed, and proclaimed common cause with the banned African National Congress.

But his strong stand was tempered with loving kindness. When political prisoners were allowed to study, he welcomed the gesture. It was in the spirit of Christian charity that he went to a meeting with P.W. Botha in 1980 to discuss racial issues, but he and his delegation could make no impression on the official point of view. Yet the very fact that he had tried to speak out was held against him by both black and white militants.

He went about the world in a blaze of publicity. The government was seriously worried by the influence of the S.A.C.C. and ordered an investigation into its funding. The commission of inquiry took over a year to find that although there was some evidence of poor book-keeping, there was no evidence of misappropriation. Desmond Tutu's appearance as a witness brought him once more into prominence, so the authorities who had sought to undermine him were instrumental in their own defeat.

In 1984, while Desmond Tutu was a visiting lecturer at an American seminary, he received notice that he had been awarded the Nobel Peace Prize. Immediately he was the centre of attention for the world's media. Far from being overcome, he welcomed the chance to use the platform he had been given to act as the voice of his beloved people. When he returned to his own country, he was welcomed by a great crowd at the airport, singing and dancing with joy. Bishop Tutu and his wife joined them as they bowed their heads in a prayerful rendition of 'Nkosi Sikele i'Afrika'. Both he and the Nobel Committee made it clear that the award was being made to "all individuals and groups in South Africa who, with their concern for human dignity, fraternity and democracy, incite the admiration of the world."

Bishop Tutu was asked to address the United Nations Security Council and one of the committees of the American House of Representatives, but in these speeches, and in his acceptance of the Peace Prize in Oslo, he refrained from triumphalism, impressing everyone with his humility and gratitude for the honour done to his people.

His election to the bishopric of Johannesburg was assured; he was the first black to hold the post. The news was not universally welcomed, but the dissident voices were barely heard above the clamour of joy. His new diocese comprised almost a third of Anglican South Africans, including many right-wing whites. He kept a base in Soweto, wishing to preserve his solidarity with the life of his black brothers. This was even more necessary, as killings had become a commonplace, not only between black and white, but also between black and black.

Owing to the longstanding government policy of 'divide and rule', the tribal frictions had erupted into open warfare. Worse, those accused of collaborating with the authorities were subjected to the infamous 'necklace' killings, which caused a great loss of sympathy abroad for the African liberation groups. While conducting a funeral service for some blacks killed in an explosion, Bishop Tutu hauled to safety a man attacked by a crowd baying for blood.

A state of emergency was imposed in 1985, and crushing restrictions placed on press coverage of such events. Unable to speak freely at home, he made speeches in England and America, unafraid to criticise the powerful – including Margaret Thatcher's and Ronald Reagan's stand on sanctions. When rioting took place in the townships, he did his best to diffuse tension.

In an attempt to douse the flames of revolt, the Immorality Act was repealed in 1986, but the first hint of approaching change caused the oppressed to call for more evidence of further freedom. Rioting continued, even when the hated Pass Laws disappeared. Then Bishop Philip Russell announced his retirement as Archbishop of Capetown, the Primate of the Anglican Church in South Africa. There was an overwhelming vote for Desmond Tutu to fill the vacancy.

Hundreds of whites attended his farewell service in Soweto, carrying flowers and making a chain with the black congregation, united in a chant of 'Peace, Peace'. A flood of progressive legislation came in 1991, and a National Peace accord was signed by representatives of the government, the African National Congress, and the smaller splinter parties.

Archbishop Tutu is now more of a Churchman and less of a politician, but wherever he speaks he insists on co-operation and non-violence. This devoted son of his country, with his vivid contemporary language and his appeal to a wide spectrum of people, sheds tears with those who mourn, and yet can utter the rallying cry: "We are going to stride into this great new future, this new South Africa – this non-racial South Africa, where people count, not because of the colour of their skins, but where people count because they have been made in the image of God."

POPE JOHN XXIII

The weekend of 26-28 October 1962 was a crucial one in the history of the world. America's first Catholic President, John F. Kennedy, and Nikita Krushchev were confronting each other eyeball to eyeball, though half a world apart. Russian ships were sailing toward Cuba with warheads to arm the missile sites nearing completion, destined to be targeted on mainland America; Kennedy had announced a blockade to prevent them from arriving at their destination. Mankind held its breath, afraid to disturb the silence of the impasse, while peace was threatened as never before.

Held in the tension, the contestants must have been as close as father and son in their lonely eminence. Pope John, the good Pope, elected in 1959 as a stop-gap, who had captured the heart of the world, had added his voice, appealing for a change of mind in the statesmen confronting one another. It seemed a forlorn hope, but it made the front page of *Pravda*, and was the first sign of the Russian withdrawal. Both Kennedy and Krushchev thanked the Pope for his intervention.

Behind it was a lifetime spent in a personal search for humility and holiness, and a public life conducted with shrewdness, tact and unquenchable optimism. Sunday the 28th was the Feast of Christ the King, and Pope John's fourth anniversary of his pontificate. To the crowds that thronged St Peter's Square he brought the news that they could exhale, breathing the spirit of love into the relationships between nations.

John XXIII was born a peasant, in a village near Bergamo called Sotto il Monte, and baptised on the day of of his birth, 25 November 1881, Angelo Giuseppe; the family name was

Roncalli. He was the fourth child and first son in a family that when complete numbered ten. That was the number of brothers and sisters, but the house also contained cousins, uncles and aunts, and it was rare that less than thirty sat down to the simplest of food; it did not go far among so many. The farm that fed them only covered five hectares, and although they used every inch to produce a living, they had to pay part of the crop to the landlords, and survival was precarious. In spite of their poverty they spared something for those they considered less fortunate, and found room for them at their crowded tables.

Angelino – as he was known during his childhood – was surrounded by love that was shown in practical ways, and never restrictive. When a new baby was delivered in the parental bed, and he had to leave it, his godfather, great-uncle Zaverio who had never married, took him under his wing. Zaverio was pious, reading the local Catholic press and devotional books, and kept the family in touch with the latest innovations in the missions at home and abroad. He was a member of Catholic Action, pioneered in Bergamo, and persuaded the family to save, and to approach the Credit Bank for a mortgage to buy their farm. It took them twenty years, but they did it. Although Angelo Roncalli was never a businessman, he was careful not to incur expenses he could not afford, and never lost an interest in the economics of rural life, since he always kept a toe-hold in his native village.

Three years education at primary level became compulsory when he was six. The system was administered by the state, and replaced a network of small Church schools. The battle for Angelo's mind had already been won by the local parish priest, Father Rebuzzini, for whom he served Mass and who saw that he was prepared for Confirmation and First Communion when he was eight; which was considered young according to the practice of the time.

He welcomed the experience with a child's innocent fervour, and confessed to a girl cousin that he wanted to be a priest – an ambition conceived so early he could not remember a time when it had not ruled his life. His openness was so apparent, it was noticed by Father Rebuzzini, who humorously pointed out the penalty of wearing a stiff Roman collar in the sweltering summer heat.

Then there was a false start when he received Latin lessons from a rather terrifying priest in a neighbouring parish, who bullied all fluency in the language out of him. Father Rebuzzini, who had kept an eye on him, came to the rescue, coaching him for entry into the junior seminary at Bergamo. At the age of eleven he set out on the long road to the priesthood, leaving home and family like the disciples of Jesus in the early Church.

The object of the junior seminary was to foster vocations and keep the young unspotted from the world. The foundation, by St Charles Borromeo, a reforming bishop in the sixteenth century, was an attempt to produce clergy of exemplary holiness. Angelo received the tonsure in 1895, the minor orders in 1898 and 1899, and started a journal to record his spiritual life. It was first suggested by his spiritual director, but he derived such profit from the act of writing about his inner thoughts that he practised it ever after. He was scrupulously honest with himself, and almost over-anxious to observe the Rule that was laid down for him.

His hobby was history. Bergamo was full of it – painters and musicians of international renown had worked there, Donizetti and Tiepolo among them. The country boy responded to the beauty on display in the churches, while carefully averting his gaze from the distractions of the town. His models were three Jesuits who had died young and been canonized for their purity: Sts Aloysius Gonzaga, Stanislaus Kostka and John Berchmans. He read about them in the pious histories of the day, in which the reality of their sixteenth century existence had almost disappeared, and decided to model himself on them. He strove to monitor his entire day for lapses from purity, and even tried to carry the practice over into his sleeping hours.

The Journal records his battles with pride and ambition, understandable in a poor boy escaping the poverty of his family by the ladder of education. Anxious relatives may well have fanned the flame, seeing in his possible elevation an advantage to themselves. Nepotism, though hardly on the scale of earlier times, was not unknown at the turn of the century; but Angelo Roncalli closed his ears, and set his mind on becoming a pastor, a carer for souls.

He created a favourable impression on his tutors, until a gossiping Franciscan friar chose to think that his mother was spoiling him during the holidays, and passed on the information to his teachers. Their subsequent reprimands, entirely undeserved, he regarded as an opportunity to practise his admired virtue, humility.

In spite of the mischief-making Franciscan, his superiors appointed him prefect over his fellow pupils and put him in charge of the newly-established Gregorian chant. While visiting in another parish in 1899, he met a canon of St Peter's in Rome called Monsignor Radini Tedeschi, a leading light in Catholic social action, who was organising pilgrimages for the following year, the beginning of the new century, which had been declared holy.

The young seminarian and the official of the Curia struck an immediate rapport, and it was settled that if he did get the scholarship at the Roman college, open to students from Bergamo, he was to join Mgr Radini's group 'Our Lady's Club', which included study and action on social questions. He returned from a pilgrimage to Assisi and Loreto to discover that his hard work had been rewarded by the scholarship, and he set off for Rome in January 1901, to be met with a friendly welcome from the college staff with whom he began to establish close ties. On his first Sunday he received a personal blessing from the Pope.

Pope Leo XIII was over ninety, but in spite of his great age he survived the long ceremonies of the Church with a dignity that impressed the young country boy, who was still uneasy on some social occasions. He was not at all uncertain when it came to study, passing his exams in the summer with the honour of a prize for a paper in Hebrew.

But he was not to enjoy these congenial surroundings uninterrupted. The civil authorities did not exempt the clergy from military service, and Angelo Roncalli received his call-up papers. When he was just twenty he reported to the barracks of the Lombardy Brigade in Bergamo. Although his term had been reduced to twelve months, the conditions appalled him, and he was deeply unhappy. It was not the physical deprivations, which were certainly no worse than he had endured from his childhood; it was the lack of time for meditation and the performance of his religious duties, as the raw recruits were turned into soldiers. In fact it was probably what he needed to keep him in contact with the robust humour of ordinary men, as they boasted of their amorous adventures and tussled in the barrack-rooms. He was deeply shocked, but he weathered the storm, rising to the rank of sergeant; popular with his superiors and subordinates alike.

When the year was over he went back to the seminary, thanking God for the preservation of his vocation; his 'motherly care' as he somewhat unusually expressed it. He applied himself to his studies with fervour, making up for his absence, and though by no means a Modernist, he was attracted to the liberal wing of the Church. Gradually he realised that he could not become a carbon copy of his admired saints, but with their help God was calling him to perfect his own distinct soul.

Leo XIII died in 1903 and was replaced by Pius X, just as Angelo was ordained into the diaconate. It soon became clear that Pius was to be a conservative Pope, and where he led the Church would follow. The young ordinand was already working out his own compromises, resolving upon a middle way. Then on 19 August 1904 he was ordained priest. Afterwards, in a state of great spiritual joy, he claimed that a statue of Our Lady near the altar had seemed to smile at him. He said his first Mass in the crypt of St Peter's, and pledged himself to "the service of Jesus and of the Church" – a vow he repeated to the Pope when received in audience several hours later. The Pope approved his intentions, asking him about his native village and commenting graciously on Bergamo.

He went home for the Feast of the Assumption to the acclamation of those who had known him all his life, then returned to Rome for further studies and made his first attempt at public speaking. His subject was the Immaculate Conception, and – conscious that he had chosen far too ornate a style – he tried to make it simpler but only succeeded in becoming hopelessly confused. The humiliation bit deep, but he was always ready to correct his faults, and he learned from the experience.

His benefactor Radini Tedeschi, once tipped as Secretary of state, was found too modern by Pope Pius X, and removed to the bishopric of Bergamo. After testing him out, the new Bishop invited Angelo Roncalli to act as his secretary. To someone as devoted to his home landscape as Angelo, this did not demand any sacrifice, and he left Rome without regret.

In spite of the suppression of the Opera Dei Congressi which had been Tedeschi's organisation for the advancement of social reform, he saw that its aims were served in his diocese. His secretary became his devoted lieutenant, and took up journalism in order to explain their point of view. Another important discovery was the numerous volumes detailing St Charles Borromeo's visit to Bergamo in order to carry out the intentions of the Council of Trent, at the time of the Counter-Reformation. These gave new impetus to Angelo's hobby of historical research, providing him with a subject that would last a lifetime. He would always approve the action of bishops to reform their own dioceses, rather than the appointment of outsiders from Rome.

In all he served his Bishop until Tedeschi's death in August 1914, just two days after the demise of the Pope who had blocked his career. At the outbreak of the First World War, Tedeschi's final breath was a prayer for peace. The new Pope, Benedict XV, announced that the end of the war would be the principal aim of his pontificate.

Italy did not enter the war until May 1915, and then against Austria, not Germany. A hefty bribe of post-war territorial gains was offered by the British, French and Russian entente, but the conflict was not popular in Italy. Don Angelo Roncalli was called up almost immediately, and became a medical orderly in Bergamo.

The hospital he was attached to receive casualties from the front. In addition to his medical ministrations, he acted as chaplain, and as he tended the wounded and dying he discovered in their simple acceptance of what happened to them, and their return to the Faith when he offered its comforts, a source of both sadness and consolation. At the end of each demanding day he returned to his room in tears, releasing his pent-up emotion. He never forgot the lessons he received from men whose uncomplaining sacrifice he witnessed. Like Jesus, they were lambs led to the slaughter, and he suffered with them.

While Russia was otherwise occupied with the Revolution in October 1917, the combined German and Austrian armies marched on Italy and occupied a great tract of her northern territory for a time, as the tide of battle turned to and fro. Don Roncalli was too fully occupied with his duties to do more than keep track of the family and hearten them. He was proud that Catholics had played a part in the liberation of Italy, but said more than once: "We are all sinners, all are guilty." It was impossible for him to take a narrowly patriotic view of war.

When it was over he was full of the prevailing optimism, destroyed his army uniform, and embarked on supervising a student hostel. He was never happier than when he was in direct care of souls, and felt that his attempts to claim them for Christ from the Communists and the Fascists was important work. But it was a speech to the National Eucharistic Congress in September 1920, that brought him into the public eye. An audience of bishops and official representatives gave a standing ovation to his discourse on 'The Eucharist and Our Lady'. He managed to avoid an excess of Mariology, while giving the Mother of God her full due, but it was his certainty of a prominent role for the Church in the post-war world that really brought him acclaim.

At that time, Benedict XV was looking for an organiser of missions in the department of the Curia known as 'Propaganda Fide', and Don Roncalli was offered the post. He was reluctant to move to Rome, but his doubts were overcome when several influential clergy declared that it was the will of God. He also accepted the title 'Monsignor'. But he had hardly completed one tour of the European states to see how they managed their missions when his mentor, the reigning Pontiff, died, to be replaced in January 1922 by Pius XI – who showed himself ready to deal with Mussolini's Fascists two years later.

When Roncalli was asked to deliver a sermon to some

students in Bergamo on the tenth anniversary of the death of 'his' Bishop Tedeschi, he was moved to announce his own distrust of the Fascists, who had just won a landslide victory in a general election. This marked him out as a trouble-maker, and his dismissal from his post in Rome was only a matter of time. He survived until 1925, but his star seemed to have set when he was offered the post of Apostolic Visitor to Bulgaria. It was presented as a stepping-stone to a more prestigious post, though he pointed out that he had no aptitude as a diplomat.

When he was convinced that his move was a matter of obedience, he agreed to it. He knew nothing of Bulgaria – an ignorance he shared with his superiors. All that was known was that a state of utmost confusion existed there, and that Moslems, Orthodox, Greek Catholics and Latins were all at each other's throats. His nomination as Archbishop did not dry the tears that his banishment caused him, and his exile continued for eight years.

Then in 1933 he moved sideways to Constantinople – or Istanbul, as the ruler of Turkey, Kemel Ataturk, had renamed the city. Catholics in Greece were also in his care, and he trod a tightrope in that mainly Orthodox country. He needed all his tact and optimism to cope with this post, but in his next he was called upon to be the Papal Nuncio to newly-liberated France in 1944, where he would be treading on eggshells. The elder daughter of the Church, France was riddled with anti-clericalism and undergoing something like another Revolution. Charles de Gaulle, a pious autocrat, led a nation plagued with guilt about its collaboration in the German Occupation. Suddenly everyone was an ex-member of the Resistance and politically 'clean'.

Among those who had really suffered imprisonment and exile were idealistic young men who drew their inspiration from the priests among them; but they did not want to serve as priests had done before the war. They proposed going into the factories, sharing the servitude of the workers. An ordination of these young men in Notre Dame was the most moving experience of Angelo Roncalli's nunciature.

But at last he was to achieve what he had always wanted:

the post of pastor, that had so long eluded him. Venice had been a close ally of his native Bergamo for centuries, and after his native landscape it was probably the place where he would feel most comfortable on earth. For a tubby gentleman just into his seventies, Venice, resplendent with jet-setting international visitors in summer, and largely left to itself in winter, was an ideal retirement home. He was as happy with the inhabitants of the palaces on the Grand Canal as with those in the housing estates of the Giudecca.

When he introduced himself to his new congregation he played down his reputation for diplomacy, but admitted that he had some experience of different nationalities and religions. Modestly, he hoped not to be over-praised, and concluded: "I commend to your kindness someone who simply wants to be your brother; kind, approachable and understanding." As an amateur historian he revelled in the history of the place; as pastor he was fully occupied in dealing with the poverty beneath the surface.

In 1954 it was revealed that the Pope was ailing. A self-appointed French prophet wrote a book, predicting that Cardinal Roncalli would become Pope, and the name that he would choose. This dubious volume was sent to him in manuscript, and he was asked to write a preface. He did his level best to denounce it as dabbling in Satanism, and more than hinted that the author was mad. He also rounded on his own nephew, recently ordained, who proposed that the fiftieth anniversary of his uncle's priesthood should be celebrated with some solemnity in Bergamo and Venice. A strong letter revealed that the projected recipient of these honours forbade any ceremony except a simple Mass in his native village.

In fact Pius XII was to live for another four years, during which Cardinal Roncalli continued to grow in wisdom, preparing for his own death rather than for the papacy. Thought about the Last Things was provoked by the deaths of several older sisters, including some who had acted as housekeepers in his various appointments. He trod a path between avuncular availability and firm leadership; as he liked to say: "Neither a tyrant, nor a doormat." On the 4 October 1958, Pius XII died, and Cardinal Roncalli left Venice to attend the conclave that would elect a successor. He was seventy-six; fit, in spite of his weight problem – and only an outsider in the papal stakes.

By the time the fifty-one Cardinals had worked out the kind of Pope they wished to elect, he was rated as a two-to-one possibility. What was wanted was a transitional Pope, neither too young nor too old, whose relatives were not ambitious (Nepotism had blighted the pontificate of Pius XII); capable of dealing with both the Eastern and Western arms of the Church, and – perhaps most emphatically – never too remote and autocratic to consult the bishops. He must also be of great personal holiness.

The Cardinals tried to find who best fitted these specifications. More and more the portly form of Cardinal Roncalli came nearest to matching them, though he was not actually elected until the eleventh ballot; the fewer votes he received, the more cheerful he became.

He recorded in his diary that when he was finally trapped by his obedience to the judgment of his peers, he echoed the words of his predecessor: "Have mercy on me, Lord, according to thy great mercy."

He was hastily robed in a cassock too small for him, the safety-pins securing it hidden under a surplice, and stepped on to St Peter's balcony, where he was blinded by arc-lights, to be greeted by a crowd of three hundred thousand cheering souls.

When he explained his surprising choice of the name 'John', the reasons became clearer. Those who had formerly taken the name were some of the least worthy holders of the office, but as his father's name it had been dear to him since childhood. Even more appropriately, it was the name of both the Baptist, 'the man sent from God whose name was John', and the disciple whom Jesus loved. This convinced many of his hearers that the Holy Spirit had not made such an odd choice after all. There was no sign whatever that during the next five years this humble, chubby figure would inaugurate changes that were to transform the Church.

He made his first broadcast, insisting that part of it was addressed to the Orthodox Churches and "those who are separated from us". His coronation on 4 November, the feast of St Charles Borromeo,(he chose it) took due notice of historical precedent, but included one innovation: a homily he delivered himself, declaring that he wished to be a good shepherd and a brother to his flock. He spoke simply, and his words touched the hearts of his hearers; through television and radio, they reached the whole world.

Later he was to emphasise the importance in Christian life of the Gospel and the Eucharist. Already in the earliest days of his pontificate he was to make more accessible the book and the chalice. It took him time to become used to hearing himself referred to as 'the Pope', often thinking that the reference was to Pius XII. Yet he took the step of creating new Cardinals to bring the Sacred College up to strength, and contrived to make them as internationally representative as possible, including the first black Cardinal. He celebrated Christmas by visiting a children's hospital, and the Regina Coeli prison, where he embraced a murderer who asked if there would be forgiveness for him. Such visits were unprecedented, and had the unexpected result of making the papacy popular again.

As for the Council – although the idea had presented itself to him a matter of days after his election – he pondered whether he was right to follow his inspiration. Anything that smacked of self-aggrandisement was anathema to him. It was nearly a hundred years since Vatican I had been interrupted by the war of 1870. He announced both a diocesan synod for Rome, and an ecumenical council for the universal Church. The news was made public on 25 January 1959, and caused a sensation. This was not what was expected of a stop-gap Pope.

He could not hurry the Curia – "I'm only the Pope around here", he remarked ruefully – but the Council opened three years later, so his influence did expedite the process. He emphasised the need for renewal, and spoke of 'a new Pentecost'. In the meantime his simple, honest stamp was introduced into papal encyclicals and official correspondence. "I cannot possibly say that" was an annotation he frequently employed.

The Roman Synod took place in 1960 and he prepared for it with greater care than he did the Council; in a sense it was his preparation for the Council. It made him Bishop of Rome like no other who had held the office before. He called on his clergy for greater holiness of life, while pledging his help for those whose vocations were lost or spoiled. He urged them to cease acting as magazine editors or parish bank clerks, if these activities interfered with their pastoral care. This contribution was not innovatory, but it was designed to bring the clergy closer to God and their congregations.

The Preparatory Commissions for the Council started work in November 1960. Meanwhile hundreds of suggestions had been made by every kind of authority in the universal Church; advice, disseminated by the media, was not lacking. With the help of a Jesuit, Cardinal Bea, who in spite of the fact that he was six months older than Pope John became his intermediary with the 'separated brethren', as Christians outside the Roman Catholic Church came to be called, and travelled extensively all over the world. It was thanks to him that Christian Unity was an aim of the Council.

In May 1961 one of the most important encyclicals of modern times was published. It reflected Pope John's interest in social questions, the things that governed the lives of his flock. It treated of their rights to a just wage, and to own property (did he remember his family's difficulties in buying their farm long ago?) and also dealt with the right of undeveloped countries to be assisted by the more affluent. But perhaps Pope John's greatest contribution to the cause of the workers was to give a blessing to the idea that the state should be a participant in the welfare of its citizens, who should have a hand in the management of their own industries. Conservatives saw this as an endorsement of socialism, but the bulk of Catholics saw it as opening up to the aspirations of the modern world.

As the Berlin Wall became the concrete barrier between East and West, preparations went on to find a bridge between the Catholic Church and its own dissidents. Addressing a meeting, Pope John stated clearly that the Council would bring the Church up to date. This was the first time it had been said openly, and it made its mark. Although he had grown in stature in the eyes of the world, in his private Journal he remained humble, almost deriding his own efforts at holiness. In following Christ, he measured himself against the highest standards of perfection, and always found himself wanting. Yet he never gave way to despair – it merely spurred him on to greater efforts. This was the darker side of the easygoing, humorous Pontiff depicted on the television screens.

On his eightieth birthday, 29 November 1961, congratulations poured in; notably a telegram from Krushchev in Moscow. The receipient of these greetings was feeling his age, but still managed to enlarge the scope of the Council to include the world and its concerns – not only the Catholic element, which he hoped, "though old, would remain ever young."

The following year the date for the opening of the Council was set for 11 October. Pope John immediately used the diplomacy he had acquired in the East to get Krushchev to agree to the attendance of bishops from behind the Iron Curtain. Krushchev agreed; the Council would be complete. One by one, and then in hundreds, the answers to the invitations to non-Catholic observers poured in, all eager to be at the centre of this 'dialogue with history', as the prime mover put it. For himself, he said in an unguarded moment that his part would be suffering.

Ever practical, he made his will and arranged that his funeral would not be subject to the disasters attending that of his predecessor. In September he submitted himself to a series of X-rays and tests that revealed a terminal illness. His reply was to go on pilgrimage to Loreto and Assisi, making him the first Pope to travel outside the Vatican for nearly a century. By the time he returned, the Council members were arriving in Rome.

He made his opening speech, the climax of a ceremony that began at eight in the morning, and to all who heard it, it was an experience they never forgot. He might be compared with Moses, pointing the way to a promised land, denied to himself.

What he asked for was a new interpretation of faith, which would not sweep away the past but enhance it. The Church would have to make a great leap forward to be fit to survive in the twenty-first century. Language and consciences alike had to be renewed, and all men should become brothers because they had the same Father. So he led on to his last great encyclical, *Pacem in Terris*, on which he was working. Not to be published until the following year, it was in his mind and would show his desire for world peace, his views on the arms race, which included the banning of nuclear weapons, and dialogue with governments of all complexions. It mentioned the rights of human beings that should be respected by everyone, and the growing influence of women in the world.

While he worked on this encyclical he was watching the procedures of the Council. Prominent amongst the Cardinals was Montini of Milan, who was to inherit the Council and complete his work as Pope Paul VI. Pope John kept in touch through a series of private audiences with the bishops, and his influence was as much felt as if he had been present in St Peter's. The conservatives were confounded when he talked of giving "freedom to follow one's own conscience". It began to look as if the Church would turn into a democracy, rather than the benevolent dictatorship it had been.

He was criticised for beginning with the liturgy instead of doctrine, but it was a happy accident – or... the intervention of the Holy Spirit. Ordinary pew Catholics were unaware of doctrine, but knew perfectly well what happened at Sunday Mass. They were to receive some salutary shocks in the following years: hearing the Gospel in their own tongue, seeing the face of the priest as he celebrated Mass. Pope John had said: "The Church has nothing to hide"; by removing the veils of mystery the sacraments were revealed in all their beauty.

This freedom was too heady for many priests and religious, who left their presbyteries and cloisters in droves, but those who remained were faithful, tried and tested and not found wanting. They had, as he had said, "a generous willingness to enter into the heart and mind of the divine plan."

When he gave his concluding speech on 8 December he was a sick man. He called on the bishops not to rest between sessions of the Council but to do their homework and come prepared. They all knew that his own preparations would be for his deathbed, and this gave great poignancy to everything he said. Controversy was to follow him practically to the end; he received Krushchev's daughter and her husband in a private audience, and was accused of encouraging communism. So far was he from this that his gift to Krushchev's daughter was a rosary.

Holy Week and Easter were a torment, and doctors were present at the long ceremonies; he somehow managed to endure them. He gave his last blessing 'Urbi et Orbi', adding messages in twenty-six languages. He spoke of life and renewal; he insisted on seeing all the documents concerning the Council.

By now he was sinking fast, and the world was praying for him; day after day, not only the religious and quality press, but the popular tabloids too, carried headlines about his progress. His request to those around him was that they should help him to die "like a Bishop, or a Pope". The priest who anointed him was so moved, he forgot the correct order, and had to be prompted by the dying Pontiff. On 3 June, the day after Pentecost, just as evening Mass was ending in St Peter's Square, he breathed his last.

Other Popes have been more learned, or better diplomats; none has ever been more beloved. His fatherly care was obvious to the most obscure congregations far across the world. He carried the Church forward on a great wave of optimism, and the Barque of Peter rides it yet.

OSCAR ROMERO

The volcanic mountains which straddle El Salvador are cultivated with the principal export, coffee, up to their very cones
– not all of which are dormant. When Oscar Romero was six
years old, Mount San Salvador erupted, damaging the city
and ruining the crops with tons of volcanic ash. The people,
some of whom had already weathered earthquakes, patiently
rebuilt and replanted.

El Salvador is the smallest country in Central America,
being just 160 miles at its widest where it borders the Pacific,
and 60 miles across where its boundaries are with Guatemala
and Honduras. Its Indian population was overcome by a lieutenant of Cortez early in the sixteenth century, and the Spanish families who settled there exploited their labour from the
first. However, they found champions in the Church that
baptised them.

Life is hard in El Salvador. Even the winters are hot,
causing thunderstorms and torrential rains in July and August,
followed by a short dry spell during which the precious crops
are sown. In the past, when wars and revolutions were more
gentlemanly affairs, they were never waged during this season, though violence brewed up in the little mountain state,
hemmed in on three sides, ever since it achieved a separate
identity from the rest of Central America in 1823.

Young Oscar Romero was the second boy in a family of
eight, and not baptised until he was two years old, which
argues a certain laxity in religious matters. It was not the only
lapse in his father's life. Oscar had an illegitimate sister who
was born in the same small town, Ciudad Barrios, and continued to live there after his death.

The official family acquired a number of skills outside the school which only provided tuition for three years. Their father was the local postmaster and telegraphist; they learned to send and receive messages, and to work on a small coffee plantation, their mother's dowry. Their house was a little more solidly built than their neighbours, and although a number of the children shared a bed, they were certainly luckier than the majority of the population.

For the most part, the families who formed an oligarchy, and were the power behind whoever happened to be President, were of Spanish origin, and intermarried with Latin-Europeans; they were talked about in whispers. Rumour made even their number uncertain, but it was calculated that 0.7 per cent of the population owned 40 per cent of the land.

When Oscar Romero was growing up during the Thirties, General Maximilian Hernandez Martinez was President, putting down a serious uprising by the campesinos (landless peasants) in 1934 with great loss of life.

When Oscar was twelve years old, his father decided to terminate his education with a private schoolmaster, and apprenticed him to a carpenter, so Oscar Romero learned the trade that his Lord had been taught by St Joseph. He was a good carpenter; a serious boy who liked to do everything well. During breaks in his labours it was noticed that he would take refuge in a nearby church. He was also fond of music, an interest he shared with his father, who passed on his skill in playing the bamboo flute. He taught Oscar to read music, and also insisted that he should learn the simple prayers of the Church: the Our Father, Hail Mary, the Creed and the Hail, Holy Queen. The seed fell on good ground. Gradually it dawned on the boy that he had a vocation for the priesthood.

In 1930 a newly-ordained priest came to say his first Mass in the town; the ceremony was graced by the presence of the Vicar General of the San Miguel diocese. Urged on by the Mayor, Oscar spoke to this influential personage of his desire to attend the junior seminary in San Miguel. Something about the boy impressed him, and soon Oscar Romero was beginning the seven-hour journey on horseback to the distant town. During this time he wrote a poem on the subject of Our Lord as teacher; there may have been more which were not preserved. He always remembered the members of the junior seminary as his adopted family.

By 1937 he had done well enough to move on to the national seminary in San Salvador. This was a pleasant place with shaded squares, a theatre and botanical gardens, reminiscent of a European provincial capital. It was also the scene of his intense grief at his father's death.

A year and a half later, he was on his way to live at the Latin-American College in Rome while he studied at the Gregorian university. Both institutions were run by Jesuits; later, his relations with the Order were to fluctuate considerably. He was noted for his calm, unruffled approach: "Like one who knows that life has to be taken as it comes – rather quiet, a bit shy" wrote a fellow-student. He was also conscientious and academically successful, his writing and speaking being especially notable.

His vacations were sometimes spent in a villa by the sea, where Oscar was put in charge as swimming instructor. He offered to race his pupils to a rock, and owing to his superior skill he arrived first. Unfortunately, as he awaited the arrival of his companions, he sat on some sea-urchins; he tried to keep his dignity by not mentioning the incident, but the infirmarian to whom he confided his plight gave him away. It is certain that this chance to laugh at a rather serious colleague was not lost on his fellow-students.

During the war rations were scarce, and even the Father Rector was not above hunting for food. Some seminaries closed because they could not feed their students, but this one survived. When Oscar received his theology degree *cum laude* in 1941, he was still too young to be ordained, so it was decided that he should prepare a thesis for his doctorate, but before this was completed he received a summons to return to San Salvador.

He was ordained priest in 1943 and embarked on a nightmare wartime journey home. He and a companion were actually interned on their arrival in Cuba, and had to be smuggled into a hospital by some Redemptorist Fathers; when they eventually made landfall in El Salvador they were given a public reception. The young priest made no delay in offering a solemn Mass for his neighbours and relatives, up-country in Ciudad Barrios.

After a few months as pastor of a mountain town, not unlike his birthplace, the Bishop appointed him secretary of the diocese, resident in San Miguel. The shortage of priests in Latin-America has always demanded a high degree of versatility in those who are ordained, and Father Romero was no exception. He became pastor of the Cathedral Church and administered two other parishes, yet found time to see that the half-finished cathedral was completed. He oversaw all the local Catholic societies, from the Legion of Mary to Alcoholics Anonymous. He visited the poor homes of the campesinos, and those incarcerated in the city jails.

He saw to it that Caritas should not merely distribute food to the poor, but give lessons to them on nutrition. Six local radio stations beamed his Sunday Mass to a wider audience, and his homilies became famous. He was also Editor of *Chapperrastique*, the weekly paper of the diocese. In addition, he was Rector of a minor seminary and confessor to various Congregations; in the Bishop's absence, he acted for him. This headlong rush was kept up for twenty-three years.

In 1959 a young man called Salvador Barraza went to hear one of his sermons, and succeeded in being introduced to him. They found that they were relaxed with each other, and enjoyed each others' company, and went on meeting from time to time. Although Father Romero had been exposed to the influence of St Ignatius by his Jesuit mentors, he did not make the Spiritual Exercises until the mid-fifties. When he did so, they made a profound difference to his life. From them he took the phrase he would later use as his episcopal motto: "To be of one mind and heart with the Church'.

This was difficult during the years between 1962 and 1966, when the Second Vatican Council was in session. New ideas and practices poured forth from Rome. Initially, Father Romero was reassured by reading Pope John XXIII's 'Journal of a Soul', and finding that the Spiritual Exercises were as important to the Pope as they were to himself. He acknowledged the need for every priest to renew his life and become a more effective vessel of grace.

But the silver jubilee of his priesthood was imminent, and he had become set in his ways. The new young priests, going about with no sign of their office, meeting women, and restless to make changes in every practice of religion, scandalized him. By now he had considerable power through his radio and journalistic work, and he made no secret of his disapproval. A new Bishop was appointed, who received many requests for his removal.

His anniversary was celebrated with great solemnity and he was given the title of Monsignor, but he was on his way out. The new Bishop was not a delegator, and was anxious to get the effective power wielded by Romero back into his own hands. In spite of protests from Romero's supporters, he was given the post of secretary-general of the national Bishops' Conference, and sent to San Salvador.

There amid the country clubs and luxurious houses the families who wielded the real power entertained each other, sending their children to be educated abroad, alienating them even further from those who served them. Tension mounted, until it was unsafe for them to travel the streets at night. In 1969 another blow fell: Honduras, where the campesinos had found a haven from poverty and unemployment, decided to expel all El Salvadoran nationals.

This threatened the precariously-balanced economy, and created a wave of anger against Honduras. The international press, which had never taken Central American politics seriously, reported that the dispute had taken place over a football match, but this trivialised a crucial problem. A flood of refugees poured into the already crowded country, adding yet more ammunition to an explosive situation.

In April 1970 Monsignor Romero was offered the post of Auxiliary Bishop by Archbishop Chavez. He was given only twenty-four hours to make his decision, and afterwards distrusted the motives for his assent; he sought their purification by making the Spiritual Exercises again. In this he showed his humility and desire for perfection. His episcopal ordination was a great event, in the presence of Church and government dignitaries, and was arranged by a priest called Rutilio Grande, who worked night and day for its success.

Mention must be made of a meeting of Latin-American bishops at Medellin, to discuss the application of Vatican II to South America. The day after Bishop Romero's ordination, a gathering of all the clergy and religious in the country was held in the capital, to bring the decisions of Medellin to El Salvador. Romero took only a small part in these discussions, which in any case were ignored by most of the bishops.

On the agenda was participation by the laity in religious instruction and Bible study-groups – as leaders, not merely followers – a provision which, if accepted, would help to relieve the pressure on the clergy, though at the time they seemed more anxious to preserve their exclusivity.

Liberation Theology, the insistence that social justice was the concern of the people of God, led – inevitably in the political climate of El Salvador – to a conflict of interest between the government and the people. It is certain that Bishop Romero really wished to co-operate with the spirit of Vatican II, but he could not help being cautious, even reluctant to adopt its recommendations. The acceptance of the prevailing injustices was engrained in him, and was part of Christian resignation to suffering. Liberation Theology turned his world upside down: he began to withdraw from close contact with the Jesuits, who were enthusiastic in their welcome of Vatican II and Medellin, and he chose as his companions and confessors priests connected with the conservative secular institute, Opus Dei.

In the autumn of 1970 his friend Salvador Barraza found him ill and unattended in the seminary where he was living. Bishop Romero was prevailed upon to move into Barraza's house, where he was nursed by Barraza's wife, Eugenia. After this he was to spend many spare moments in the family. Barraza was a self-employed shoe-merchant, and could take time out to chauffeur his friend on holiday, and contribute to his comfort and well-being. No doubt this contact with an ordinary family counterbalanced the constant company of clergy – not always well-disposed toward him.

Archbishop Chevez invited him to edit the archdiocesan

newspaper, replacing an editor who had dealt controversially with social questions. Bishop Romero chose to attack drugs, alcoholism and pornography, which were safer targets. Then in 1973 he wrote an editorial drawing attention to the 'Marxist' tone of leaflets circulating in a school run by Jesuits.

His editorship was criticized, and he felt misunderstood and isolated. He took a long vacation in Mexico and derived great benefit from it. After all, he had been overworked for a quarter of a century, and suffered from the resultant irritability and nervous strain. A psychologist described him as "a compulsive, obsessive perfectionist", and he spent three months in therapy, seeking warmer relationships with his colleagues and greater security in making decisions.

A year later he was made Bishop of Santiago de Maria, which he considered an endorsement of his editorship, including his criticism of Liberation Theology. But events were to herald a change in his thinking. There were several incidents which involved the army and police attacking campesinos and even priests, beating and humiliating them. In June 1975 one of these incidents took place in Bishop Romero's own diocese, and six campesinos were hacked to death. The Bishop went immediately to comfort the bereaved, and wrote a letter of protest to the President, although it was couched in respectful terms. But alongside his timidity in approaching the authorities there was a real care for the workers and for the sick.

Invited to attend a meeting of the Political Commission for Latin-America in Rome he delivered a memorandum on the – to him – regrettable preoccupation by priests in El Salvador with politics; particularly the Jesuits. As always, there were willing ears to listen to criticism of the Order. He admitted that the government was militaristic and repressive, but disapproved of opposition to it. Yet on 30 July 1975, troops in San Salvador massacred some forty students, demonstrating against the closure of the university in Santa Ana. Still Romero, ignoring all signs of conflict, sought harmony between government and people. He wanted more piety and less politics in the life of the Church.

Fearful of the chaos threatened by the success of Liberation Theology among ordinary people, it was decided that

Romero's moderation would keep the precarious balance which the Church strove to achieve. He was appointed Archbishop of San Salvador.

But before he could take charge of his Cathedral, tragedy was to strike a close friend. For several years, Rutilio Grande, a Jesuit priest who had arranged his episcopal ordination, had been part of a team running a parish at Aguilares. Like most of the Order he was concerned to use the directives of Vatican II and Meddelin to transform the life of his parish, and he had been called a Communist for his pains. One Saturday in March 1976 he was shot dead with two campesinos as he went to celebrate an evening Mass in an outlying church.

His murder had a profound effect on Romero. Not only had he lost a friend, the priestly office had been desecrated. But in his eulogy he quoted the Gospel: "Father, forgive them, for they know not what they do." What Rutilio Grande stood for was the identity of the Church with the poor, and Archbishop Romero was not quite ready to follow him. Yet from now on it was noticeable that he not only prayed about decision-making, he consulted with everyone whose opinion was relevant, lay and clerical. He became accessible to the lowliest of his flock, and established a dialogue with them.

It was as the head of the Church that he came again to the stricken parish of Aguilares in June 1977, installing a new priest to replace three who had been exiled by the Army. The soldiers had also gone on a hunt to kill unoffending towns-people, and had desecrated the Blessed Sacrament in the Cathedral. Five thousand gathered for the Mass, and listened to his sermon.

He told them: "It is my lot to gather up the trampled, the dead, and all that the persecution of the Church leaves behind", and reminded them that those who lived by the sword would die by it. Such was the power of this shy, timid man when stirred by the suffering of his people, that wave after wave of applause broke out, and the effect of his words was indelible.

He was attacked by the government newspapers and radio stations, and retaliated by using his own propaganda weapons – the archdiocesan newspaper and the radio station which gave air-time to his weekly sermons and a regular programme at mid-week. He also took a step toward protest by staying away from the inauguration of his namesake, President Romero, though insisting that this should not preclude the possibility of dialogue with the authorities. He received support from various bodies abroad, including non-Catholic Christians. Fanmail poured into his office – some letters written on the cheapest paper and signed with thumbprints. He was rapidly becoming the voice of the people, and they expressed their love and gratitude to him, confiding their problems and sufferings to a ready listener.

In a pastoral letter published in August 1977 on the Feast of the Transfiguration, celebrated in El Salvador as the patronal feast of the nation, he urged his flock to revere the gospel. He called on everyone to partake of the sacrament of salvation, and to seek conversion. He quoted the conference of Medellin, when it pronounced that temporal tasks should not be excluded from sanctification, and welcomed at last the evolution of the Church as 'The body of Christ in history'.

Persecution of the Church in El Salvador was the subject of a sub-committee of the United States House of Representatives; the voices of the murdered and 'disappeared' were beginning to be heard. Archbishop Romero agreed to meet the President, making clear to him that no dialogue could be fruitful unless the government showed that it would force those responsible for crimes against humanity to confess and make reparation. The President made some small concessions concerning the intimidation of priests, but he blamed most of the excesses on the capitalists in the country, over whom he claimed he had no power.

At this time Archbishop Romero took up residence at a cancer hospital for patients without means, where he was cared for by the Sisters in charge until his death. He had no wish to live in the luxury of a palace while his flock were for the most part miserably poor. At the grass-roots, a revolution had taken place; teams of priests and lay catechists were evangelising the townspeople and campesinos, who were responding with fervour. The blood of the martyrs was once again nourishing the Church, as it had done long ago after

Pentecost. But in the new situation, new methods were necessary, and these same evangelists were preaching Liberation, along with the Word.

Meanwhile the Papal Nuncio and some of the bishops were still trying to paper over the cracks in the relationship between Church and state, making Archbishop Romero more isolated at the apex of the hierarchical pyramid. Added to his broad support amongst parish clergy were a number of groups abroad, and in January 1978 he was awarded an honorary degree by Georgetown University of Washington D.C. In his acceptance speech he spoke of it as "a gesture and a voice of solidarity that inspires and gives hope to those who here suffer violence against their fundamental rights in so many and such humiliating ways."

A series of massacres and arrests during Holy Week led the popular parties to occupy the Cathedral and several embassies in retaliation. Such things became increasingly frequent as one of the only gestures open to the people. Romero supported the victims of oppression and denounced judges who ignored signs of ill-treatment in those who appeared before them. He never ceased to bring before the authorities cases of people who had 'disappeared', demanding to know their fate.

In June, on a visit to Rome, he strove to bring the plight of his clergy and people before various secretariats, and correct the erroneous impression they had received from the Nuncio to El Salvador. In an interview with Pope Paul VI he received commendation for his stand; afterwards he described how, taking both his hands, the Pope spoke "words of encouragement and understanding, and made me the messenger of his great pastoral affection for our people."

Later in the year the Latin-American hierarchy gathered in Puebla, Mexico, for their third general meeting. One of their declarations was that "the fear of Marxism keeps many from confronting the oppressive reality of liberal capitalism". It could not have summed up Archbishop Romero's previous fears better; but now he refused to be intimidated, and chose the path of patience and courage and solidarity with the oppressed.

By 1979 relations with his country's bishops had deteriorated so much, Pope John Paul II suggested the appointment of an Administrator for the archdiocese, leaving Romero as a figurehead; but when the Archbishop outlined his objections, the Pope – who had experienced similar difficulties in his own country in confrontations between Church and state – was sympathetic .

When he returned to El Salvador, he was met with the news of further violence by the Army, and the retaliatory occupation of churches and embassies. Archbishop Romero offered himself as a mediator and called upon his flock to respect foreigners, asking for international understanding of his country's problems and diplomatic influence in establishing human rights within its borders.

However highly thought of he was abroad, in El Salvador opinions were divided. Among the people, who heard him on the radio and attended his celebrations of the Mass, his stock was high, but the Church was so split that a number of bishops wrote a joint letter to Rome, decrying his ministry as 'Marxist-inspired'. Still he went on trying to unite the right and left wings amongst Christians, fearful that division would make them more vulnerable to persecution. The climate became more electric when civil war flared up in Nicaragua; the Archbishop prayed for the sister republic, now liberated, and sent what aid he could. Without identifying itself with the new Sandinista government, the Church in Nicaragua was soldily behind the people, and so enjoyed its confidence.

Those close to him noticed that he drove himself on and worked relentlessly; even when relaxing with the Barraza family he would be monitoring the government television, listening to the diocesan radio station, eating a meal and conducting a conversation, all at the same time. But the show of energy was deceptive; at the heart of his activity was a deep peace that could not be broken, even by the most virulent misunderstanding of his motives. He was centred in Jesus Christ, and his spiritual life was never neglected. It sustained him against the death threats he was beginning to receive from right-wing organisations.

Later, after a coup d'etat in October 1979 that put in a

more moderate government, the threats also came from the left, suspicious of his call to wait and see if the new promises would be honoured. By the end of the year, the military members of the government were again looking for allies, and some members of the Christian Democratic party joined them. Archbishop Romero was again in evidence as mediator. He called on the oligarchy, the power that was blocking reform, to "share their power and wealth with all, instead of provoking a civil war that will bathe us all in blood."

An attempt to demonstrate on the anniversary of the 1932 massacre of the campesinos was savagely put down, and the authorities jammed the only source of unbiassed news, the radio station that broadcast Archbishop Romero's homilies. On returning from a trip to Europe, during which he had another endorsement from the Pope, he discovered that the United States was giving military aid to El Salvador, including crowd-control equipment; the label 'Christian Democrat' had deceived the naive state Department. Archbishop Romero read a letter to his flock, outlining the true situation to President Carter, and when they thundered their approval, he despatched it. The reply was courteous, but the policy remained unreformed.

His Lenten homilies had the nation glued to their radio sets, and when the station was blown up by right-wing extremists, donations flooded in to rebuild it. Warnings of death threats came from Costa Rica, and he was offered sanctuary in Nicaragua, but replied that he could not leave his people. He made his Lenten retreat, aware of the possibility that he would meet a violent death; he feared it, but was comforted by the thought that God had been close to the martyrs. He was human enough to be rather abrasive with his fellow-retreatants and suffered remorse because of it.

The Christian Democrats left the government, and the killings continued. A suitcase crammed with sticks of dynamite was found when Romero celebrated a funeral Mass for a murdered Christian Democrat. On 23 March he preached his longest homily; though it lasted an hour and three-quarters, it held his hearers' avid attention, and was punctuated by applause. All over El Salvador it was heard on short-wave radio by people crowding into open doorways or taking their radios out into the streets.

He said: "We want the government to understand seriously that reforms are worth nothing if they are stained in so much blood. In the name of God, and in the name of this suffering people, whose laments rise to heaven each day more tumultuously, I beg you – I beseech you – I order you in the name of God – stop the repression."

He was treated almost as a saint by those who approached him on the steps of the Cathedral. He ate his midday meal with the Barrazas and relaxed, watching television while sipping a drink, and playing with the children; the rest of the day was taken up with his religious duties.

The next day – Monday – it had been announced in the newspapers that he would say the 6 p.m. Mass at the Cancer Hospital where he lived; an anniversary Mass for the mother of a journalist friend. It was simple, and in the homily he asked the congregation to profit by the example of a mother who had always encouraged her children. He introduced the bidding prayers – and the sound of a shot tore through the silence. Behind the altar, Archbishop Romero slumped to the ground, his life blood gushing out and staining his violet vestments. He died in hospital without regaining consciousness.

The funeral took place on Palm Sunday among a crowd that included representatives from all parties in El Salvador, and many from around the world, but he was not to rest in peace. A bomb exploded, shooting was heard, and he was buried hastily as the gathering broke up in chaos. On his tomb was his episcopal motto: "To be of one mind and heart with the Church". When Pope John Paul II visited El Salvador, he knelt beside it in prayer.

Two weeks before his death, Archbishop Romero had said: "As a shepherd I am obliged by divine mandate to give my life for those I love – for all Salvadorans – even for those who may be going to kill me... A Bishop will die, but God's Church, which is the people, will not perish."

EDITH STEIN

By the early twenties Germany – only unified in 1871, in the blaze of glory after she had humiliated her great neighbour France in battle – was in eclipse. The memory of internal strife during the Revolution of 1918, which had accelerated her defeat in World War I, was still near and painful. The Allies were demanding reparation payments; unemployment was high, and the country had not managed to turn round the economy to compete in peacetime markets. On a memorable day, 15 November 1923, one dollar was worth a billion marks. Barter replaced currency, and a fear of inflation was to haunt the country for decades to come.

People lived from day to day, and couples found that they both had to work in order to support their families. Women had received the suffrage in 1919, but it was economic necessity that completed their emancipation. One notable feminist and philosopher, Edith Stein, was working at Speyer in the Rhineland as a teacher of history and German literature at St Magdalene's, a training college run by some Dominican Sisters. She was thirty-two years old, and had become a Catholic the year before, after a long and sometimes turbulent journey.

Her native place was Breslau in what became Poland, and she was born on the Day of Atonement, 12 October 1891, into an orthodox Jewish family of extensive size – she was the youngest of eleven children, seven of whom survived childhood. Later she wrote of the beauty of the Jewish year, with its festival liturgies and observances. Not all her relatives were equally devout, and among her numerous uncles, aunts and cousins there was a variety of belief and unbelief.

The story of her earliest years is overshadowed by an

event that took place in July 1893. She and her mother were waving goodbye to her father, a lumber merchant, who was off to the forest to survey some timber. The little girl called him back for a final kiss, and he went on his way into the forest. Later a passing postman saw him lying on the ground; it was a very hot day, and he assumed that Siegfried Stein was taking a nap. In fact he had been overcome by heatstroke, as the postman discovered on passing the same way several hours later. Turning him over, he found that he was dead.

His widow was distraught, but the family rallied round, together with friends they had made by their generous hospitality in happier times. Edith and her sister Erna, to whom she was as close in love as she was in age, were drawn together as their mother decided to take over the lumber business and run it herself, so her growing family might be kept together and enjoy any advantages she could provide for them. She was an excellent businesswoman, with abundant energy, and although she worked long hours, she was never too tired to greet her beloved youngest daughter on her return home.

The elder sisters who looked after Edith found her quite a handful. She was precocious, almost hyperactive, and like all small children she considered herself to be the centre of the universe. This illusion did not long survive in the the hurly-burly of the large family, and she became biddable and co-operative – not however before she had joined her elder sister at school, after rejecting a sojourn at a kindergarten as being unworthy of her talents.

She requested that the present she wanted for her sixth birthday would be entrance into 'Big School', and threatened that she would not be mollified by any other. Anxious not to disappoint her, her sister Rosa, who had just passed her teaching examinations, approached the authorities, and it was largely due to Rosa that Edith was accepted – though she could not yet read or write. It was sink or swim in the new environment, but she floated through it, acquiring the new skills. She still had some of the fear of being ignored that occurs in the younger members of a large family, and would gallop down to the front of the class, waving her arm frantically to capture the teacher's attention.

As far as possible she was treated exactly like her fellow pupils, though her work was outstanding. This pleased her and made her feel she was being taken seriously. At home, she was not able to avoid being singled out, when her consistently good marks were noticed. Perhaps she was afraid of being teased, which was only too likely.

The family provided a backdrop to her mental life which would always be of vital importance to her. But she enjoyed the round of births, marriages and deaths that provided opportunities for getting together, feasting royally, and welcoming the new additions to the ranks since their last gathering. Family life gave her a constant outlet for that empathy which irradiated her nature, and prevented her from being a one-sided intellectual.

There were seven of her co-religionists in class, and they did not have any religious tuition, but the example of her pious mother was sufficient education for her. Her school career was distinguished; the 'report book' which chronicled it was full of the longed-for Grade I (A) results, but these did not necessarily lead to employment.

Her sister Else had passed all her teaching exams, but because of anti-Semitic feeling in Prussia, she could not find a place in the school system and had to content herself with taking private pupils. She was very beautiful, and had become engaged to a Catholic law student who boarded with the family – but the parents would not consent to a mixed marriage, and it was broken off. Later Else succeeded in getting a post at a private school in Hamburg, where she met a young dermatologist, Max Gordon, and married him.

For Edith, a summer trip to Hamburg was eagerly anticipated every year. The young husband was musical, and at first well-liked in the family, but he had a cantankerous side which became more apparent as he grew older.

When Edith left school at the age of fifteen, it was decided that she should make an extended visit to Else, and learn something from her about running a home and looking after children. Although her ticket was for a return in six weeks, she proved so useful that she stayed for ten months, becoming a dependable prop for her sister and – when Else was away from home – taking sole charge of the household, which now included two young children.

One negative result of the stay in Hamburg was that no longer surrounded by the faith of her mother, she succumbed to the atmosphere of her sister's household where all religious practices had been abandoned. Worse than that, she made a conscious rejection of the faith, and resolved not to pray.

In 1907, her beloved sister Erna went to university, studying to become a doctor. She met her future husband on the day they registered, and they were soon inseparable. At that time they did not think of marriage, because Hans Biberstein was the adored only son of a widowed mother who had carefully impressed upon him that his first duty was to her. Edith was instrumental in helping Erna to enter the university; although she was younger, she coached her sister for her final exams at the high school, thus showing her own talent for tuition – she always insisted on the answers to questions on English or French history being given in the appropriate language.

It was in sharing Erna's work, and in some cases improving on it, that she realised she wanted to return to school herself. Although there seemed to be insurmountable difficulties in reaching the required standard, her mother and siblings encouraged her, and she had private tuition to make up for the three years of classes she had not attended. She enjoyed working at full stretch, and described this later as being the first time when she had felt completely happy.

She was tutored in Latin and mathematics, taking to both like a duck to water. There was no doubt in anyone's mind except her own that she would succeed in reaching her goal; she worked as if her life depended on it. Among the golden opinions she won from her tutors, she inspired another, more tender passion in a grown-up cousin, Fritz. He had been forced to give up study before reaching university entrance standard on account of illness, and had to enter a bank. Sitting opposite Edith as she studied, he fell in love with her, and made the most tentative proposal.

It is easy to see why she captivated him. Photographs taken of her show a full-lipped, rounded beauty with a dimpled chin. But it is her eyes that are so extraordinary; large, dark and luminous, they seem to be so deep that they probe to the very heart of what they see. Gently, she informed Fritz that she was determined to carry on with her studies, and he faded from her life. Was she proud of this conquest? Years later, she mentioned it with some tenderness, and noted that her 'knight' never married.

Despite her nervousness in the examinations, she was exhilarated, finding them less difficult than she had anticipated, and she passed with flying colours to take her place at the Grammar school. Her career there was a meteoric rise to the top of the class, with no challengers coming within reach of her attainments. When the class above hers was told publicly that she was more gifted than any of them, she feared she would suffer from their envy, but it never seemed to happen. She was generous with her time in coaching fellow-pupils, and did not hide her work from anyone who wished to copy it.

Always sensitive, she was in tears when, during a game of 'Truth', one of her teachers said that she was given to gloating over the misfortunes of the other girls. The actual 'truth' was that she had laughed, when some of them made absurd answers to questions, and this gave rise to the more wounding accusation. Any fault worried her seriously; there is no doubt that she was a perfectionist. She always retained her sensitivity; any mention of violent crime made her ill. People instinctively censored themselves in her presence, and she retained a shining innocence.

When her homework was out of the way, she read widely, and as the leaving examinations loomed she gave some thought to a career. Her chosen subjects were literature and philosophy, with a view to taking up teaching. With her entrance to the university assured, she was given the task of writing a light-hearted playlet to be performed at the farewell party for students who had completed their course; she also appears to have directed it.

At university she joined her elder sister Erna, who was a year or so into her medical training. Not only were they distinguished by their brilliance and the seriousness with which they studied, but they interested themselves in questions of the day, like co-education and feminism. They tackled difficult texts, and gained from one another's interpretations of them. In summer they rambled through the surrounding countryside; in winter there were entertainments at the Students Union, although Erna and Edith considered these rather frivolous. More and more, Edith took on tutorial work, though not to the neglect of her own.

She was studying the psychology of thought, and one of her tutors recommended an out-of-print textbook by a philosopher called Edmund Husserl. She found it in the library of the Philosophy Department, and spent her vacation studying it. It so excited her, that she resolved to go to Gottingen and sit at the master's feet as soon as she felt sufficiently informed to profit by it. Her mother usually put up a determined opposition to any of her daughters living away from home, unless they were leaving to marry someone she approved of, but fortunately for Edith, a cousin had become a lecturer in mathematics at Gottingen, and her mother relented.

Once there, she lived and breathed philosophy, with the ardour generated by the lectures of her heroes, 'The Gottingen School', who were famous throughout the country.

With them, she learned to select the phenomena that were various manifestations of being, and examined them with her own mental tools through an intuitive perception of their essence. She was enjoying herself.

Adolf Reinach, whose lectures she hoped to attend, welcomed her kindly but passed her on to the master himself, Edmund Husserl. She was amazed to discover that despite his fame, he was very accessible to his students, setting aside one afternoon each week to talk to them informally at his home. Edith was able to tell him that she had read his latest work, '*Ideas*' which seemed to contradict some of his earlier conclusions. Not everyone could go along with these, and lively discussions resulted.

The cream of his students formed the Philosophical Society, and Edith and her room-mate soon joined it. They did not join in social events, as the senior ladies in the group showed a certain amount of reserve towards them.

In Edith's second year, Max Scheler's work was under discussion; he was thought to be closer to the spirit of Husserl's early intentions than the master himself, and Edith considered he had true genius. He was the complete absent-minded professor, which endeared him to her, and he was the first Catholic she had met and admired, as his religion had a real bearing upon his work.

Her relationship with Doctor. Reinach was very close, especially when he read part of a thesis – 'The Problem of Empathy' – with which she was having some difficulty. He praised it and encouraged her to persist, however unwieldy the task seemed to be. With his encouragement she finished the thesis, and on its completion he agreed that she should submit it for her State Boards Examination.

In 1914 the peaceful tenor of their lives was shattered by the shot of the assassin at Sarajevo. Ever afterwards, there was a gap between those who had lived in the stability of pre-war Germany and those who had not. The students assembled in Reinach's study for the last session of the seminar; one of them ventured to ask the question on all their minds – would he have to go to war? He replied: "I am permitted to go", disclaiming any idea of compulsion.

Gradually the young men disappeared from the scene, leaving women and older men. Edith enrolled in a nursing course for women students; she felt that the university life she had embraced so warmly was trivial compared with the calamity which had fallen on them all. Then came news of the first casualties.

Though she grieved, like her friends, her life was full. Her theses were finished and submitted to the examiners. She was to take her orals in January 1915, and stayed over Christmas to prepare for them. It had been a habit of hers to go and listen to the sermons at Protestant churches, but she found that their faith was too much mixed with politics to make any impression on her. She passed her examinations, and learned from Husserl himself that she had received the notation, 'Passed with highest honours."

But she felt the call to help those caught up in the war, and asked if she could be accepted for the nursing service. Her mother was bitterly against this, as the only vacancies were far away in Austria, but no-one opposed Edith for long when she was really determined. After the most elementary training, she was assigned to a typhoid ward, and soon gained experience of the course of the illness. When the hospital staff decided to celebrate the admission of their thousandth patient, Edith – who did not drink, though she had learned to smoke – was the only sober member of the party. Dismayed that her colleagues should abandon all thoughts of their critically ill patients within the building, she was rescued in a state of shock by a Polish nobleman.

During the night, she had sixty patients to look after, and with only the scantiest training she undertook to give them their injections. She grew familiar with deaths, both easy and difficult. Over the months, better preventative techniques gradually dried up the stream of patients, and when Edith asked for a more demanding assignment she was allocated to a small operating theatre. Though she was merely an aide, she took a full part in the team, being put in charge of the instrument table; she even found herself able to give instructions to an inexperienced lady surgeon. Later she was put in complete charge of two wards of young soldiers in traction, who had to remain immobile. The caring aspect of the work pleased her, but it was physically demanding, and at the end of each duty she was often too tired to eat. When the time for her leave came round, the Matron left it to her to decide when she should return.

All the time she was in the hospital she had kept up a correspondence with Husserl, and with Reinach at the front, who welcomed her as a comrade in arms. Now she was free to work on her Ph.D. Back in Gottingen for a visit, she was able to attend a birthday party for Doctor. Reinach, who was home on leave, and his students revived the past. This led to other social occasions, in which Husserl and his wife also figured.

Then she received a summons from the Principal of her old school in Breslau, offering her a teaching post. She had no certificate to teach languages, which the position required, but it was wartime and this was overlooked. So as a stop-gap she began her teaching career. But the work was very tiring, and fatigue brought on an illness – probably nervous exhaustion – which was to plague her for many years to come.

She went to Freiburg where Husserl was now teaching,

and with the aid of his wife persuaded him to read her doctor's thesis. He gave an enthusiastic endorsement to his colleagues, and she attended his lectures. But he was ageing now, and needed an assistant. There was a great deal of discussion as to who this might be; his male students were involved in the war and Edith hesitated to propose herself until after the results of her examination, but he offered to publish her thesis, and she was emboldened to put the proposition to him. When the results were known, she received her doctorate *summa cum laude*, and Frau Husserl and her daughter wove her a beautiful victor's wreath which she wore in her hair at the celebration dinner. Her reward was to become her master's assistant for two years.

In 1917 she received the shocking news that Adolf Reinach had been killed in Flanders. His widow asked Edith if she would deal with his papers, and the two women met. Edith, who did not at the time believe in an afterlife, felt completely disoriented by his death, and was amazed that his wife Anna should be able to remain serene and full of hope. Edith took comfort from her, and grew to realise that it was Anna's Christian faith that sustained her.

Although she did not lose her intellectual doubts for years, this encounter with real faith was the dawn of her belief. As with so many, the experience was not of the head, but of the heart. She began to read the New Testament, and to understand the triumph that could come through the Cross.

While she worked with Husserl in Freiburg, there was a growing mood of pessimism in Germany. The suicide rate soared, and the statistics took on a ghastly reality when one of the young phenomenologists succumbed. Edith wrote: "We may not survive the war... but we stand at a turning-point in mankind's spiritual development."

She saw in the art and music of the time a struggle between sense and nonsense, between good and evil. Everyone was bewildered, and found life too complicated to apply a single plan for world improvement. She later wrote that communism and Fascism were not the answers, and foresaw that it would take many years before the atrocities could be purged from the countries that experimented with them.

Her work with Husserl was made difficult by his increasing intolerance, and she resigned as his assistant in 1918. Returning to Breslau, she got on with her own work, financing it by private teaching. Here she was able to explore the question of faith, resting in God and waiting for his call, believing in Christ, but stopping short of conversion.

It took a dark night of the soul before she surrendered. First of all she had professional setbacks when she applied for professorships which she was entitled to with her academic qualifications. She was not only a woman; she was a Jewess. She also suffered a psychological freeze of mind and heart. She hints at an experience of human love which may have set off this complete inertia: "I can immerse myself in the greatness of someone's character without being able to offer him the recognition he deserves", was how she put it.

Unable to think or act independently she surrendered to the Divine Will. While in Frankfurt she took refuge in the Cathedral, and saw a woman with a shopping basket making a brief visit as if calling in on a friend. She had never seen such a sight in a synagogue or a Protestant church, and the unknown worshipper decided her on the Catholic faith. Another influence was the Danish religious philosopher Kierkegaard, with his insistence on the necessity of choosing Christ rather than adhering to dogma. She also picked up the autobiography of St Teresa of Avila and read it all through one night, declaring in the morning: "This is the Truth."

When she chose Christ, she believed with "the most interior and personal part of the soul", and said it was "something that could light up inside us and become actually perceptible." The call had come, and she answered it eagerly, going out to buy a catechism and a missal; she read them with the eye of faith. For the first time she went to Mass, and followed it perfectly. Thinking she had conquered all the obstacles in the way of being received, she found her way to the sacristy, demanding immediate baptism from the celebrant.

He was rather taken aback by her request, and insisted that she should wait and receive some instruction. She persisted, saying that she understood the thinking behind the dogmas she had read about. The scholar in her demanded to be examined in the faith. Eventually her importunity wore him down, but the first date he would consider for her reception was New Year's Day 1922.

Her family's reaction to her conversion would make no difference to her resolve, but she was worried about its effect on them. Her brothers and sisters accepted the situation calmly. Her sister Erna, who was closest to her, had married in 1920 the young doctor she had loved since her student days. The ceremony took place when Edith's spirits were at their lowest ebb, but she recovered almost miraculously and danced with the bridegroom several times. She said later that this was the last time she ever danced. Her grief may not have been entirely for the loss of her sister; it was about this time that she decided marriage was not for her.

She had chosen 'Teresa' as her baptismal name, thus acquiring St Teresa of Avila as her patron – a good choice for a doctor of philosophy. When she could no longer defer the confrontation, she told her mother that she had become a Christian. She expected an angry tirade, but Auguste Stein wept bitterly. Edith had never seen her mother, the driver of hard bargains and manager of her large family, in tears before. It seemed that the sight of Edith's radiant face cut her to the heart; she had gone where her mother could never follow. On the spot Edith decided that, although she felt a vocation to the religious life, she would defer answering it until she could approach her mother with the idea.

Inevitably, her life changed. She taught in a girls' school in Speyer and a Teacher-Training College; she also wrote and lectured. Her first task was to translate the speeches and writings of Cardinal Newman before his conversion. Her ready empathy made her particularly suited to the work, and made German readers feel close to Newman in his journey – the one she had made so recently herself.

Her lectures were arranged by the Association of Catholic Women Teachers and the Association of Catholic University Graduates. Covering sociological, psychological and philosophical fields, she gave her audiences a new Catholic feminism which fully acknowledged the special place of women in the Church, and their unique talents for vocations in the world. She believed that they were not only fitted by their psychology to excel in caring professions, but they brought a special feminine genius to all forms of work.

Speedily she gained an international reputation as the lectures were acclaimed in all parts of Germany and Switzerland; she also spoke to the radio audience. At the same time, she was preparing to take a University Chair when one fell vacant. In 1932 she became a teacher at the German Institute for Scientific Pedagogy in Munster, but a new personality had emerged on the political scene – Adolf Hitler.

In 1933 he became Chancellor of Germany, and under the race laws all Jews were banned from prominent positions in the country, including those in education. This was Edith's chance to answer the call she had first heard nearly twenty years earlier. Still her mother opposed her decision, applying all her powers of emotional blackmail to prevent her from entering the Carmelite Order. She had decided to join them after stopping in Cologne to spend a Holy Hour at their convent. The homily was so dull, she began to meditate, and spoke silently to Jesus about the trials of the Jewish people, saying that she wanted to share in carrying their Cross.

Her name in religion was Sister Teresa Benedicta a Cruce, remembering her patron, St Teresa, and her devotion to the Passion. After entering the Cologne Carmel on St Teresa's feast in 1933, she made her final vows on the 21 April 1938, to live the hidden life of an enclosed nun. But there were many to remember her; one of her friends informed her that her old master, Edmund Husserl, had died six days after her profession, having turned happily to God in his old age.

On the last day of the year 1938 she moved to the Carmelite convent at Echt in Holland to avoid the authorities disturbing the Sisters at Cologne. She was joined there by her sister Rosa, who had also become a Catholic; they had two years of the traditional Carmelite life until 1940, when Holland was invaded.

An attempt to transfer them to a convent in Switzerland came to nothing. The members of their family who had not escaped to America were rounded up and sent to concentration camps. Edith had always wanted to share the fate of her people; when she saw Jews being beaten up in Münster in 1932, she had said: "All this must be atoned for." She had equated the holocaust with the Cross, and told her confessor: "You don't know what it means to me to be a daughter of the chosen people – to belong to Christ not only spiritually, but also in the flesh."

It was as a bride of Christ that she was present in the chapel at five o'clock on the 2nd of August 1942, for the evening hour of mental prayer. She read a poem, the point from which meditation would begin, and in the silence that followed it, the heavy boots of soldiers could be heard approaching the choir. Sister Teresa and her sister Rosa were carried away, as their Lord had been, like lambs to the slaughter.

A few days later a message reached the convent that they were well, and in the transit concentration camp at Westerbork. There was one possible sighting of them in a cattle truck, on their way to Auschwitz.

The Nazis kept the records of their victims meticulously: Edith Stein and her sister were recorded as having been admitted to Auschwitz from Westerbork on 7 August. The grim pictures of the concentration camp, with the railway line leading to the entrance from which so few returned, are familiar to us now. At the time nothing was known of their fate. After the war, the Dutch Red Cross managed to produce a document saying that Edith Stein was considered to have died on 9 August 1942.

But that was far from being the end of her story. Her writings are valued throughout the world, and have influenced many, and the cause for her beatification was introduced in Rome in 1972. It is not unlikely that her life will be crowned by being named among the company of the saints - saints of the Church she graced with such holiness, erudition, and compassion.

PIERRE
TEILHARD DE CHARDIN

In 1623, there was born in Clermont-Ferrand a boy who, as Blaise Pascal, mathematician, inventor and physicist, was to dazzle the French court presided over by Richelieu. His attacks on the Jesuits – the 'Lettres Provinciales' – were to be the model for Voltaire's masterly invective. An overnight conversion changed his life, and amongst his papers after his early death at the age of thirty-nine were found the *Pensees* which were to inspire so many in their spiritual lives.

Two hundred and fifty years later, Voltaire's great-grand-niece Berthe-Adele Teilhard de Chardin gave birth to her fourth child – almost within sight of the lights of Clermont-Ferrand, the capital of the Auvergne, surrounded by its extinct volcanoes. It was a son, baptised Marie-Joseph-Pierre in the shell-shaped font of the village church at Orcines. His birthday was May Day, and he would grow up to have a great devotion to Our Lady; but his mother, of an age to remember the general institution of the feast of the Sacred Heart, pressed upon him devotion to that image of Jesus's love. Like most boys, he was influenced by things concrete, fastening quickly on to what he could touch and see.

In his spiritual autobiography, *The Heart of the Matter*, he tells how he worshipped a piece of iron, the lock-pin of a plough; it impressed him with its smoothness, its seeming indestructibility. This was in the summer countryside, under the shadow of the Puy de Dome. Winter months were spent in the city, where the object of his devotion was a metal bolt in the nursery floor. Watching the fire destroy a lock of hair, he

129

felt vulnerable, needing as the centre of his world something more powerful than iron, which could wear away and become tarnished; then he saw pictures of Jesus with his heart exposed, and found in them the solidarity he needed. He focussed upon the Sacred Heart and it became an almost incredible source of energy – the fire of love. It was the beginning of an intuition of the God-Man in splendour, which irradiated everything within himself.

Growing up against the background of the ancient conical mountains, Teilhard was very conscious of his frailty, but he loved them, and would return to them all through his life. He was educated at home until he was eleven, his father encouraging him to collect insects, birds and rocks. There was all the joy of discovering the fossils and semi-precious stones in the area. Life was simple, modelled on the hunting, shooting and fishing pastimes of the English landed gentry; his father was a regular subscriber to English magazines.

Like the other sons in the family, Teilhard went to the Jesuit school at Villefranche-sur-Saone, where he was academically outstanding. His First Communion and Confirmation days were duly celebrated, though he was somewhat argumentative during religious instruction – no doubt a reflection of the lacklustre and narrow teaching. One of his masters complained that he was more interested in rocks than in his formal studies. His health deteriorated – probably he felt the deprivation of his previous outdoor life – and after he graduated in 1897 he spent some time at home, recovering his former vigour. He had already decided he wanted to be a priest, and believed that joining the Society of Jesus was the best way for him to reach perfection in the spiritual life.

But the Jesuits were the prime target of the laws banning religious orders from France, and after a novitiate in Aix-en-Provence, he and his fellow-seminarians were forced to flee, wearing a motley collection of civilian garments, and take refuge in Jersey. He made his first vows in 1901 on the Feast of the Annunciation, and directed a Greek play to entertain the community. Jersey possessed a rich vein for the embryonic palaeontologist to mine, and he developed scruples about his passion for it, which were dispersed by the Novice-Master, who assured him that "...my crucified God looked for a natural development of my being, as well as its sanctification."

Sent in 1905 to teach physics and chemistry at the Jesuits' secondary school in Cairo, he made expeditions into the desert to discover mineral deposits and fossils. He found these journeys had a spiritual content; the clean bare miles with their landscapes of sand reminded him of the Desert Fathers, and their temptations and triumphs. He enjoyed this exhilaration more than teaching, and his young pupils felt somewhat overstretched by his lessons. Publication of his findings began in 1908, and many rare specimens enriched his collections, some of which were named after him. Although his scientific curiosity was excited by his studies, he also wished to proclaim the mastery of Christ over prehistory. Already, with his thought only half formulated, he was feeling its direction.

At Ore Place, near Hastings in Sussex, he spent four years leading to his ordination in August 1911. His parents received Communion from him at his first Mass; a just reward for their devoted care and example. His sister Françoise, who was a Sister in a missionary order in Shanghai and with whom he had conducted a loving correspondence, died of smallpox, leaving a gaping wound in his emotional life. Intellectually he was stimulated by reading Bergson's book *Creative Evolution*, which set his mind racing. Alongside this he came to the realisation that matter and spirit were one.

After his sister's death, the void in his life was filled by a cousin, Marguerite Teilhard-Chambon, who came to represent the feminine influence in an existence that was very much male-orientated. She was cultivated, indeed a writer herself, and they exchanged manuscripts, ideas and family gossip until the end. This friendship was a release, guarding him from being too absorbed by the impersonal, generalising mode of masculine thought.

At this time he conceived a great interest in the Wealden bone-beds, rich in fossil teeth, which were easily accessible. Thanks to the liberal views of the Rector he was allowed to develop what was becoming more than a hobby; he had chosen to serve God as a scientist. His superiors sent him to study his subject in Paris, but he kept his contacts in England, though the Parisians were also very important to him. He studied with Professor Boule of the Paris Museum, one of the great specialists on Neanderthal Man, who welcomed good scientists, whether left-wing sceptics or clerics. Marcellin Boule was also from the Auvergne, which gave Teilhard another point of contact with him. The Abbé Breuil, with whom he visited the cave-paintings in Spain in 1912, was a great influence; they argued as equals, and in later years the Abbé became a close confidant.

The saga of Piltdown Man began when Charles Dawson, a solicitor and amateur geologist – whom Teilhard had welcomed when he was in Sussex and like-minded friends were thin on the ground – walked into the Natural History Museum in London. He laid before the curator of the Geology Department a collection that consisted of fragments of cranial bone, hippopotamus teeth, elephant fossils and flint tools. Dawson claimed they had been found in a gravel pit at Barkham Manor, Piltdown. Further finds included an eye-tooth which was apelike in appearance but with the marks of wear associated with human teeth, and part of a jawbone; they were pronounced to be human remains, Lower Pleistocene, and an important link in the evolutionary chain. Although Professor Boule refused to believe a word of it, Teilhard joined his friend on the site and had the heady experience of digging up one of the eye-teeth found in 1913. He lived long enough to see Dawson posthumously exposed as a fool or a fraud, and was glad that the truth had been established, even though this had been one of his brightest and earliest palaeontological memories.

One missing element in the character of the scientist and dedicated priest was added by the devastating war of 1914-18. When it began he was still studying in England, at Canterbury, but when religious were called up, he attended a medical board that certified him fit to serve. He was attached to a Moroccan regiment of light infantry as a stretcher-bearer; they were crack troops, and served in all the principal engagements of the war. To associate himself with the North Africans he adopted their dress, which included a red fez, and refused to be promoted to the post of Chaplain, with the honorary rank of Captain. "Leave me among the men", was his response to the suggestion. He was proud of his Corporal's stripes which he gained in 1915, and when advised to put down a heavy pack because he was fatigued, he said: "A Corporal does not set a bad example."

In spite of his background as a gentleman's son and a priest, he developed a rapport with the men, gaining the confidence of Moslems and atheists alike, many of whom expressed a wish that he should attend them when they were dying. He said Mass as the shells ranged about the network of trenches, fortified by sandbags, that were home to thousands. All around was a sea of mud; the soldiers shared their shelters with rats, and were infested with lice. It was a life almost as primitive as that of the early cavemen that were his passion.

When he was unable to say Mass, he made a spiritual offering of the sufferings which were like a palpable vapour over the battlefields. In July 1918, just after he had taken his solemn vows (in spite of the opposition of those who considered that war was not a suitable apprenticeship for the religious life) he wrote down his very beautiful meditation: 'The Mass on the World'. Afterwards, he would say it aloud when he was on his travels without the elements of the Mass.

His unit entered Germany in January 1919, and he ended the war with many citations for bravery, the Croix de Guerre and the Medaille Militaire. Though life was dear to him, he was cool and detached under fire, which gave him a feeling of extraordinary freedom. He expressed this in a piece written in July 1917: 'Nostalgia for the Front', in which he described the shared life – being an individual yet part of a whole – the conviction that men who had been under enemy fire were different from those who had merely escaped accidental death – the moment of deliverance that gave an exhilaration like no other. There is no doubt that this held the seeds from which all his future life would grow.

Demobilised in March 1919, he immediately returned to his studies, finding, like other men who returned, some difficulty in adjusting to the academic life. This was reflected in the results of his Natural Science degree which were merely 'good' as opposed to 'excellent'. He was made a Chevalier of the Legion d'Honneur in June 1920. He went back to Marcellin Boule at the Museum, and tried to interest him in making contact with German scientists – but Boule, who had not seen service, was adamant in his refusal. His doctorate thesis was on the mammals of the Lower Eocene period in France, and it was accepted with an honourable mention, later appearing along with other work in geological publications. After five years in the trenches under fire, he made light work of spending seven or eight hours a day on a dig.

Through an introduction by Abbé Breuil, he became a teacher of geology at the Institut Catholique, a post he held from 1920 to 1923. He was highly thought of by his students, who appreciated that he did not talk down to them.

His complete conversion to Evolutionism took place about this time, though there had been stirrings as far back as his sojourn in Hastings when he pored over fossils, including that of the 'Dawn Man'. His expression of his ideas was startling and original. Already he was looking beyond matter to its spirit, seeing in both different aspects of the same phenomena, though the spirit always took precedence over the physical and chemical.

In 1922 a Jesuit priest, Father Emile Licent, who had been working as a scientific observer in Central China for nearly ten years, asked Teilhard to visit him at his museum in Tiensin where he had assembled a rather unorganised collection of zoological, botanical and mineralogical specimens. He sent some of these to the Paris Museum, and Boule gave them to Teilhard to examine; he was intrigued enough by some fossils among them to agree to travel to China.

Father Licent was quite different from Teilhard in his haphazard way of collecting, and in his temperament, which was decidedly dictatorial. He even tried to boss Teilhard, who was better qualified, but Teilhard took it in good part, deferring to the older man. Licent did not like working with foreign expeditions, whereas Teilhard made good friends with his Swedish, American and Chinese counterparts, co-operating with them and exchanging information. But Father Licent's knowledge of China and practical help were invaluable, and though their paths diverged, Teilhard felt grateful and affectionate towards him.

Their first dig in Western Mongolia yielded a rich harvest of Palaeolithic deposits that seemed to prove once and for all that prehistoric man had lived there. Teilhard found life in these remote places similar to life at the front – perhaps unexpectedly so, as bandits proliferated. China had become increasingly nationalistic and hostile to foreigners. Teilhard never learned Chinese, though he was a better-than-average linguist, and was later to use English as a second language. His prejudice against the materialistic and unstable elements in Chinese society caused him to underrate them initially, although he made friends among the Europeanised upper classes.

In a series of letters, many to his cousin Marguerite, he described his travels, making vivid word-pictures of the countryside. Part of the landscape consisted of extinct volcanoes, similar to those which had loomed above his childhood home. He returned to France in 1924 and spent some time trying to define his view of the cosmos. His experience of the war, and of the vast spaces of Asia, was distilled into a book: *Le Milieu Divin*. He wrote:

"To Christify Matter: that sums up the whole venture of my innermost being... A grand and glorious venture (and I tremble often as I pursue it) but I found it impossible not to hazard myself in it, so powerful was the force with which the levels of the Universal and the Personal came together and gradually closed up over my head, to form one single vault."

It was a vision that beckoned tantalisingly all his life; but when the manuscript began to be circulated, word got about that his theories of evolution had resulted in his not being doctrinally sound on the question of original sin. His superiors decided he must leave the Institut Catholique and only publish on narrowly scientific subjects. He was convinced that he could only grow spiritually within the Church, and specifically in the Society of Jesus, and accepted the ban without complaint.

During the years from 1926 to 1929 he divided his time between Paris and China. The contrast between one of the most sophisticated capitals in the world and war-torn China was not lost on the creative artist that lurked in him. He foresaw the triumph of the Communists and predicted that China would reject all Western influence. He was delighted that he was trusted by his Chinese contacts, and was allowed official status with them – the only Catholic priest to be so honoured. He loved Peking, which he said reminded him of Paris for its air of civilisation amid the chaos in the rest of the country.

It was in Chou-Kou-Tien, some thirty miles south-west of the city, on the edge of a series of limestone mountains with fissures of red clay, disclosing a seemingly inexhaustible supply of fossils, that an authentic human tooth was found in 1927. Teilhard was sceptical at first – he would always be cautious before accepting the authenticity of phenomena – but once he had, his intuition took wings and he built solid structures of thought upon them.

Although he felt tense in Paris – the French atmosphere was febrile after the relaxed exchanges with his international friends in China – he wrote papers for scientific journals and made contacts with students, who joined with others in using him as a spiritual director. In China he was given an office with the official Geographic Survey, and virtually led the research at Chou-Kou-Tien.

They were not the first on the scene, and they owed a great deal to their predecessors at the dig. It was a team effort in 1928 that first found two fragments of jawbone that had belonged to 'Sinanthropus', as they called him. Then on 28 December 1929 they sent a telegram to Boule at the Museum in Paris: "New Year Greetings. Recovered Chou-Kou-Tien uncrushed adult Sinanthropus skull entire except face." It filled in another link in the evolutionary chain, and they were justifiably jubilant. They had to wait until April 1931 for tools and traces of fire to be found, and deduced that 'Peking Man' (as he came to be known) had a primitive form of speech.

Although he was taken up by Americans working in China who provided much of the funds for these excavations, he was also financially dependent on France since the car manufacturers Citroen decided to sponsor a trans-Asian journey, the

'Croisiere Jaune', which was to travel as far as Hanoi, and Teilhard obtained permission from his superiors to accompany the expedition. Before joining the party he had time to visit France, to stay in his beloved Auvergne, and gave talks to a wide range of students in small groups, outside the ban that still existed on his teaching. He made his first visit to America, where he was assured that he could have a post at any university for the asking.

He also began gathering material for his treatise: *The Phenomenon of Man* in which he considered man "no longer as an exception in and something extrinsic to the universe, but integrated with and intrinsic to it, and thus serving as an interpretation or a key." He thought that all the phenomena of mankind should be studied together, with the 'noosphere' – as he named the envelope of thinking and feeling that hovered over the earth. He thought this would be a step towards a cosmic view of man's situation, believing that spirituality was still evolving, and that God had prepared a new revelation for the time when men would be ready to receive it. Then there would be an explosion of energy when the world would die, to be reunited with Christ, the All in All, in his second coming.

Teilhard's body was as active as his mind, and the 'Croisiere Jaune' took him to many parts of China previously unknown to him. By the time it was completed he had perhaps a clearer picture of its geography and geology, and its place in Central Asia, than anyone on earth. No-one on the expedition was a practising Catholic, and several of them tried his patience with their obtuse questions about religion, but they all attended the Mass he celebrated on New Year's Day 1932. His homily gave them credit for their devotion to their work and he offered the Mass for their realisation of their place in the universe, and for their families. The latter intention was all the more poignant because his own father and mother had died during his absence.

In 1935 he had the great joy of a visit from his friend and teacher, Abbé Breuil, and together they stood before a statue of the Buddha that had a particularly serene and joyful expression. Teilhard spoke softly: "I am very fond of this head, because it says something to me. It tells me that here is something that Christianity should adopt." There was no question of his 'going native', but he did believe that the Church should not restrict itself to Mediterranean culture and modes of thought, but take the best of philosophy and mysticism from the whole world. Yet there were those who called him racist when he said that oriental detachment was negative, and that Christianity's mysticism, proceeding through matter, was superior.

On a visit to Paris in the same year he sensed that the new warring elements, Fascism and Communism, would diverge still further, and that the next few years would be crucial in man's history. He never seemed to doubt that the world would achieve rejuvenation even as it suffered, which was why he appealed so much to idealistic youth. The following year the Japanese invaded China, and he was occupied with a hasty clearing of the Chou-Kou-Tien site. He was much concerned with the stages by which men had evolved, and the order in which the discoveries appeared. So many of the intermediate steps were lost that he despaired of making a complete record, but he did see in the laboratory fragments of the skeletal bones of 'Peking Man', although he had to wait until May 1938. In the August of that year he wrote the first chapter of *The Phenomenon of Man*, which was to be one of the foundations upon which his fame rests. Through the Thirties he travelled South-East Asia – on foot, by palanquin, on horseback, by sampan, steamer and aeroplane – and he built up an international network of scientists, assisting one another.

He was absent from France in her dark hours from 1940 to 1945, trapped in China after Pearl Harbour by the Japanese occupation, bitterly regretting his powerlessness to help except by heartfelt prayers. He was restricted to working over old material, and took the opportunity to finish *The Phenomenon of Man*, and completed a bibliography of Chinese fossil mammals with a fellow worker, Pierre Leroy. He did his best to preserve the Sinanthropus skulls by putting them in the hands of some American soldiers, but they were intercepted by the Japanese while they were pulling out, and the chest containing the scientific treasure was probably kicked into a watery grave at Taku by an ignorant Japanese NCO.

Those who knew him at the time speak of his spontaneity, which was infectious, and his willingness to explain his work in simple terms so that people untrained in science could understand it. His courtesy and holiness were legendary, yet it is evident that he was not as unfailingly serene as these qualities would suggest. He was no stranger to the dark night of the soul; scorning the orthodox explanation that it was a privilege God gave to his most favoured to test their fidelity, he explained that God worked with all his power to give happiness and light, but that "our eyes are unable to see him yet. Is not the whole course of centuries needed, in order for our gaze to accustom itself to the light?" He was on good terms with his fellow Jesuits, describing himself within the privacy of their houses as 'Founder of the Congregation of Divine Fantasy'.

The question of the publication of *The Phenomenon of Man* was considered by Rome in 1944, and permission was withheld. For Teilhard it meant that its contents were lost, perhaps for ever, and this caused him acute suffering. Yet somehow he recovered, and was even amused to hear a report on an illicit BBC news bulletin that he had been murdered by bandits in Tibet. When he reappeared in Paris at the end of the war he found himself a celebrity. The citation for his promotion to Officer of the Legion of Honour described him as one of the glories of French science. Titled hostesses and intellectuals arranged for him to debate with Marxists and Communists, and representatives of other Christian schools of thought; he put them all in the shade with his clarity and modesty. There was nothing elitist about his ideas, but he was unable to contact the masses because he observed scrupulously the ban on his lecturing or preaching to larger gatherings. The Society had the dilemma of having a genius on its hands, with no idea what use to make of him.

In 1947 he suffered a heart attack and battled with death for fifteen days. He recuperated at his brother's house in the Auvergne, and rejoiced in the sight of the setting sun gilding the mountains. Here he made his retreats and planned his autobiographical and philosophical work 'The Heart of the Matter'. People in the Church were turning him into the centre of controversy, which he deplored, though he did allow his manuscripts to be mimeographed and passed from hand to hand like the dissident literature in Russia.

The following year he made a visit to America, cementing his friendships there, and worked at the American Museum where he complained humorously that the most delectable fossils left him lukewarm; he was out of love with the past, and wanted to concentrate on the future of man. The virulent anti-communism amongst all classes shocked him, but he had no difficulty in making his more tolerant views heard. His fluency in English was extraordinary; he could even write learned papers directly into the language.

Suffering from nervous exhaustion, he returned to be hospitalised in Paris, where honours of all kinds, from many sources, were heaped upon him. His election to the Institut de France caused great rejoicing, even in the Jesuit Order. He wrote about computers and Super Brains, and praised man's ability to make such machines serve him, greeting this as a new stage in evolution. During a visit to South Africa in 1951, there was an attempt to persuade him to spend what, in the light of his increasing frailty, would be his declining years in its wonderful climate, but he resisted this and settled on America as his final place of exile.

There he divided his time between the Wenner-Gren Foundation and the American Museum. The lights of Broadway delighted him, and the excitement of the Christmas shopping rush, but he sought simplicity in his living-space. He got on well with Americans, meeting everyone of any eminence, and made converts among them – mainly by his example, for he never proselytised. He came across a para-psychologist, and proved he could keep up with what was being explored in that field. Although he detested occultism, he thought there might be some profit in the examination of what evidence existed of extra-sensory perception, which he believed might be allied with the physicists' electro-magnetic field.

The cyclotrons at Berkeley fascinated him, and he used them as an object of meditation; they were the image of his 'noosphere', which he believed would coil in on itself until it formed a single enormous cyclone, whose property was to produce not nuclear energy, but psychic energy in a continuously reflective, ultra-human state. For him, all forms of scientific advance meant a return to the centre – God himself. He covered America from coast to coast in a couple of months, calling on scientists to integrate physics, biology and sociology to create a unity of human knowledge, wishing them to think in terms of the whole universe, not merely their own disciplines – to abandon Aristotle's static cosmos in favour of one permanently evolving upward to reflect the Creator.

In 1954, when his relations with Rome were in a temporarily relaxed phase, he was allowed to return to France. As usual he maintained a frantic pace; meeting too many people, he felt his age. A lecture he gave seemed to close observers to have lost the old momentum. He visited the cave paintings at Lascaux for the first time during another stay with his brother in the Auvergne. There was something valedictory in his manner as he looked at the church where he he was baptised and his ancestors buried. It was not a false premonition; he was visiting France for the last time, having been ordered back to America by his superiors.

He was homesick for Europe and increasingly frail, yet he asked his friends not to think of him as persecuted. He always saw the vital necessity of the Church, and was never within sight of leaving it. A friend was moved when Teilhard asked him to pray that he would not die embittered. He felt more and more alienated from other thinkers, as he had been long ago from those who had not shared his war experiences – because, as he wrote, "only at the front, lit up by flares after a day of intense work, could I sense the oneness of all men; their collective, yet individual future."

He had a spiritual vision of "the divine spark that leapt from God, creating an explosion that recast the whole face of the world in an instant." In his own time there was no-one to share that vision. Now, due to his persistence and loyalty to it, many have been privileged to share what he was the first to put into words, leaving posterity to make what they could of it. This was his missionary work, and he always believed that work was a source of grace. In his last days he lived in a Jesuit house in New York, still trying to gain the world for Christ.

He was not so much tolerant of others' frailty, as blind to it. He did not fear death, only the decline of his powers, as he set himself to reflect on old age and so turn it into a friend. His end was to be swift, and came when he wished it, because he had always wanted to die at the time of the Resurrection. On Easter Sunday 1955 he went to High Mass at St Patrick's Cathedral, and to a concert in the afternoon. Afterwards, about to have a cup of tea with some friends, he suffered a rupture of the coronary artery. He knew it was mortal, and died within minutes. His Requiem was simple, and there were few mourners.

Theodore Mond said he was one of the rare believers who had really tested Christianity. Another described him as: "A radiant soul that knew no frontiers; full of joy himself, he could transmit it to others" – and those others included people of all beliefs, from Muslims to Marxists, who held him in high regard. What he said of himself showed true humility: "In all my work I am conscious of being no more than a kind of sounding-box, amplifying what people around me are thinking. Take from me what suits you, and build your own structure."

The father of his biographer, Claude Cuenot, was a biologist and an unbeliever; when he was dying, he expressed to Teilhard his doubts about his unbelief. The one thing he was certain of was his science, and he was trying to complete his last testament as a scientist. Teilhard, who had Christianised evolution, wrote him a moving letter which concluded: "And so I pray for you, as I do for myself, that we may be given the vision (as keenly reasoned, and yet as warmly felt as possible) of a universe fundamentally loving and lovable, and that after working so long for it we may at last close our eyes and abandon ourselves to it. That is how I too, before very long, shall try to end."

May he rest in peace.

MARTIN LUTHER KING

In 1929, the year of Martin Luther King's birth, the American Stock Market crashed, creating a national anxiety-neurosis that would last for a decade. His father, 'Mike' Martin Luther King, did his best to see that his three children should be untouched by it. As the pastor of a thriving Baptist Chapel in Atlanta, Georgia, inherited from his father-in-law, he was well placed to cushion the blows of life. He had built up his congregation until it numbered several thousands, and the building had to be enlarged to accommodate them all. Six choirs lashed the listeners to a frenzy, preparing them for their pastor's inspired preaching. It was not surprising that his daughter was fired to pledge herself to Jesus Christ at a revival meeting. Five-year-old Martin Luther King Junior, his elder son, was swift to follow her, not to be outdone by his sister.

The dancing and clapping of black gospel worship created a heady atmosphere, although Martin afterwards confessed that he was sometimes embarrassed by his father's robust style in church. Mike King was equally robust in disciplining his children, being an advocate of not sparing the rod. M.L., as he was known, bore this stoically, but with fierce inner anger. His demeanour moved his grandmother to tears, and she became his favourite person; once, when he and his brother knocked her over when they slid down the bannisters, he was so afraid he had killed her that he threw himself out of an upstairs window.

At five, when he started school, he quickly showed academic promise, though he lost his best friend, who was white; it hurt him deeply when the boy's parents broke off their friendship. Schools in Atlanta were segregated, and M.L. was told about the colour bar, that he was restricted to black seating in the cinema and on buses, that he had to slake his thirst at a black water-fountain, and urinate in a black lavatory.

There was also a division in the culture of the day, which took its ethics from the movies. The great event of 1939 was the premiere of *Gone With The Wind* which took place in Atlanta, when all the stars and leading socialites came to see a replica of the town burnt on screen. It revived the simmering colour question that had lingered in the South since Lincoln emancipated the slaves: whites walked tall and waved Confederate flags; the black population looked on sullenly or angrily, according to temperament. M.L.'s father was proud and insisted on his rights, such as they were, though he called on his children not to have hatred in their hearts, even as the lynchings and beatings by the Klu Klux Klan went on unchecked.

Harlem negroes had a successful boycott of segregated buses in 1941, which did not go unnoticed by one small black boy in Atlanta. When he was fourteen, his voice broke, and the treble pipe that had delighted the ladies in his father's congregation turned into a golden baritone. He became a flirt and a dandy, finding that the change of register intrigued a new section of the available females.

As older negro students were called up, he was allowed to qualify for college at the age of fifteen. Before taking up his place at Atlanta's Morehouse College he spent a summer working in the tobacco fields of Connecticut, experiencing his first taste of unsegregated life. Temporary freedom made him more aware of the restrictions in the south, but at college he learned from his teachers how to hold up his head as a negro, as well as getting a good grounding in English and Sociology, his chosen subjects. His nascent doubts about fundamentalist religion were confirmed, and he began to see how myth and legend served religion. The president of the college was a convinced modernist, determined to turn out moral and rational men, capable of bringing honour and prestige to the black population, allowing them to meet whites as equals.

Toward the end of his time at Morehouse, when he was seventeen, he decided to become a Baptist minister. Mr King Senior did not relax his stern attitude to his son, despite his inward delight; he arranged for him to preach a trial sermon which was such a success that all Mike's hopes for his son were realised. Martin, as his friends began to call him, was now reading widely, and he came across an essay called *Civil Disobedience* by the American poet Thoreau, written a century before, which had influenced the Indian leader Gandhi during his tussles with the British rulers of his country. In 1947 the principles of non-violent action were brought into play in the western hemisphere for the first time when A. Philip Randolph threatened to call a mass protest if the armed services were not desegregated; the move was an unqualified success. Martin also became aware of the National Association for the Advancement of Coloured People (the N.A.A.C.P.) whose ranks he was to join. They brought legal actions to resolve the rights of negroes, and recruited from black professionals and progressive whites.

When he was nineteen Martin graduated from Morehouse and settled on the non-segregated Crozer Seminary in Pennsylvania for his degree in Divinity. Determined not to appear to the white majority of the students as the stereotype black, he dressed conservatively and cultivated a rather stern and unyielding expression, resolving to work harder than any other student and taking extra lessons in Philosophy at the university of Pennsylvania. He was seeking to hammer out his own philosophical method that would steer a middle course between capitalism and communism, the great ideologies of the time. He gave a sermon on 'The Challenge of Communism to Christianity', saying that communism had only got a hold because Christianity failed to be Christian enough, but he was equally critical of capitalism for having too materialistic a view of the world.

A racist student from North Carolina accused him of ransacking his room and threatened him with a pistol, but Martin stared him down, refusing to press charges against him. If there had ever been any doubt about his integrity amongst his fellow students, it was dispelled by this incident. What particularly pleased him was that he won the friendship of his adversary. Here in miniature was the triumph of the Gandhian ideal. At that time he had hated whites, but during the confrontation he had come to know and love his opponent. As Gandhi had overcome his own violence, he had learned to deal with other people's violence. By organising boycotts, strikes and protest marches – all of them non-violent – he had gained the respect of the British and ensured that there would be no enmity between their nations after the British left India. To the young black student, this suggested his own course of action.

He graduated from Crozer in June 1951. He was top of his class and gave the graduation address, proving that he was more than equal with whites. There was an open scholarship waiting for him, to choose his own school, and he settled on Boston University School of Theology, prepared to conquer the heart of Ivy League country and obtain a Ph.D.

A year later he became increasingly aware of his own sexuality. While at Crozer, he had fallen in love with a white girl and wanted to marry her, but their parents stepped in and prevented the match. The only honourable path for a Baptist minister was marriage, and Martin set about looking for a suitable partner of his own colour.

A friend introduced him to Coretta Scott, a music student at the New England Conservatory. She was a farmer's daughter from Alabama; a young woman with a mind of her own, determined to make a career as a singer. He made no secret of the fact that he was looking for a wife, and was determined that she would have to be a full-time one; he had no intention of bringing up 'latch-key' children. Their relation seemed deadlocked, but their difficulties melted away as they grew to love each other, and they were married in June 1953. They spent their wedding night in the house of an undertaker friend of the Scotts; it became a family joke that they had honey-mooned in a funeral parlour.

The young husband was undecided whether he wanted to teach, or work in the pastoral field. Several jobs in academe offered themselves, but he decided to gain some experience of preaching before committing himself to scholarship. The Dexter Avenue Baptist Church in Montgomery, Alabama, was quick to offer the young man a post as pastor. Coretta knew the area and was unenthusiastic; it meant returning to the segregated south. His father also disapproved; he had always wanted his son to take over his parish, which had become almost hereditary. But Martin felt the call to return to his oppressed people and, with a sinking heart, Coretta agreed to the move.

Hope seemed to be on the horizon when the United States Supreme Court ruled that all public schools should be open to students of all races, but in the south a white backlash was gathering momentum. The Klu Klux Klan burned its fiery crosses in their rage against the decision, and the Montgomery Educational Board bowed to the storm and put off desegregation for a year. The state of Alabama went further, and declared the Supreme Court ruling null and void.

By rising at 5.30 in the morning, Martin found he could fit in work on his thesis. He swiftly became the confidant of his congregation, giving counsel on complicated moral questions from the eminence of his twenty-five years. He began by preaching the theology he had learned in college, with illustrations drawn from his extensive reading, but discovered that what really touched the hearts of his hearers was the kind of dramatic sermon his father had preached. He soon learned to conduct a dialogue with his congregation which reached a climax in tears, laughter and applause.

He became a leader in the local branch of the N.A.A.C.P. but this was largely ineffectual, as the majority of blacks had been rendered apathetic by continual deprivation. No court would uphold black complaints of rape and murder, and blacks who offended against the 'Jim Crow' laws enforcing their inferiority in housing, transport and education, were given summary sentences.

In December 1955 a test case was presented to the N.A.A.C.P. that seemed to have some hope. A member called Mrs Rosa Parks refused to give up her seat to a white man on a city bus, in spite of the law obliging her to do so. At Martin's church, a meeting was hastily called to discuss a bus boycott. This was called for 5 December. and the date leaked to the local paper, who accused the N.A.A.C.P. of deliberate provocation. After a sleepless night – his first daughter Yolanda was barely a month old – Martin came down at dawn to keep watch over the buses passing his house. Usually they were crowded with negroes on their way to menial jobs, serving the town's whites; today the buses trundled down the road empty – and a great wave of joy and relief filled his heart. Everywhere, the same story emerged; the boycott was complete.

When Mrs Parks was tried, the city judge rose to the bait and she was fined fourteen dollars and costs. The way was open for an appeal to the federal court, and the Montgomery Improvement Association came into being, to organise matters arising out of the boycott. The surprise nomination for chairman was Martin Luther King, mostly because he was too young to be identified with any particular group. Realising that he would be held responsible for the actions of the Association, he nevertheless accepted, then faced Coretta with the news that she had a protest leader as a husband, with all the absences from home that this would entail.

"You know that whatever you do, you have my backing", was her reply.

He had only twenty minutes to prepare a speech at a mass meeting to discuss the future. He worried away five minutes, and then prayed he would be given the right words. A crowd numbering several thousand had been gathering for hours; police cars and television cameras were covering the event. Martin had the heady experience of speaking to an enraptured audience, and they took fire from each other. In framing his call to action he insisted that it should be in the light of Christian principles.

"If we protest courageously," he said, "and yet with dignity and Christian love, when history books are written in the future, somebody will have to say: 'There lived a race of people – of black people – who had the moral courage to stand up for their rights; and thereby they injected a new meaning into the veins of history and civilsation.'"

In sixteen minutes, the youthful, scholarly pastor changed into a man with the power to move and educate an excited audience, without allowing it to erupt into violence. As the crowds streamed away, Martin was left with his destiny as an unparalleled leader.

He was the spokesman for the M.I.A. when it met representatives of the City Fathers and the bus company in an unsuccessful attempt to end the boycott. He hoped that because the black clientele made up seventy per cent of the total, financial pressure would tell in the end. Twice a week meetings were held as morale boosters; his speeches were the focal point. He expounded the philosophy of non-violence, using the rhythmic cadences associated with gospel-singing that had made slavery bearable with its promise of eternal glory – but this was a message that God promised freedom here and now. Sometimes he quoted philosophers they had never heard of, or systems of thought they could not follow, but they loved and trusted him and that was enough. The white liberal press began to write about his spellbinding oratory.

Along with the fame came efforts to undermine his influence with his people. He was accused of using M.I.A. funds to buy expensive cars for Coretta and himself. These smears were bad enough, but the mail brought letters full of hate, and telephone-callers uttered obscenities. After threats to Coretta and the little girl, he was tempted to stand down as President of the M.I.A; as he plumbed the depths he found that his intellectual concept of God was no comfort. But he discovered a new strength in an aspect of God he had never known before – a real and personal presence, as vivid to Martin as he was to the simple, pious people who were his flock. The fear and panic left him and were replaced by a new assurance that he would never be alone again.

On the 30 January 1956, the eighth anniversary of Gandhi's assassination, he was speaking at one of his meetings when he heard that his house had been bombed. Numb with shock, he stood amongst the rubble and broken glass, hardly able to take in the miracle of Coretta's and the baby's escape. A crowd of negroes gathered, baying for vengeance against the mayor and police chief when they arrived on the scene. Martin's magic oratory turned aside their anger, as he called on them to obey the Christian commandment to love their enemies.

"We must meet hate with love", he said. Then the full horror of what might have happened struck, and his voice faltered as he went on: "Remember – if I am stopped, this Movement will not stop – because God is with this Movement."

Later, in February, after the Rosa Parks case had failed to find a place on the federal courts' list, thus blocking the M.I.A.'s tactics, an obscure law forbidding boycotts was dredged up, and used to indict eighty-nine negro leaders, twenty-four of them – including Martin – ministers of religion. He took Coretta and the baby to stay with his parents, then gave himself up with the rest of the offenders. The local jail was almost festive as they were booked for a future trial. No southern court would have given them a fair hearing, and Martin was found guilty and fined, but the case had brought the world's press to Montgomery, and it endorsed Martin's popularity.

On the back of this publicity the legality of segregated buses was discussed through all the available courts. Finally the Supreme Court ruled on 13 November 1956 that Alabama's state and its local laws for the segregation of buses were unconstitutional. This was victory, total and unequivocal, and set every negro in the south dancing and singing. Still Martin urged the Christian viewpoint: there were to be no jibes at white passengers – they were to behave immaculately, with love, not hate. To show them how, black leaders from all over the Union joined him in riding the first integrated bus, sitting in the white section. The boycott was over.

But the powerful white backlash was not. Militant whites ran amok on the buses and bombed black churches and parsonages, but the time had gone by when they could do this with impunity. The state Governor intervened to offer a reward for information leading to the arrest of the perpetrators. Martin felt that by his stand he had brought vengeance on his own people.

At one meeting he broke down, after praying: "I hope no-one will have to die as a result of our struggle for freedom in Montgomery. Certainly I don't want to die – but if anyone has to die, let it be me."

His devoted people roared their dissent, but he never lost his conviction that there would have to be a scapegoat to bear his people's wrongs.

The pace of his life quickened, and ate into his sleep. He was increasingly in demand as a speaker, and he received the accolade of a *Time* profile; even *Playboy* interviewed him. He joined the Ghanaian Independence celebrations; although he loved Africa – "The home of my father's fathers", he called it – he poured cold water on the aspirations of 'Back to Africa' movements, insisting that black Americans must be made equal partners in the American heritage.

The south lacked an effective organisation to act on specifically local interests. Martin called a meeting of all negro leaders in the area on 7 August 1957; they named the alliance 'The Southern Christian Leadership Conference', and it was decided that their first assignment should be to encourage blacks to register throughout the south so that they could exercise their voting rights. The deadline was the Lincoln Birthday holiday in February 1958. Martin did his best to make his flock responsible; he harangued them about their shortcomings and said they had to prove themselves frugal about money – not given to drunkenness and crime – and when they achieved professional status, they were not to rest on their laurels and fall behind white practitioners. There was also jealousy and bickering among some negro leaders, which he knew only too well, having been a target for their ill-will. Surprisingly, his audiences took his criticisms to heart, and he had so many speaking engagements, he nearly missed being present at the birth of his son, Martin Luther King, in October 1958.

At what some would consider the early age of twenty-nine he wrote his autobiography; most of the royalties went to the S.C.L.C. which was in a bad way financially. Indirectly, the publication led to his narrowest escape from death yet. He was signing books in a department store when a negro woman put a volume in front of him. As he glanced up at her, she thrust a sharpened Japanese letter-opener into his chest. It lodged near his heart, touching the main artery, and he was literally within a sneeze of death. But he did not sneeze, and the blade was removed successfully. It showed what a precarious existence he led, but it was Coretta who feared most for his life.

He gave up his pastorship of the Montgomery church, as he could no longer spend enough time there, and felt this was unfair to his flock; but he remained an active minister in his father's church in Atlanta. The south was stirred by student sit-ins at 'Whites only' lunch counters in department stores, and it was at Nashville, Tennessee, in February 1960 that they began to sing an old Labour Union song – 'We Shall Overcome'. It spread spontaneously, to echo round the world, wherever freedom was threatened. Martin showed his solidarity with the students by sharing their jail sentences, although this violated a probation order he had received for a trifling traffic offence. On retrial he was given a four-month sentence without the option of a fine, and was deliberately degraded in prison. His release was gained on the personal intervention of the would-be president, John F. Kennedy. King, as a prominent black leader, had been asked if he would endorse Kennedy's candidacy. Although he had only described himself as "neutral against Nixon", the black vote went to Kennedy and before he became too taken up with the Cold War, he did enact some negro-friendly legislation.

In 1963, the centenary of Lincoln's Emancipation Proclamation, at King's request Kennedy initiated a new Civil Rights bill, but it died in Congress. Robert Kennedy, his brother's Attorney-General, blamed lethargy on the part of the public, but King was determined to prove him wrong. He marshalled his forces carefully, giving them training in non-violence, removing any weapons they had, and by role-playing taught them to sing in the face of insults, and endure being beaten without retaliating.

Then he led them to sit in at lunch counters in Birmingham, Alabama, which claimed to be the most entrenched bastion of white supremacy. A state injunction was out to prevent the demonstration, and he was accompanied by hundreds of well-wishers, along with ghouls who wanted to see him humiliated and jailed. They had their hopes fulfilled when he was led to prison for the thirteenth time. On this occasion he was placed in solitary confinement, and he took the opportunity to write a moving document: 'Letter from a Birmingham Jail', in which he traced the history of his people from their transportation from Africa as slaves, to their present state as prisoners of the system. It was issued as a pamphlet by a group of Quaker sympathisers, and reproduced in many magazines. Copies went to the White House, and reached the mass of Americans, proving that the pen had once again been mightier than the sword.

When the older students failed to keep the sit-ins going in Birmingham, he appealed to enthusiastic high school students to take over. Joined by their brothers and sisters from junior schools, they marched on 2 May 1963. This was a controversial move, and King hesitated to give his consent. The column was attacked and routed by police with dogs and water-cannon, watched by the television cameras; the pictures caused revulsion all over the world. In the peroration of a speech, King warned the opposition:"We will wear you down by our capacity to suffer. In winning victory, we will not only win our freedom, we will so appeal to your heart and your conscience that we will win you too."

The situation in Alabama was electric, and when a bombing campaign began against the King family, the President went on television to tell the nation that he was sending in federal troops – not before time, as negroes were taking to the streets with rocks and knives. King pleaded for non-violence, but he was up against another leader, Malcolm X, and his Black Muslim movement which attracted the most disaffected and reckless in black society. King resolved to have a great march on the seat of government in Washington to support the President's bill, ensuring Civil Rights to every American.

The date selected was 28 August 1963. Coretta joined him, though she rarely left their children, who now numbered four. Almost a quarter of a million people gathered near the White House to march to the Lincoln Memorial. The seething thousands included many white sympathisers and almost all the most famous entertainers of the day. They joined together to sing the old Negro spirituals and wave aloft their banners, asking for the freedom that had been promised a century ago – and an army of television cameras beamed pictures across the world. King was the last of many speakers, and before he addressed them the crowd had begun to thin, milling about and looking for picnic places, but when he was introduced as 'The moral leader of the nation', they regrouped and prepared to listen.

He was the focus of universal attention, and as usual it inspired him. He started his carefully tuned and worked-over speech by echoing Lincoln's Gettysburg address, and flung a challenge to the administration to act immediately, not in some unspecified future.

"We can never be satisfied," he said, "as long as a negro in Mississippi cannot vote, and a negro in New York believes he has nothing to vote for."

The vast audience roared and clapped and shouted. He was at one with them, his heart beating with theirs, every word echoing their spirit. Then he abandoned his notes and launched into a sequence that was a prose poem about his dream – "Deeply rooted in the American dream" – of black and white sitting at one table of brotherhood. His rich, honey-sweet voice threaded lines from the psalms and the national anthem into the texture of his address, and he ended: "When we let freedom ring – when we let it ring from every village and hamlet, from every state and city we will be able to speed that day when all of God's children, black and white men, Jews and Gentiles, Protestants and Catholics, will be able to join hands and sing in the words of the old Negro spiritual 'Free at last! Free at last! Thank God Almighty, we are free at last!'"

The shouts and applause rose in the sunlit air to the vault of heaven. If he had never done anything else in his life, that one speech would have ensured that his memory would live in his country's history. But it was only the culmination of all that had gone before – his people's struggle, his faith, his humiliations, all summed up in one tremendous torrent of words. And the man at the centre of this flood of emotion was numb. He sat through a reception at the White House, receiving the accolades of the President and his own party. Back at his hotel, the rejoicings continued; Coretta left the scene of her husband's triumph to go back to the children, but he remained – on the high of a lifetime.

Those were the Sixties, when sexuality had its own liberation theology. A tape of the proceedings at the party found its way into the office of the F.B.I, and it indicated 'sexual activity' in King's room. It was rumoured that this was not an

154

isolated occasion; malicious gossip reported that his partners were both black and white. It seemed that the segregationalists were right – had they not warned what would happen if niggers were allowed to get uppity?

Tragedy put an end to speculation. In Birmingham, Alabama, four negro girls had been killed by the bomb-blast in a chapel. In his eulogy at their funeral, King spoke movingly of the redemptive value of their deaths, and hoped it would bring life to their dark city. Then he went to Atlanta to write the history of the Birmingham campaign; that was where he heard the news of President Kennedy's assassination. As he waited by his TV set, like the rest of the nation, he said sombrely: "I don't think I am going to live to reach forty... This is a sick nation, and I don't think I can survive either."

Coretta and the children gathered round him, aghast at his words, their devotion casting aside every other consideration.

Martin Luther King was nominated '*Time's Man of the Year*', but his intelligence was insulted by having to give the same speech over and over again. Every move he made was monitored by friend and foe alike; he was a man in a straitjacket, which he tore at blindly. Ordinary blacks idolised him, which made him feel unworthy. He gave way to depression, and turned from it to the outstretched arms of women, anxious to share momentarily in his fame. Gleefully, the F.B.I. recorded his lapses; his feelings of guilt had physical effects on him – sleep became elusive. Sometimes he felt that another Martin Luther King existed, over whom he had no control.

On 2 July 1964 the Civil Rights Bill was signed by President Johnson. King was in St Augustine, Florida, standing by helplessly as a thousand white demonstrators frenziedly attacked any negro in sight, but the law now existed to prosecute them. It was another milestone passed, and he set his sights on a solution to the problem of poverty amongst his people, which he formulated in a Bill of Rights for the Disadvantaged. The summer heat saw riots breaking out in the negro ghettoes of the northern cities, and he found himself unable to control their violence. This was a new generation of young men, nourished on the slogans of Black Power. This, and the constant calls on his unique talents as a speaker, wore him down. His detractors called him "De Lawd" – instead of turning it aside with a laugh, he allowed it to hurt him.

Exhausted, he entered hospital for a rest in October, where Coretta telephoned him to say he had won the Nobel Peace Prize – at thirty-five, the youngest recipient. Congratulations were far from unanimous, but he accepted it on behalf of his people. On his way to Norway to receive it, he preached at St Paul's Cathedral in London, the first non-Anglican to do so. The young people of Oslo showed him that they knew the anthem of the Civil Rights movement: "We Shall Overcome".

Ten years after Rosa Parks had refused to give up her seat to a white man on a Montgomery 'bus, King led a march from Selma, Alabama, to the state capital fifty miles away. The intention was to present a petition to Governor Wallace, one of the most virulent segregationalists in the legislature, calling on him to guarantee negro voting rights. The marchers suffered imprisonment, and an ordeal by tear-gas and clubbing, but they reached their objective. The Washington Post wrote: "King has proven himself a master organiser of demonstrations, and has exposed the plight of the negro in the south as has never been done before" – and pointed to his use of television to "make racism in the south come alive".

After a speech that roused his hearers to applause, on the scale of the 'Dream' speech in Washington, the words of the Civil Rights anthem were rewritten:

"Deep in my heart, I do believe
We have overcome, today."

In spite of renewed death threats and the bugging of every hotel room, car and aircraft he used, he led another thirty thousand people to City Hall in Chicago to ask for their rights. The battle was won on 6 August 1965 when President Lyndon Johnson completed the work of his predecessor J.F. Kennedy by signing the Voting Rights Bill. King was present at the ceremony.

When he spoke out against the Vietnam war he lost Johnson's regard, and was told to stick to his own territory, combating racism. There were more violent riots in the black ghettoes; one in Watts, L.A., left thirty-four dead and thousands arrested. Sick at heart, he visited the city. In Mississippi he held a joint march with the Black Power movement; their threatening slogans caused renewed force against them, and he did not repeat the experiment. His influence was waning with the young people who took up arms against the authorities, and against one another. A battle in Chicago, unprecedentedly bloody, lasted for days, and King narrowly escaped a knife thrown at him.

But the burning issue that divided America in 1967 was the Vietnam war; guilt for the conflict united black and white alike. King pointed out that young Americans unable to live on the same street were allowed to butcher Asians together. To those who begged him to be less vocal about the war, he replied: "Injustice anywhere is a threat to justice everywhere."

He had plans to head an inter-racial march on Washington, reviving his great days. In March 1968 he was asked if he would go to Memphis, where some refuse disposal workers were striking to unionise, and better their wages and conditions. It was not in him to withold his support. As a march got under way, with King receiving the usual adulation, there was a flurry of activity at the rear. Unknown to him, youths were smashing windows and looting. When he became aware of what was happening, he tried to call off the march. From the Rivermount Holiday Inn, he and his aides watched, powerless, as the police waded into the crowd, using tear-gas and clubs and finally guns – a negro boy of sixteen was killed. King saw it as his own failure, but he would not accept it, and promised to return.

In the first days of April he redeemed his pledge. He spoke to a crowd at an evening meeting, telling them he wanted to be with them in spite of a bomb threat to his plane, and the rewards that were promised to anyone who murdered him. The rich voice wrought its old magic and the crowd roared back at him; this was the south as he understood it, that understood him. A dialogue developed, and they inspired each other. He had always been called 'The Black Moses', and this time he said:"I have been to the mountain-top. And I've seen the Promised Land."

Later, in his hotel room, his brother visited him and they talked until the small hours. Waking late, he received a visit from some young militants he hoped to win over to non-violence, but they were unco-operative, and he sent them away. He was dining with friends, and he waited on the verandah for someone to fetch him a topcoat as the air was fresh after an overnight storm.

As he stood alone, a shot rang out, fired by a white ex-convict called James Earl Ray. It shattered the right side of his face and neck. His friends got him to a hospital, but he died during an operation that was very nearly hopeless.

His death bred rumours that triggered riots in a hundred and ten cities; the fires in Washington could be seen for many miles. It was the final irony that the Nobel Peace Prizewinner was the unwitting cause of the deaths of thirty-nine people, mostly of his own colour.

A day of national mourning was announced by President Johnson, and his widow led a silent march through Memphis in his place. Tributes poured in from prominent people all over the world; even the militants came to his funeral. Fifty thousand mourners followed his coffin, mounted on a mule-cart, and millions watched the television broadcast. He was laid to rest in the South View Cemetery in Atlanta, where the memorial tablet reads: "Free at last! Free at last! Thank God Almighty, I'm free at last!"

His wife and children have dedicated themselves to perpetuate his work for the poor and oppressed. The Martin Luther King Jr. Centre for Non-Violent Change is maintained in Atlanta, where the texts of his books and speeches, sermons and personal papers are preserved, and the continuing history of the movement he initiated is set out in a splendid display.

The whole world owes him a debt of gratitude for proving that non-violent demonstration can alter oppressive regimes. The marching feet were not only successful in his own country; they were echoed in Moscow, Warsaw, Budapest and Tallinn – above all, in Berlin, where, in the words of the spiritual "The Walls Came Tumbling Down."

BILLY GRAHAM

North Carolina, where Billy Graham was born on 7 November 1918, was at that time overwhelmingly rural, and he was a farmer's son. In the Civil War, both his grandfathers had fought on the Confederate side and been wounded; his parents taught the Shorter Catechism and the fear of hellfire, and if that did not result in good behaviour his father enforced it with a strap. In spite of this formidable education, young Billy was taken to the doctor because "he never seemed to run down"; he was not only hyperactive, he was also a nail-biter. He helped out with the haymaking and milking, but did it without enthusiasm. What really occupied his every spare minute was reading; anything printed was grist to his mill, including an abridged version of Gibbons's *Decline and Fall of the Roman Empire.* As time went on he elongated into a skinny youth, and his rather large head was filled with thoughts of baseball (at which he was not as good as he would have liked to be) and girls (whom he kissed robustly, but never went any further).

In 1935, during the Great Depression, a bank-failure having resulted in the disappearance of his savings, and a bad accident on the farm, caused Graham Senior to turn to the Lord, and he frequented revival meetings led by an evangelist of the old school, Mordecai Ham. These went on from Harvest to Thanksgiving, and at one point a prayer was offered up that someone from Charlotte – the district where Billy was born – would preach the Gospel to the ends of the earth. Totally unaware that he would provide an answer to this petition, Billy stayed on the sidelines, using his father's truck to ferry members of the congregation to the Tabernacle. One evening, out of curiosity, he entered and was immediately struck by the preacher, who seemed to know all the sins he had contemplated without actually committing. He joined the choir, though he would always be far from musical, and sat next to a pair of cheerful, enthusiastic brothers – Grady and T.W. Wilson. So began a friendship for life.

On the 6th of November that year, when the evangelist issued the invitation for those who felt the call to go forward, Billy went with the rest. An immediate neighbour was a woman with tears streaming down her face; Billy envied her deep feelings – for him it was not an emotional matter, just a sober conviction. Actually he made his submission alone in his room at home. He wanted to witness to Christ, but only felt capable of listening to others. Grady Wilson wanted to be a minister, and started his preaching career with a sermon of one and a half hours. He timed it by Billy's watch – a symbol of his father's prosperity in those hard times – and managed to overwind it. It was a sign of Billy's easygoing character that he did not hold this against him, and still admired him greatly.

Billy graduated without distinction in 1936, and was destined for Bob Jones College, a Fundamentalist stronghold in Cleveland, Tennessee. The summer before he entered, an employee of his father's initiated him into the mysteries of selling brushes, door to door. He became carried away with enthusiasm for the product, which he sold with missionary ardour. By the end of his stint, he held the record for sales in the two Carolinas. He found life on the road an eye-opening experience, and had some encounters with sin, though they left him him with no desire to emulate the sinners. After his day's work he studied the Bible and prayed, and followed his favourite preacher Jimmie Johnson on his circuit.

One day they arrived in the city jail at Munroe. With the pious chicanery sometimes practised by itinerant preachers, Johnson called on Billy to testify how Christ had changed his life. He rose to the occasion, exaggerating his faults, and ending with a moving account of his awareness of salvation. What the prisoners made of this is not recorded, but Billy left the meeting with a new, urgent ambition – to become a preacher himself.

Bob Jones College proved to be a false start; the location was bleak, and his health suffered. On doctor's orders, he transferred to the Florida Bible Institute. The campus had once been a country club, and was now a resort for good Fundamentalists. The students earned money, caddying for guests, acting as guides, and washing dishes. Billy also made an unexpected use of the golf course. After a disappointment when a girl turned him down for a better prospect, he suffered depression and went for long, lonely walks. Around midnight, he found himself at the eighteenth green and knelt down, pledging his life to preaching.

His first sermon was a disaster. Invited to preach by one of his teachers at Palatke in the north of Florida, he gave an address based on what he remembered of a book of sermons he had read. In eight minutes his memories were exhausted, and his mentor had to take over.

This setback made him more resolved than ever to perfect his technique, and he could be found in quiet corners haranguing inanimate objects and threatening them with hellfire if they persisted in their sins. He was not averse to self-promotion, occasionally putting his exploits in a rosy light to ensure full houses when he was invited to preach. Every invitation was accepted with alacrity, no matter how far-flung the venue. He did not always trouble to check his facts, but he generated so much energy, and spoke in such mind-numbing decibels, the cynics were silenced.

In the summer of 1938 he held his first revival meetings at East Palatke Baptist Church. Finding that he was a Presbyterian, a hasty immersion was arranged at nearby Silver Lake. His ordination took place some months later. So successful had his mission been, some visiting talent-spotters from Wheaton College, Illinois – at that time the leading Fundamentalist College in the country – considered him to be good material. They took back news of the rising star to their principal, who offered him a year's free tuition as his parents were unable to afford the fees.

A fellow student introduced him to Ruth Bell, the much-travelled daughter of missionaries, born and brought up in China. She had been a solemn and slightly morbid child who had set her heart on going to the mission field in Tibet, and gaining a martyr's crown. As a young woman, she had lost none of her whole-hearted dedication, and was startlingly pretty. Her early adventures made her fascinating to stay-at-home Billy, and he soon wrote to his mother that he intended to marry Ruth, though as yet he had not even asked her out on a date. When he did so, he behaved with a mixture of arrogance and naivety. Something about him intrigued her, and she continued to go out with him. Their respective 'calls' – hers to the missions and his to itinerant preaching – seemed incompatible, but they agreed to pray about their relationship.

Billy was happy that God proved amenable to his plans, and Ruth consented to an engagement in July 1941. It was to last for eighteen months, to enable the young couple to finish college and Billy to obtain gainful employment. A wealthy printer and publisher heard him preach in the college chapel and offered him a pastorship at Western Springs, Illinois. Typically, he accepted the post without consulting his future wife, who not for the last time had to accept his assurance that it was the will of God. Such was her love and belief in his gifts, she subordinated her life to his, though she never felt bound to restrict her criticisms, and was a strong influence on his decisions.

He made a success of his ministry – so much so, the church had to be enlarged. He also inherited a radio programme from a popular pastor who was overstretched. Quickly realising that he needed musical items, he prevailed upon a well-known bass-baritone, Bev Shea, to perform on air. The time was paid for by listeners' contributions, and by selling sheet-music of the songs. Bev Shea continued to perform for the Billy Graham Organisation for over forty years.

Religion had a revival in the war years; all sects were seeking to minister to young people drafted into the Services, or working in defence plants. The Evangelicals' campaign was called 'Youth for Christ', and Graham was invited to join the Chicago branch. On a late May evening in 1944 he paced backstage in a hired hall that seated three thousand, listening to the excited buzz of a full house. He suffered a crippling attack of stage-fright; nevertheless, his swift delivery and the certainty of his reiteration of "The Bible says..." caused forty-six of his hearers to declare for Christ. At the time, the Y.F.C. had no follow-up plans for them, but the numbers told in Graham's favour and he was asked to join Youth for Christ International, which hoped to mount worldwide campaigns. He was soon on his way, doing a series of one-night stands all over America. In September 1945 he even missed the birth of his first child, a daughter called Virginia, while his wife shared a home with her parents.

The following spring he made a tour of Europe, including the British Isles, scarred by the war and suffering material deprivation. To the natives, the young Americans with their fresh faces and colourful clothes seemed like visitors from another planet. Some were suspicious of their brashness and their recourse to sentiment. In particular, Graham's machine-like delivery was hard to follow, but he made friends with a young Welsh preacher called Stephen Olford. On his next visit to England, he sought him out and Olford shared with him the great spiritual benefit he received from observing a period of quiet. There had been no time for silence in Graham's headlong existence, and as his friend described his experience, he replied with tears: "Stephen – I see it; that's what I want; that's what I need in my life."

The two young men prayed together, and then Graham sprang to his feet and paced about, laughing and crying out: "I have it... I'm filled! This is the turning-point in my life."

Afterwards he seemed to speak with a new authority. Not with more confidence – he had always had that – but now he talked of Jesus as if he knew him in a personal way. The next test of his ministry was to organise a revival campaign in his home town, Charlotte. He accepted the challenge with some trepidation, fearing those who had known him since childhood would be sceptical. He tried to ensure the success of his visit with every kind of publicity – telephone-calls, news handouts, leaflet bombing, stickers on every kind of surface, personal appearances and radio spots. Grady Wilson, who was part of the team, wondered if Graham had gone over the top, but when he saw the number of young people responding to the invitation at the end of the first meeting, he acknowledged that Graham had judged correctly. Middle America was ready to receive his message.

In 1948 he left the shelter of the Y.F.C. and set out on his own. The parent body had enabled him to develop his particular talents, and he was ready to walk forth on a wider stage. He saw the prime enemy as communism, together with the twin sins of sexual promiscuity and financial fraud. During his first independent campaign he called together his closest associates and asked them to draw up a manifesto for dealing with the scandals that had brought down other evangelists. At the top of everyone's list were sex and money. They resolved upon the highest standard of clean living; not only would they be above reproach, they would be seen to be. Even casual meetings with women alone were ruled out; they set themselves to chaperone each other.

Money was dealt with by handing over all the 'love offerings' of the faithful to the sponsors of the campaigns, who paid them what they considered to be their due; the labourers were worthy of their hire. They also agreed to take independent estimates of crowd attendances rather than be accused of exaggeration. Graham made a return trip to England, and others to Miami and Baltimore, none outstandingly successful. Then came Altoona, Pennsylvania. It was so disastrous that it became the 'low' by which all other campaigns were measured. There were mitigating circumstances, but Graham felt his star was setting before he had had a chance to testify to the Lord.

Doubts began to loom large in his mind, and these were reinforced when he found himself engaged to preach with an old colleague from Y.F.C. days, Chuck Templeton, at a student conference at Forest Home, a retreat house in the mountains near Los Angeles. It was generally conceded that Templeton's sermons had the edge, but Graham was the more successful coaxer of converts. Templeton proposed that they should both take a sabbatical and study theology at Princeton.

The arguments for and against liberal theology and Bible criticism went back and forth between them. Every time his friend made a point Graham felt threatened. If the Bible was not the literal truth, how could he preach it to those who needed his clear message? He admitted he was not an intellectual, familiar with complicated ideas and shades of meaning. Further education would only confuse and undermine him. When he listened to his friend's talented preaching, and the discussions it provoked, his feeling of uncertainty returned. To dispel it he took a walk in the pinewoods. He turned off the main path and sat down on a large stone, balancing his Bible on a tree stump. There he heard an inner voice, and recognised it as his own, appealing to heaven in an act of humility: "Oh God, I cannot prove certain things. I cannot answer some of the questions Chuck is raising, and some other people are raising, but I accept this Book by faith as the Word of God."

Henceforward he did not hesitate to point to the Bible and reiterate with complete confidence: "The Bible says..." He used it as a key to unlock men's hearts and consciences, and bring them to surrender as he had. There was no further confrontation with dangerous ideas; nothing but the pure light of faith shining out like a beacon, and attracting others who flew to him for reassurance. Today a stone, suitably inscribed, marks the spot where he made his decision.

In 1949 some lay people in Los Angeles approached him to conduct a crusade in that most extrovert and volatile of cities. It would be easy to point to the sins of its people, and call for repentance, but he took no chance of the message going unheard. Nine months before the commencement, hundreds of prayer groups were organised to pray for success. Helpers were trained to look after enquirers, and guide them to a Bible-orientated church. He hired a huge circus tent from Ringling Brothers, seating six thousand people, and pitched it at the junction of two busy streets. In spite of a twenty-five thousand dollar pre-publicity drive, the first three weeks brought only modest returns.

For many years his style of preaching changed little. He paced the platform, walking as much as a mile, it was claimed, during the course of an evening. His arms were raised in supplication, and he used his hands like pistols; his rich voice poured forth in denunciation. He could detect a blink at the back of the tent, and change tone to capture flagging attention. President Truman had recently announced that the Russians possessed the atomic bomb, which was calculated to concentrate minds wonderfully, and this gave a weighty boost to his thunderings against communism. He warned that Los Angeles was a hotbed of fellow-travellers, and he saw the wrath of God poised over the city.

It was heady stuff, but the Canvas Cathedral – as the publicity christened it – remained only two-thirds full. The conversion of a minor radio-presenter was the first windfall of a wider harvest and, more importantly, the intervention of William Randolph Hearst, the newspaper tycoon. He had heard of Graham's attitude to the Communist threat and sent telegrams to his editors, tellihg them: "Puff Graham." The result was that articles appeared about him nationwide.

This paid off when he came to Catholic and Episcopalian Boston in the unfamiliar territory of New England. Crowds packed his meetings to the doors and many were turned away. Graham begged his team to pray for him. To face the adulation of capacity crowds night after night had turned the heads of many an evangelist, but Graham somehow stayed on an even keel. He had all the gifts of a super-salesman, but claimed no credit for them. He was the first to admit that the secret of his magnetism was hidden from him.

Ruth helped to keep him well-anchored in the ground. He was given to acting out the roles in the Old and New Testament stories he loved to tell, receiving widespread acclaim for the punchiness of his dialogue, and the vivid quality of the characterisations.

"As an actor, you're pretty much of a ham", was Ruth's comment. "Bill, Jesus didn't act out the gospel, he just preached it. I think that's all he has called you to do."

The press loved to interview her, and she provided them with some quotable lines. When asked if she was lonely due to Graham's travels, she said: "I'd rather have a little of Bill than a lot of any other man."

Another daughter was born into the family in 1950, and a son in 1952, who was named after his father and grandfather. In their infancy, the babies were never quite sure who Graham was, but Ruth read his letters to them, led prayers for him every evening, and they listened to his radio programmes together. By the time the children numbered five, Ruth had made a home for them at Montreat in North Carolina, where their father could rest between campaigns, in the heart of a loving family.

A crusade in South Carolina brought him to the notice of Henry R. Luce, publisher of the influential *Life* and *Time* magazines. Luce came from a missionary background and approved of Graham's message, as well as his politics. In July 1950, a protracted effort to be asked to meet President Truman at the White House was successful; Graham manoeuvred the President into praying with him and his aides, which delighted them so much that they babbled of it to the waiting press. The great man was not pleased by the leak, and indicated that no further interviews would be given to Mr Graham.

As always, Graham learned from his mistake and never again divulged the details of his many meetings with world leaders. He continued with his crusades and inaugurated a nationwide radio programme, 'Hour of Decision', which had an audience of some twenty million. A television version was launched in 1951, but lasted only three years, owing to the difficulty of finding enough material for the greedy maw of the medium. A syndicated newspaper column, 'My Answer', followed in 1952, and 1953 saw the publication of the first of many devotional books, *Peace with God*.

By this time he was getting fifteen to twenty thousand letters a week, most enclosing small sums of money. He was persuaded by an associate to soft-pedal still further his requests for 'love offerings', and instead relied on a mailing-list of stalwarts, who received a tactfully mild hint that the time for a donation had come round once again. An office was opened to deal with mail, which became the headquarters of the Billy Graham Evangelistic Association. There were also two films in 1951 – *Mr Texas* and *Oiltown* – which could be described as Christian Westerns. The faithful supported them, and the making of other films was undertaken, but their quality was not high in the eyes of the critics.

The President might have been turned off by Graham's brand of piety, but Congress passed an act permitting him to hold a meeting on the steps of the Capitol. It was the highlight of a five-week takeover of Washington and gained a crowd of forty thousand, including a large number of the legislature.

The Korean war brought many letters from servicemen at the battlefront, and he visited them at Christmas 1952. He went out as a private citizen, but was later sponsored by the Pentagon and given V.I.P. treatment as he toured the forward positions, meeting the troops and being shown the grimmest evidence of the tragedy of war. He also met South Korean Christians who had suffered for their faith, and was humbled by their gratitude for his visit. He came home to assist in the inauguration of Dwight Eisenhower, and afterwards baptised the President in the White House.

On two of the most divisive questions of the Fifties his stand was at first ambiguous. He refused to condemn Macarthyism, though he did not endorse it either. Racism he deplored, though until the Supreme Court ruled against segregation, he permitted it at his rallies in the South. It was his practice to be ruled purely by local custom, but as time went on he acquired many black friends and associates.

His cool reception by Harry S. Truman seems to have been an isolated incident. Hostility did not survive a meeting with him. This was nowhere more apparent than in his Harringay campaign in London during 1954. The press was almost entirely hostile, having gained the impression that he was coming to make a condescending attempt to convert the British. It was February, the dreariest month of the year; the building was vast and gloomy, and unknown to most Londoners. Yet the phlegmatic British packed it and responded in much the same proportions as their American counterparts. There were two innovations; free double tickets, so each recipient was encouraged to bring one enquirer, and land-line links that relayed the services to local rented halls and churches. A headcount of the combined audience numbered two million. Churchill offered him a five-minute interview that stretched to forty, as he listened to Graham's optimistic answer to his question: "What hope do you have for the world, young man?"

The critics ate their words, and the Archbishop of Canterbury blessed the final meeting at Wembley Stadium which comprised 185,000 souls.

In deference to the British character, Graham divested himself of his more extrovert behaviour. He was less abrasive and more static. It was noticeable that he refrained from giving the exact dimensions of heaven, and expressed doubt about the precise heat of hellfire; his genuine humility made him capable of change. And England was a gateway to the Commonwealth. After a visit to Europe, during which he appeared at the Olympic Stadium in Berlin, speaking to larger crowds than Hitler attracted in the same venue, he made his way to India.

If he had been a novelty in war-ravaged Europe, with his blond good looks, he stood head and shoulders above the inhabitants of the sub-continent. Hindus, much to his alarm, were prepared to add him to the number of their gods. An interview with Prime Minister Nehru was a success when he abandoned the subject of politics and fell back on Evangelical Christianity.

Back at home he cemented a friendship with Vice-President Nixon – brought up a Quaker, but converted by an Evangelical preacher. During the 1956 election campaign, Graham led the Evangelical vote into the Republican fold, and future Presidential candidates had to reckon with him. As far as the politics of religion were concerned, he ceased to make common cause with the Fundamentalists, and his New York crusade of 1957 was ecumenical, being backed by Episcopalians and Modernists. There was a further imnovation – phone lines for people with problems. Live transmissions of his Saturday night services reached millions of homes, and the numbers of decision-makers escalated.

He was worried that he was practically ignored by the black population, until he invited Martin Luther King to join him on the platform at Madison Square Gardens. This acknowledgement of their revolutionary hero pleased his followers, and the two leaders appreciated that they needed each other. Graham was exhausted after dealing with huge crowds every night, but it was only when he failed to recognise his wife in an elevator that he decided to rest during the day. The concluding rally in Times Square on Labour Day was attended by over a hundred thousand people, including many who would never have gone to a church. One of the most rewarding signs of success was the number of young men electing to go into the ministry, ensuring good leadership for the future.

The year 1959 saw him in the uttermost parts of the earth; Australia, New Zealand, Russia and Africa received him with varying degrees of enthusiasm. As he grew older he became more tolerant of liberals and Catholics, and they in their turn began to appreciate him – not without some envy of his triumphant use of the media. It was his belief that if St Paul had been alive in the twentieth century, he would have used its techniques to spread the faith.

He succumbed to the Kennedy charm, and met the President after his election in 1960, but never came as close to him as he did with Lyndon Johnson, when he took over after Kennedy's assassination. They were both farm boys without academic honours, and formed a mutual admiration society. It did Johnson no harm politically to be associated with Graham, and he also seems to have needed his rock-sure faith in the troubled times of his presidency.

Graham backed his welfare programmes, calling on audiences to help the underprivileged in America and the Third World, citing Jesus's care for the poor and the sick. He was not over-ready to welcome the Civil Rights Bill for negro equality, and thought legislation was not as effective as the conversion of individual souls to eradicate separatism. He went to Los Angeles during the Watts riots, surveying the smoking chaos of the suburb from a helicopter, and was shocked into pronouncing it a Communist plot to seize the hearts and minds of the black population.

The Sixties as a whole gave him ammunition for many new sermons on the dangers of the permissive society. Sex, drugs and the psychedelic culture all received the thunder of his denunciation, and he did not hesitate to blame lack of parental control for the misdemeanours of the young. He shook his head over his country, claiming that only the Second Coming could remedy its ills. His distress was beamed through closed-circuit television to meetings in selected cities over the whole country, reaching millions of people.

He called a meeting of worldwide Evangelical leaders in Berlin in 1966. It lasted ten days, and in his opening address he outlined his traditional values yet again, insisting on Bible Christianity and individual salvation. Not surprisingly, there was no criticism from the assembled company, which included Orthodox and Catholic observers; even Vatican Radio proclaimed it a great event.

At Christmas he tested the water for a visit to the troops fighting the Vietnam war, which was at its height of unpopularity at home. His attitude was coloured by his friendship with Lyndon Johnson, who gave his blessing, knowing that Graham would not take a stand against American involvement. He and Cardinal Spellman of New York, who made a similar visit, reported back, praising the troops highly but agreeing with the President that only a speedy end to the conflict would pacify public opinion. The Cardinal called for a mighty military onslaught, but Graham admitted that he had no solution to the problem.

After Martin Luther King's assassination in 1968, it was hoped that Graham might take his place as the exponent of non-violent action against racism, but he chose not to commit himself, relying instead upon his influence on those in power. He reckoned that if he could persuade them to act as Christians, the country would become redeemed as well. The next election saw the triumph of his friend Richard Nixon, whom he had endorsed whole-heartedly. He cannot be blamed too harshly for his misreading of a character that was extraordinarily complex, since Nixon managed to confuse so many voters into giving him the victory.

But in 1972 the home political situation was far from being his only commitment. Crusades in Northern Ireland and the Republic, as well as South Africa, brought him face to face with conflict. He preached co-operation and non-segregation, and showed great courage in situations that could have become dangerous. But perhaps his greatest success was in his Organisation bringing together the rapidly growing Christian body in South Korea where three million people heard him in the space of five days. On the last day, with Ruth by his side – for her it was a return to the country where she had

171

received part of her education – he preached to a crowd of half a million. When he watched them waving up at his departing aircraft, he said with awe: "This is the work of God. There is no other explanation."

He also drew large crowds in Russia and China, both countries having given him a warm welcome. Simple curiosity might explain the size of the turn-out, but he was certainly used by the authorities to emphasise their tolerance of religion – a tolerance which did not in fact exist – but his meetings were a chance for the faithful to worship openly.

Vietnam and Watergate – the two scars on the American psyche that persisted until the time of Ronald Reagan's presidency – left their mark on Graham too. Everyone knew he spent most of the war either defending the hawks or evading the issue, and he backed Nixon until his malpractices were irrefutable. In this he was at one with all those who believed in their country, right or wrong, and he always found it difficult to see any fault in those who were his friends.

At the beginning of the Seventies he laid careful plans for the Lausanne Congress of Evangelicals in 1974. Their numbers and influence had grown steadily throughout the world, and he thought they should come together and show their strength. Although he was not anxious for his own Organisation to have too high a profile, its brilliant use of technology was a pattern for the rest. By now, every part of the globe could be reached by the Gospel message.

The Lausanne Covenant drawn up by the Assembly was said to be "one of this century's exemplary statements on Christian beliefs, concerns and commitment." The delegates went back to their own ministries enriched and refreshed.

As the decade drew to a close several television Evangelists overtook Graham in capturing public interest. Most fell by the wayside, unable to match his record on sexual and financial probity. None of them ever succeeded in becoming, as he did, the friend of Presidents, so that his visits abroad had almost ambassadorial status.

Almost – but not quite. He remained his own man about nuclear weapons, and backed every move to have them reduced or eliminated. This made him welcome in countries behind the Iron Curtain, which initially invited him for propaganda purposes. When taxed with this, he said: "Wanting to preach in Russia is not my ego; it's my calling."

He would go anywhere and do anything to gain a hearing for the Good News. In fact, by the late Eighties he had the technological knowhow to make a simultaneous transmission to most of the world, but drew back from this final step. His contributions in money and effort to the evangelisation of all for Christ far outstrip any other single person's. He would, however, be the first to point out how much he owes to a disciplined and effective team of workers. His ability to choose and delegate to his helpers is an outstanding part of his ministry. They have hammered out formulae that fit every situation an evangelist could face, getting the maximum help from the most primitive organs of dissemination as well as the high technology of the most advanced nations.

After forty years, the crusade machine rolls on oiled wheels, but its central core remains the number of people responding to the invitation Billy Graham holds out to every listener, to make a decision for Christ. His ability to do this makes him unique. For the rest, he is an ordinary man, who appeals to the best in ordinary men. He enables them to find the Saviour in whose company he walks, and he may be considered a true vessel of grace.

JACKIE PULLINGER

Croydon, a London suburb that proudly preserves its own identity, was under fire from flying-bombs in 1944, and staked its claim to be the most bombed borough in the country. In spite of this there was a great feeling of optimism. The battle of Normandy was going well, and people were turning their minds to the reconstruction of Europe and the creation of a new, better and peaceful world. Jackie Pullinger was born, one of twin girls, in a comfortably-off middleclass family. As only one child had been expected, her father was granted compassionate leave from the Services. He was greatly out-numbered by the women in his life; the twins had two sisters, and it was to fill what she believed to be a void that Jackie decided to be a tomboy, and cultivated an interest in rugger.

One of her early memories of Sunday School was being pointed at by a missionary of the old school, who declaimed: "And could God want you on the Mission Field?" Although she had very little idea what was meant, she claimed to have been called – but learned to keep quiet about it, as people only remembered when her behaviour was less than perfect. In answer to questions about her ambition, she said she wanted to be the conductor of an orchestra, or join the circus, or to be the first woman to climb Everest, as Hillary had recently done, in 1953.

A career in music was the most lasting of these ambitions, and when she left the boarding-school that she attended with her twin, she went on to the Royal College of Music, to study the piano and oboe. While still at school she had heard Billy Graham speaking on the radio, and been impressed, but when she passed a remark about this, one of the revered seniors dismissed the evangelist as a purveyor of 'mass emotion'. Jackie fastened on to the expression and for several years trotted it out whenever the talk turned to religion. At the R.C.M. she became a groupie of the brass players, and neglected her own instruments to follow them round their engagements and listen to their rehearsals. It was the very beginning of the silly Sixties, and though permissiveness had become the norm, it did not touch her. She found the men at the parties she went to resistable; she failed to be turned on by the Christians either, finding them unattractive and dull.

Commuting to London, one day on the train she ran into some old school friends who told her they had met some Christians who might be more to her liking. They introduced her to a Bible Study group; the members dressed normally and shared her interests. They told her that the route to God was through his Son, so she made a commitment to Jesus. This did not elate her; it was the result of logical thought. If Jesus had said he was the way to the Father, she had a choice of believing it or not – and she believed him. The group met one Sunday, and when she looked round she saw on every side people with a rather smug certainty that they were going to heaven. Jackie alone felt sorry that there were others who would not be going. She remembered afterwards that they had a supper of risotto she could not bear to eat.

Then she passed up a Rugger International to play the piano for an Evangelical tea-party; this was after she had left college with her diploma and a degree in music and started teaching. Suddenly, in the middle of the sausage-frying and the excited talk, she felt an impulse to offer her life to God. He seemed curiously unaware of her gift. None of the African missions she applied to wanted musicians. She tried every one of her Church contacts for advice and they all said: "Pray." Following their counsel, she raced for the post every morning, to see if the answer had come by mail.

Dreaming she was poring over a map with her family, she saw Hong Kong, shimmering pink. She felt called to go there, and wrote to the government of the Colony, offering her services. Again she received a negative answer, and had another from the mission to Hong Kong, who would not look at her until she was twenty-five. As she was twenty-two, the next three years seemed an age. Later, in a little village church, she had a vision of a woman holding out her arms to her. Like a rolling caption, words accompanied it: "What can you give us?" She felt this was not a request for material help, and what was really wanted was the love of Jesus.

A factory worker knew of a charismatic group at West Croydon which he felt could help her out of her dilemma. He took her along, warning her that odd things sometimes happened. Jackie thought there was nothing extraordinary when two people started talking in tongues, which were later translated. She heard a voice from God telling her to trust him. To show her trust she gave up her teaching job. Using her leisure, she went to help a minister called Richard Thompson in his Shoreditch parish; she sought a private interview with him, and began by staring tongue-tied at the carpet. Gradually she got up the courage to put her problem to him. God seemed to be calling her, but she didn't know where.

The answer took her breath away: "If I were you, I would go out and buy a ticket for a boat going on the longest journey you can find, and pray to know where to get off."

The idea of absolute trust seemed difficult and dangerous, but she felt it was right. Her parents did not see things in the same light, her father taking the liberal view that the people of the Third World had their own religions. Nevertheless he respected her decision. Many of her generation felt the call of the East, but they wanted to take from Eastern culture; Jackie wanted to give what was lacking in it. Her last glimpse of England included Richard Thompson charging down the platform after the boat-train, gasping: "Praise the Lord!"

Her ticket entitled her to a one-way trip from France to Japan. When she came to Hong Kong harbour, its beauty spoke to her. She packed her bags, gripped her guitar, and queued up to see the Immigration officials when they came aboard. They were wary and vigilant; Hong Kong was crammed with refugees from mainland China – they had been coming since the late forties, and the Cultural Revolution had recently sent a further influx. In just over ten years the population had grown from under a million to over five, and still they kept coming, to pack the tiny British island and the New Territories.

Jackie had to explain that she knew no-one, had no work, and only about six pounds in HK dollars. Not surprisingly, she was refused permission to land. Just in time, she remembered that her mother had spoken of her godson in the Hong Kong Police. The Immigration official was suitably impressed and returned her passport, advising her to obtain work quickly because her money would not last more than three days in such an expensive place.

Fortunately she found a teaching post – mornings only – in a primary school. But of course her real objective was to work as a missionary. She made the acquaintance of an elderly lady who ran a nursery school and church in the Walled City of Kowloon. Thinking it would be poor but picturesque, she was utterly unprepared for the reality. The answer to the quest for living space was to build upward; tall blocks of one-room apartments that were constantly being added to, and so close that there was just room for an open drain to run between them. The light was shut out, giving rise to the Chinese name 'Hak Nam' – the City of Darkness.

The stench from the refuse and sewage under their feet was appalling. Jackie was never to get used to it; walls and pathways had a patina of slime. Around them was the cranking of presses producing plastic flowers and cheap toys, and the cries of dogs being butchered to provide meat for restaurants. Jackie learned later that the police were almost helpless to keep law and order in the Colony, owing to a dispute about the ownership of Kowloon between the Chinese and English Governments. This meant it had become a centre for smuggling gold and drugs, illegal gambling and prostitution. The vacuum left by the police was filled by the Triads, two rival gangs who organised crime and battled between themselves over territory.

Mrs Donnithorne, who speedily became Auntie Donnie to Jackie, had found the Chinese parents were grateful for her attempts to educate their children. They permitted them to attend her nursery school, and allowed them to do their homework before they began helping in the cottage industries that were carried on in their homes. This was a real sacrifice, as the rates of pay were minimal and even the tiniest children had to be used to boost the family income. Auntie Donnie extracted a promise that Jackie would form a percussion band, organise group singing and English conversation classes, and play the harmonium for Sunday services.

The English conversation classes were particularly soul-destroying. All the learning was done by committing to memory, parrot-fashion. Jackie tried to get them to act out stories, but the unaccustomed freedom to move went to their heads, and they ran riot. Unable to speak Chinese, she lost control and they had to return to learning by heart. There was a system of frequent examinations too, that restricted any innovations.

The Sunday service was attended by older women, their babies strapped to their backs, who looked upon it as a chance to learn to read. There was also Bible Study in Cantonese which Jackie could not understand. She had no intention of making the difficult journey from her room every week, but an old vegetable-woman with a half-blind husband in tow buttonholed her and started talking to her rapidly. When she managed to get the words translated, she discovered that the woman was saying: "See you next week", over and over again. The knowledge that one person would be looking out for her persuaded her to return.

It was Auntie Donnie who pointed out the first drug addict she saw. In England the drug culture was just coming into fashion, but the West had profited by the drug trade to China for over two hundred years. Jackie believed addicts were violent, but soon found most of them were too ill to be anything but apathetic. She grew to know that the marks on the backs of their hands meant that they had proceeded from smoking ("Chasing the Dragon") to mainlining. The teenagers were closest to her generous heart. Walled City children had no chance of secondary education; there was no legal work for them – the boys were recruited by the Triads, and the girls went into prostitution. The drugs blunted their senses so they were less aware of the misery around them.

It was to salvage just one life from this dead-end existence that Jackie announced to Aunt Donnie: "I think the Lord would have me start a Youth Club."

The boy she wanted to rescue was called Chan Wo Sai, and came to her notice when he danced toward her, writhing sensuously, while she was trying to teach her primary class "Ten Green Bottles". He was fifteen years old. She found out where he lived – a bad place even by Walled City standards, being the remaining half of a crumbling room that he shared with his whole family. He spoke no English, and her Chinese was confined to a few phrases. She made contact with him by giving him a mute drum pad and sticks, and persuading him to practise on it. He was not musical, but she persisted because she could not get him out of her mind.

Finally she acknowledged that she loved this pathetic waif. Nothing in her life had prepared her for this rush of emotion. She supposed that love was romantic and, for a Christian, led to marriage. It seemed to have nothing in common with what moved her now – a love so deep that she could have laid down her life for Chan Wo Sai. As she was pondering what to do about the situation, in the sweltering heat of the summer of 1967, the Red Guards were terrorising mainland China, and a new flood of refugees was crowding into the already tightly-packed Colony. Inevitably there were riots, fomented by those who profited from them, and it was to prevent Chan Wo Sai from joining the boys who were being hired to throw stones that the Youth Club was born.

She planned to take the boys out for hikes, picnics, and visits to roller-skating rinks and forestry plantations. On week-day evenings she borrowed a room in the school, for darts and table-tennis. So she sublimated her emotion, and was enriched by a love that asked for nothing in return.

The children's parents thought Jackie ought to be giving vocational training, but she wanted to give them something like an ordinary adolescence – a break in the endless round of work. The 'good Christians' also criticised her because she made only brief references to Jesus; but though she longed to share her knowledge with them, she had no wish to produce 'rice Christians' – those who made their declarations of devotion in exchange for food and privileges.

She 'adopted' two girls who were at risk of going into prostitution, and shared her flat with them. Gradually she began to learn the family situations of the children, and discovered that if they could find work their parents pocketed their wages. The only way for them to keep their money was to move into a hovel with their peers, but more often than not they drifted into vice rackets. The more spirited boys were recruited by the Triads, which gave them a standing in the community and a sense of being part of a brotherhood. These were the enemy she had to fight, because of their influence over the boys. Many of them expected her to leave the Colony and go back to England. They could not believe that she had no money from her parents, or that she was as powerless as they were when dealing with the bureaucracy that governed the issue of identity papers and school admissions. But they began to accept her, and gave her a Chinese name: 'Poon Siu Jeh'.

In some ways she was more able to help them because she was not part of an established mission. Most of her missionary friends were middle-aged and hidebound. They did not reach the drug addicts, and much as she wanted to, she could not get through to them either. Help arrived unexpectedly when a Chinese couple came to take a service at the Chapel one Sunday. She did not understand the sermon they gave, but she knew they had a power that she would have given anything to possess. Afterwards she did her best to explain her need to them. "You haven't got the Holy Spirit", they said.

Without understanding what they meant – surely she had received it at her Confirmation? – she made an appointment to go to their flat. In the sparsely furnished room, there was a table, and conspicuous upon it were two plates; one with oranges, the other with wet towels. She thought the wet towels might be to cry into when she received the power, but it seems more likely that they were to mop up after the oranges had been eaten in celebration. The couple asked her to sit down, and prayed over her. Presently they said in English: "Now you begin speaking!" – very urgently, again and again.

In an agony of embarrassment she shut her mouth firmly, getting hotter and hotter. She didn't want to disappoint them, but she felt out of her depth in these un-English waves of enthusiasm.

A desperate prayer – "God help me" – came to her, and the moment she opened her mouth to voice it, a flood of speech burst from her. It was in no language that she knew, but it had cadences and rose and fell in patterns, as if she did. There was no accompanying exhilaration, yet she articulated with perfect confidence. Afterwards she remembered feeling glad that the unfamiliar sensation had not come when she was with people she knew. Her mentors wept with delight, and she had the feeling that they expected equal emotion from her. The very thought made her want to escape.

"You can expect the other gifts of the Spirit now", they assured her.

She had heard of the gifts of healing and prophecy, and realised there were others, and wondered how they would manifest themselves. Still embarrassed, she left as soon as she could; she was still failing to help people as the Bible had promised she would if she received the Holy Spirit. All her enquiries about it were met with blankness or evasion, though she contacted every religious group in the Colony. Then she heard that some newly-arrived Americans, Rick and Jean Willans, were holding a prayer meeting, and that it would be charismatic. She was very reluctant to go, yet her need was great and she decided to try one last time.

The first thing they asked her was if she spoke in tongues; she explained that she had done so, but had almost given it up because it seemed useless. Jean Willans took a firm line, and said she was doing the equivalent of throwing God's gift back in his face. A unique language had been given to her, and she must persist; Jean suggested she should start immediately. Again Jackie felt uncomfortable, speaking in this way, but it came into her head that she must not mind being a fool for Jesus's sake, and she carried on. After the Willanses had interpreted her prayer of praise and desire that God would make use of her, she realised that the gift was not frightening or involuntary, but under the direction of her own will.

Setting aside a quarter of an hour each day by the clock for speaking in the Spirit, she confessed her ignorance and asked to be led to the people she could help. After about six weeks she found that when she talked to the cases who had seemed hopeless, they responded to her. It was, she decided, because she had surrendered her will completely to God.

Christopher, one of her boys from the Youth Club, began to be absent from the meetings, and Jackie heard on the grapevine that he had succumbed to the temptation represented by the Triads. There were two gangs in the Walled City: the 14 K and the Ging Yu; they had parcelled out the district between them, never trespassing on each other's territory. The Youth Club was in 14 K's patch, and Jackie had learned all the exits and entrances to it, so she was more adept at getting about than the gangs, who only knew their own domain.

She pursued Christopher through the narrow streets and cornered him in a passage that she sealed by wedging across it an accordion she was carrying. Standing in his path, she put him through a catechism, seeking to prove that Jesus had come to save poor boys like him. He was helpless to argue, and admitted that he wanted to be a Christian. He did more: he went back to the Youth Club and testified to his resolution in front of his jeering companions.

The books of the Triad initiation rites – the secret signs and handshakes – the poems and ceremonies in which blood was drunk – all these he sent back in a courageous gesture. It was unheard of, and even the Triad brothers themselves were stunned.

Christopher's life was changed. He gained promotion in his factory and gave up gambling. His example was infectious, and served to attract other boys to the Youth Club and prayer meetings. One of the boys began to speak in tongues, and Christopher sang a beautiful translation in English – a language with which he was unfamiliar. Another boy made an identical translation in Chinese. Jackie began to think she was making progress, and this was confirmed when a full member of 14 K became a Christian. He was called Ah Ping, and he stuck by his resolution even when held down and beaten by seven gangsters, then left for dead with a terrible wound in his neck. He persuaded his friends to pray for the gangsters instead of seeking revenge, and the gash in his neck was healed with miraculous swiftness.

Jackie had difficulty in persuading the more respectable members of the Church to accept her boys. Eventually a wise priest convinced her that the Church was not ready for her converts, and that she must nourish them separately until the time was ripe. She held more prayer meetings in the evenings, as well as at weekends. It was not only children who had reformed their lives that she helped; when those who were arrested appeared in court, she stood by them whether they were innocent or guilty.

After four years of doing what she called "unstructured youth work", something happened that looked like a disaster. One of the boys who attended the Youth Club brooded on an imaginary snub he believed she had given him. He incited others into wrecking every item of furniture and equipment on the premises, and daubed the walls with excrement. When Ah Ping heard about it in the early hours of the morning, he alerted Jackie immediately. She stood in the wreckage, stricken by this rejection of herself and her work, tempted to give up and go home. Remembering in time the Christian duty to forgive, she set to work with a bamboo broom to clean the place up. She even managed to praise God, though it was between clenched teeth.

When she was ready to open the doors of the Youth Club again, she found a completely strange boy leaning against it. He made it clear that he was there to prevent further trouble, admitting that 'Goko' had sent him. It was like being told that the Devil had taken a personal interest in the affairs of the Club. Goko was the boss of the local branch of the 14 K, and held sway over much of the Walled City and the surrounding area. She tried to send a message – thanking him, but explaining that Jesus looked after them, and that they didn't need Goko's help. The guard thought she was mad, and remained at his post.

Upon further acquaintance he confessed he was addicted to opium. She told him the alternatives: 'cold turkey' – being locked in a room for a week without the drug, suffering the agonies of withdrawal, which could end in his death or permanent damage – or surrender to Jesus's healing power. It was really no contest; he decided to try the gentler method. One night he came into the Club and started to sing one of the hymns he had heard during his spell as guard. His voice was terrible, but he seemed happy and eventually prayed in tongues for half an hour. By the time he finished he was cured of his addiction without any withdrawal symptoms at all.

In the fullness of time Jackie met Goko himself. He invited her to a meal in a restaurant, and there on neutral territory they had a frank exchange of views. He equated her with himself in her power over people but admitted that he could not get his men off drugs, and that she could. He offered her his addicts if she wanted them. It was tempting to accept right away, but she wanted to be sure that he would not reclaim them when they were free of addiction.

He said: "You can have the rotten ones, and I'll keep the good ones for myself." Jackie agreed, explaining that it was the rotten ones Jesus had come for.

Each reclaimed boy brought another for treatment. Jackie's method was to lay hands on them and pray. Soon there were too many to be housed in her flat, the only safe environment for them; and so the Well came into existence – named for the Well of Salvation spoken of in Isaiah. Clean and bright, it was painted a calming green, and lifted them out of their slavery in the filth of the Walled City. When more accomodation was needed, she secured a series of apartments called Houses of Stephen, the first of which was opened in 1972.

In 1975 the Vietnamese refugees from the war zone began to arrive in great numbers, and Jackie's work-load increased. Fortunately the authorities were aware of her needs, and gave her spaces for rehabilitation units at two prime locations in the Colony. When the addicts came, they spent their first few days apart from the rest of the community, lovingly watched over by helpers who attended to their every need. Then they were ready to take their place in the community, joining in all the recreational activities as well as helping in the day-to-day running. Jackie preferred them to stay in the sheltered environment for eighteen months.

Goko, the old enemy, was losing his best men to Jackie.

184

He admitted the truth of the gospels, but said he could not give up his extortion rackets; if he did, he would have no money. He offered her his sons instead, but she refused because they were recalcitrant unbelievers. Instead she asked him why he did not set them a good example.

Months later, Jackie heard he was in prison on a 'possession of opium' charge, and went to see him. While in jail, he was not allowed drugs; she begged him to pray before the onset of withdrawal pains – and he did so, speaking in tongues and praising God. She made herself responsible for his appeal against sentence. During the break before this was heard, he was let out on bail, and took the opportunity to be baptised in Repulse Bay. His followers chartered a bus to witness the event. A year later he was attacked in a restaurant and his hand and arm were nearly severed by a knife. He forbade his friends to seek revenge, and prayed for healing, and for the surgeon who operated successfully on the wound. He celebrated his embarkation upon a changed life by taking the name 'New Paul'.

Jackie sent up a heart-cry to the Hong Kong Housing Department for more accommodation, and was offered a run-down collection of tin huts that had been used as temporary housing, called Hang Took Camp. The homeless from the Walled City learned new skills as they transformed it into a rehabilitation centre. She wanted the best for them, and they achieved it by their own efforts. People of substance in the Colony saw this, and came to help; not in a spirit of patronage, but because they appreciated the feeling of equality before God.

Today, apart from heroin and opium addicts, it is home to prostitutes, drunkards and street dwellers, all seeking a new way of life. To reach those who have escaped the efforts of the government to re-house them, Jackie and a band of helpers go out into the streets with blankets, food and clothes, to help them where they lie, and a troupe of dancers, singers and actors bring worship to life for the derelicts. Helpers, mostly former addicts and crimimals, are sent to the poor of India, Sri Lanka, the Philippines, Malaysia, Indonesia and Australia, and even Western countries like Germany and Britain, where poverty wears a different face. Jackie is constantly looking for more volunteers, hoping they will come because they want to share their faith, not because the media has made it fashionable.

For although this was the last thing in her mind, the television crews found her in the Walled City. Two programmes about her work were made in 1976 and 1978, and a book – *Chasing The Dragon* – followed, which became a best-seller. Curiosity about her was such that another – *A Crack in the Wall* – brought her story up to 1989. She has also received the M.B.E. Through what she would certainly call the power of the Holy Spirit, she talks to groups around the world about her perception of God, and her labours in his name.

When the British Government of Hong Kong decided to improve the lot of the inhabitants of Kowloon Walled City, it was proposed that the old buildings should be demolished by 1989; the weight of misery in its tight-packed streets would be lightened in a new and better environment. In its few remaining years the Walled City became a place of pilgrimage for outsiders who would not believe, until they saw it, that so much good could come from so much evil. The girl who has spent over twenty years of her life in bringing Christian compassion to the poor and outcast serves an ever-expanding mission, nourished by the prayers of all the world. Where it began, a park has been planned, to give pleasure to the citizens of Hong Kong. The Christians among them will need all the support possible in order to keep their faith under Chinese rule. If they do so, it will be due in no small measure to Jackie Pullinger's dogged endurance, and her shining vision.

DIETRICH BONHOEFFER

If the secret of a happy life is to have a happy childhood, Dietrich Bonhoeffer was destined to enjoy a rosy future. He and his twin sister Sabine, two of the youngest children in a family of eight, were born on 4 February 1906, in the disputed area of Silesia which was at that time part of the German Empire. Wilhelm II and his consort, the beloved daughter of Queen Victoria, ruled over a rapidly expanding commerce and industry, but the entrepreneurs held themselves aloof from government. The working classes, although organised so that they had a certain say in the management of the workplace, were not involved in politics. The Kaiser took a personal interest in the expansion of the high seas fleet; this was frowned on by foreign governments – an attitude the Germans regarded as censure on their attempts to arm in self-defence. They had all the touchiness of a newly-emerged nation, unification having taken place comparatively recently in 1871.

Against the current trend of mainly conservative policies, Dietrich Bonhoeffer's parents were liberals. His father was the director of a psychiatric hospital, and held professorships at the University of Breslau. His mother was a qualified teacher, directing the education of her children at home, with the help of a governess as the family filled the schoolroom. They were quite self-sufficient, making few friends outside their siblings. In later life Bonhoeffer was to regret this. At the time he enjoyed the security derived from these strong ties and the cultured atmosphere.

He and his twin sister had an unusual interest. From their window they could see the Catholic cemetery, and were avid watchers as funeral processions approached and burials took place; Dietrich even planned his own obsequies. Speculation on death was probably fuelled by the numerous accounts of infant mortality in the literature of the day. In 1912, these meditations came to an end with a move to Berlin, where their father had been offered the most prestigious professorship in his field, and the young Bonhoeffers were sent to school. Dietrich was six, the pattern of what would one day be called an Aryan, with intense blue eyes and blond hair, high forehead and determined chin. At first he was tentative and shy, but as he found that he excelled academically, his confidence grew, and he proved to be quite pugnacious. He revelled in his physical strength and improved it by practising gymnastics.

When war came – unexpectedly to liberals of his parents' stamp – the younger members of the family joined the crowds outside the Imperial Palace, cheering their sovereign. The shortages of food brought out Dietrich's ingenuity in tracking down supplies and seeing they did not pay inflated prices. Deep within him, he was aware of the cost in human misery, as the lists of casualties grew until no German home was untouched by grief. His own mother was bowed down when his brother Walter was killed in 1918 after only a fortnight at the Front, and his eldest brother Karl-Friedrich was wounded. Dietrich recognised that the war had separated those who had experienced it from those who had not.

His grandfather on his mother's side was chaplain to the Kaiser, and it was no surprise that Dietrich chose to study theology at the university; he was never attracted to science as his father had hoped. As the German war machine was broken by the Allies, and the blockade caused greater hardship, the Bonhoeffers were sheltered from the worst effects. Even after the German defeat, when unemployment and inflation added further deprivation, his father's international contacts softened the blow. Yet the effort to take his dead brother's place caused Dietrich to act in a responsible way. It almost seemed that his nature was unspoilable.

Along with most liberals, the Bonhoeffers saw in the Weimar Republic a lesser evil than the communism exported

from Russia or the extreme nationalism that sought to minimise Germany's defeat and circumvent the crippling provisions of the Treaty of Versailles. The two surviving soldiers
in the family came back from the war and gave their brother a
hard time. To them, with the scepticism born in the trenches,
his ambition to become a country pastor seemed a waste of his
talents. The Church was poor and badly organised, in spite of
the fact that education was largely in the hands of Church
schools, and the teachers were civil servants. His reply to his
brothers' denigration of the institution was: "If the Church is
feeble, I shall reform it."

He also felt a youthful helplessness in fighting off their
criticisms of his beliefs and cried out: "You may chop off my
head, but I shall still believe that there is a God."

Opposition in these arguments served to intensify his resolution, and he began studying at Tübingen in 1923, the year of
the great inflation. The whole of Germany was drinking the
cup of defeat to the dregs, and Bonhoeffer was a patriotic
German.

At Tübingen he joined a student association that formed
discussion groups and provided occasions to meet like-minded
people. More seriously, it was a disguised cadet corps that
went on manoeuvres with the small army permitted under the
Treaty of Versailles. Bonhoeffer enjoyed the spartan nature of
military life; he responded to its discipline, just as he was later
to hanker after the ordered life of the monastery.

The summer of 1924 saw him enter into serious theological studies at Berlin University, where he undertook a three-
year course. Quite early, he decided on the subject of his
doctoral thesis, which was 'The Communion of Saints' and
concerned the structure and theological basis of the Church,
and he worked on this during his academic career. He was
only nineteen when he was asked to substitute for another
preacher at the Stansdorfer Church in Berlin in October 1925.
His text was from Luke's gospel: "We are unworthy servants;
we have only done what was our duty." He prepared a swinge-
ing attack on the complacency of comfortable Christians,
pointing out that Jesus came to shake the core of conventional
piety. His mother was there to hear him, and she must have

taken back a favourable report to the family. His father, who had been disappointed when Dietrich told him he wished to become a pastor, came round to his view that the Church was in crisis, and that he had found a worthy calling.

By now his sisters were forming emotional ties with interesting young men: Sabine was engaged to a lawyer of Jewish origin – Christine married the son of the Hungarian composer Dohnanyi, also a lawyer – and Ursula, Doctor Rudiger Shleicher, a career civil servant attached to one of the Ministries in Berlin. Their brother Karl-Friedrich, a physicist, worked on research into the splitting of the hydrogen atom and often made visits abroad. Klaus also worked in the international field, as a lawyer at the League of Nations.

After his graduation in 1927 Dietrich had to spend a year as an assistant pastor and was offered a post with a German-speaking congregation in Barcelona. He began work on a new thesis which dealt with the subject of conscience in theology, and completed it in February 1930; it was later published as *Act and Being*. This entitled him to lecture in the university of Berlin and he lost no time in giving his inaugural discourse. Already at the age of twenty-four his attainments were impressive, and he was offered a Fellowship at the Union Theological Seminary in New York. Knowing he would meet international scholars there, he hastened to accept.

While he was crossing the Atlantic, the German elections had returned over a hundred National Socialists to the Reichstag. He had also left the remains of the Weimar Republic fighting for its life. Things seemed no better in America, which was suffering a deep depression; there was fighting in the streets, and a general air of gloom. A young negro student, Franklin Fisher, guided him through the black community; Bonhoeffer deplored exhibitions of racism and left a restaurant that refused to serve his friend. He devoted himself to youth work in the black ghettoes, and was moved by black culture, especially its gift to the country's Church life, the negro spiritual. The vigour of the preaching in black churches impressed him, together with the welcome it received from the congregations.

A trip to Cuba, which reminded him of Spain, led to the

first of his great Advent sermons. Every year he would return to the season with joy, and in a spirit of repentance.

"Out of the hoping, waiting, longing world," he declared, "a world of promise will arise."

He spoke of the individual responses as people approached Christmas, and called on his hearers to remember the poor and oppressed through the world. He shared his countrymen's devotion to the ceremonies of the season, and he missed his family. Letters from his twin sister Sabine, now married to a Jewish lawyer, kept him in touch with the political scene at home. The party had an answer for those who smarted under the humiliation of defeat in 1918 – a Third Reich would arise, purged of Jewish influence, and overcome the world that conspired against it. Sabine and her husband were aware of the dangers the Nazis held for them, and it was becoming more difficult for liberals like Dietrich to remain ignorant.

During his time at the seminary, he made many friends; one of them, an American called Paul Lehmann, said of Bonhoeffer: "One did not notice the solitude that prepared him for fellowship, the discipline which sustained his abandon, the quiet piety which nourished the acumen of his lively mind."

He also became a mouthpiece for the philosopher Karl Barth, who attacked the liberal theology of the day and was practically unknown in America. One of the lecturers was Reinhold Niebuhr, with whom he kept in touch after his return to Germany. He had been impressed by the way the American Churches involved themselves in practical social questions, though he thought them lax in theological discipline – but he had absorbed more from this year in the west than he realised at the time.

His championship of Karl Barth led to a meeting with the master, who heard Bonhoeffer had quoted Luther to the effect that "sometimes the curses of the godless sound better in the ears of the Almighty than the hallelujahs of the pious." The report intrigued him, and he invited the young man to dinner. They had an immediate rapport, and discussed the series of lectures Bonhoeffer was committed to give in Berlin.

A chance to prepare candidates for Confirmation in one of

the most run-down parishes of Berlin was eagerly accepted, and he took up residence there so that he could visit each of the fifty young men he was instructing. Here, amidst the stark realities of deprivation, the favoured son of a middle-class family learned to appreciate their quality. In spite of their background they were open to his message, which he developed by the use of simple Bible stories. Although they were wild and undisciplined at first, they repaid his efforts with acute attention once he had adjusted to their wavelength. He was honest enough to wonder how he would have fared, given their circumstances.

Although some of them could not resist the siren song of Nazi propaganda, they kept in touch with him for many years.

In 1931, he made contact with the World Alliance for Promoting International Friendship through the Churches, by attending an ecumenical conference in Cambridge, where he was elected co-secretary for Germany and Central Europe. The conference showed its solidarity with the work of the League of Nations and passed pacifist resolutions about reducing armaments, promoting cordial relationships between nations and helping those under attack. Later, at a meeting of the Youth Peace Conference in Czechoslovakia, he made an urgent plea for the ecumenical Church to formulate a theology on which to base its practical work. Without this, he believed it would be defenceless against outside forces like those of Nazism in his own country.

Two days after Hitler's assumption of the post of Chancellor of Germany on 30 January 1933, Bonhoeffer was giving a radio talk in his role as youth secretary. In it he outlined the dangers of idolising the leader. The switches were pulled almost immediately – Hitler had made known his wishes about opposing voices – and Bonhoeffer's warning message was lost. On the same day the Führer pronounced himself ready to take Christianity under his 'protection'. Most of the ministers, either by conviction or threatened intimidation, joined the German Christians under an archbishop favoured by the regime. The opponents formed a group called the 'Confessing Church', pledged to keep itself independent of the state.

After the Reichstag fire had been the excuse for agitating

anti-Jewish feeling, some students drew up a declaration that allowed Church membership to people of any race or social class, saying that its only binding commitment was an understanding of the cross of Christ. Bonhoeffer signed the manifesto, and what was more preached it. In return he received the accolade of Gestapo threats; but this this was not the reason he decided to accept an invitation to take charge of two expatriate congregations in England. As he explained to his old hero and mentor Karl Barth, he could not take work as a pastor in a Church that would not admit Jews. He delayed sending a letter to this effect until after he had taken up his London appointment. Barth's reply was that his place was on the battleground in Germany, and it caused Bonhoeffer a great deal of distress.

He seems to have undergone a personal crisis at this time; it was not so much a diminution of faith as a failure to reach the high standards he set for himself, a rejection of God's will for him, and a loss of direction. He even reached such a low point that he considered the ethics of suicide. One thing he could do was to interpret the situation in Germany to the world outside. He found a willing listener in Doctor George Bell, Bishop of Chichester, who was to be a good friend and ally. Otherwise he used the freedom of action given him by his residence in England to publish letters and articles defending the independence of the Confessing Church. He saw to it that the National Synod of the Confessing Church in May 1934 had its resolutions published in *The Times*, and these became the charter of resistance to the Nazis.

Addressing an Ecumenical Conference at Fano in Denmark, in his very creditable English, he called upon those present to commit themselves to work for peace. The conference went on to recognise the Confessing Church in Germany, in spite of the arguments of an official delegation of the German Christian movement. Then in 1935 came a call he could not resist – the position of director at a seminary for priests of the Confessing Church. He was still under thirty, and well able to understand the students' idealism.

Temporary accommodation was found for the new seminary at an old Bible school on the Baltic coast, until a more salubrious location was found at Finkenwalde, near Stettin. One of the senior students was Eberhard Bethge, who become a close friend and later married one of Dietrich's nieces. The regime was more spiritual than that practised in most Lutheran seminaries. The simplicity of the life was in some measure dictated by their poverty; there was a communal dormitory, and the furnishing of the other rooms was scanty. Bonhoeffer's own books formed the basis of the library, augmented by those of the students.

He made the half-hour of meditation in the morning the key to the rest of the day, and set one biblical text which was the sole source of contemplation for a week. The students were unused to the practice, and grumbled openly; only later did they come to realise its value. Apart from the usual lectures, he encouraged them to pray aloud in community, and confess to one another before Communion, but stopped short of censuring those who refrained. Every Saturday night there was a pastoral talk, after which the whole group shared their experiences of the week. He found in this plan of community the material for a book: *Life Together*. He also wrote at this time *The Cost of Discipleship*, based on his lectures on the meaning of grace and the use of prayer, and other allied subjects in the spiritual life, as well as a very beautiful description of the Sermon on the Mount.

He proved to be a good fund-raiser for the seminary, when their poverty threatened to end the work. In 1936 the Führer made the first of his international coups, securing the Olympic Games for Berlin. He was anxious to give the impression that there was freedom for all religions, and invited members of the Confessing Church to give lectures at St Paul's, in the heart of the city. Bonhoeffer knew the occasion would be used for propaganda, but it was a good opportunity to show that the Church still lived, and when Pastor Niemoller accepted, so did he. They drew huge crowds, and overflow meetings had to be held.

It was a solitary candle, for the darkness of persecution engulfed the Confessing Church the following year. Many arrests were made, including that of its leader, Pastor Niemoller. His parish prayed for him, and services of intercession were held for all the detained of the Confessing Church: these included lay people who attempted to worship in the churches, although mass arrests of whole congregations proved to be impractical and the authorities gave it up. In tribute to his fellow pastor, Bonhoeffer dedicated *The Cost of Discipleship* to Pastor Niemoller. In it he took the old Lutheran theology of salvation by grace alone and showed this was not to be obtained cheaply, but at the expense of Christ's death, a tremendous gift that must be treasured. In the course of the book he also looked forward to a day of liberation when the remnant of the German Church – that of the Confession – would lead the country back to a pure faith.

A blow to this hope came in September, when Bonhoeffer heard that the Gestapo had broken into Finkenwalde. The students were on holiday, but the Director of Studies and his housekeeper were told to leave, and the doors were officially sealed. Bonhoeffer knew that his students were in danger; they could easily be traced to their parishes and arrested. To circumvent the loss of the seminary, a plan was devised to place students in parishes with pastors who would teach them. Those in Pomerania were in particular danger, so that is where Bonhoeffer went, setting up what he called a 'collective pastorate'. The students were registered as pastors in training, and in this way he managed to disguise the function of seven or eight candidates at a time. He supervised their work, and gave them leisure to enjoy music and literature, and sport to stretch their scope as human beings.

Bonhoeffer made a friend of Ruth von Kleist-Retzow, an aristocratic lady with a keen interest in the renewal of the Church. She offered him and his students hospitality at her estate near Kieckow. Her grandchildren enjoyed their company, and one of them – thirteen-year-old Maria von Wedemeyer – was to become very important in Bonhoeffer's life. But it was her grandmother who impressed him now, combining as she did true Christian charity with the sense of duty cultivated by the Prussian nobility.

The husband of his sister Christine, Hans von Dohnanyi, was in the Foreign Office of the Abwehr, the military intelligence branch of the Army, where resistance to Hitler was focussed among the Generals. They were already plotting against him when the war began in 1939, and only a professional appreciation of his early victories caused them for a time to draw back. It went against the grain of traditional loyalty to the state, and in the circumstances their opposition was remarkable. It was also a tribute to their organising abilities that Hitler, who had crushed all his enemies at the outset, making a clean sweep of communists, socialists and trade unions, should have ignored these powerful figures who were so close to him.

Already, Bonhoeffer had taken a strong line against the Aryan laws that prevented Christian Jews from worship with the Church, but after the notorious 'Crystal Night' in November 1938, when a concerted attack left shops and synagogues in ruins, many saw that he had been right to speak out in their defence. He devoted himself to rescuing Jews and doing what he could to ease their lot, but it was impossible to do all he wanted. The boundaries were closing in around them like a trap. Among the escapees were Sabine and her family, and Bonhoeffer used his influence with Bishop Bell to get them accepted in England.

At last Hitler began to mobilise Germany for the war he had courted for so long. The class of 1906-7 was ordered to register for military service. Bonhoeffer did what he could to avoid being called up, knowing he would have to take an oath of personal loyalty to Hitler. There were other underlying problems; he was a patriotic German, and approved the Generals' conspiracy against the dictator as the best thing for his country. How could he equate this with his Christian duty to love his enemy? He needed to get away and think. He expressed this wish to Bishop Bell, and managed to see him and consult him in the spring of 1939. He also renewed his acquaintance with Reinhold Niebuhr who hoped to get him some lecturing engagements in America, so that he could carry up-to-date information to people over there.

On the boat to America he confided his dilemma to his diary, pleading with his brothers at home to render a true judgment on his defection. He was too honest to ask for what he called 'blind mercy', and said that both he and those he had left behind were in God's presence, but added poignantly: "Or have I missed the place where he is? Where is he for me? No – God says 'You are my servant'."

Fortunately, he believed that God worked through man's doubts as well as his certainties. Wherever he went, the situation in Germany haunted him. He felt torn in two; news from home was hard to come by – he was dependent on the newspapers and missed his native language, feeling shackled by his inability to express his deepest thoughts in an alien tongue.

On 26 June he read Paul's request to Timothy – "Do your best to come before winter" – and saw in it a signal that he should return home, whatever persecution might follow. He was accompanied by his physicist brother, Karl-Friedrich. His American hosts, who had been more than generous in their fund-raising for refugees, could not understand his decision. In a letter to Reinhold Niebuhr he said: "Christians in Germany will face the terrible alternative of either willing the defeat of their nation in order that Christian civilisation may survive, or willing the victory of their nation and thereby destroying our civilisation."

The Americans urged him to stay and help to galvanise their Churches into action, but his mind was made up. He came home to war. One of his students was killed in Poland, and he broke the news to those who had shared the Finkenwalde experience. He wrote to them: "Death has again come among us, and we must think of it, whether we want to or not."

But he was already being silenced. On 4 September 1940, he was forbidden to speak in public and ordered to report to the police whenever he moved. The following year he lost his right to have anything published.

It was at this point that he resolved to become a double agent. He appealed to Hans von Dohnanyi, who still held his position in the Abwehr, and asked about the possibility of work within the organisation. His friends were shocked to hear him supporting Hitler, but it was a ploy to hide his true work of undermining the Nazi influence in neutral countries, and helping Jews out of Germany. A place was found for him in the Abwehr, and he would take it up in February. Until then, he spent some months in the Benedictine Abbey of

Ettal, shedding his Lutheran view of the Catholic Church, and revelling in the orderly life and the liturgy. But this was only a respite, during which he examined the implications for a pastor and a pacifist of his resolution that only Hitler's assassination could bring relief to his country.

The Abwehr was not subject to scrutiny by the Gestapo, so it constituted a pocket of freedom within the state. Its agents were in touch with Britain through their man in the Vatican, but the British were only interested in them as double agents, not as people with whom they could negotiate peace. This did not stop them from accumulating evidence of Nazi crimes against humanity. With his new status, Bonhoeffer was able to visit Switzerland twice in 1941. His guarantor was Karl Barth, and he visited old friends, receiving news of his twin sister and her husband, who had found refuge in England.

His role in the conspiracy was to urge his English contacts, especially the Bishop of Chichester, to change Churchill's mind about the unconditional surrender of the German Forces. The conspirators showed great faith in a British victory, though at this time the signs of it were few.

In the summer of 1942 he became part of a plan to free a small number of Jews who were sent to Switzerland, ostensibly for propaganda purposes. He also went to Norway where the ministers of the Norwegian Church had laid down their office in support of a Bishop who had been put under house arrest. Once there, he found his Lutheran brothers would make common cause with the Confessing Church. When he visited Sweden in May he met Bishop Bell, who promised to contact the British Foreign Office and put forward the proposals of the conspirators. It was not his fault that the Foreign Office sent no reply.

Something else happened in this busy year. Dietrich fell in love with Maria von Wedemeyer, now an exceptionally beautiful girl of eighteen. As a man in danger, and twice her age, he regarded his chances of marrying her as less than favourable. But her father was killed in Russia, and in comforting the bereaved family he grew closer to her. The engagement was put off until January 1943 to mollify her mother's qualms about Bonhoeffer's suitability.

Meanwhile several plans were drawn up to assassinate Hitler, but the Führer seemed to bear a charmed life. In fact, although they failed, the conspirators were undetected, and it was the plot to send Jews to Switzerland that was their undoing. This was uncovered by the Gestapo, and Hans and Christine von Dohnanyi were arrested, together with Bonhoeffer. He had time to destroy incriminating papers, and thought they might be acquitted of the charge – 'subversion of the armed forces' – of which they were accused.

He was protected by Hans von Dohnanyi, who took most of the blame on himself, and by a skilful defence they managed to have the charge reduced from high treason. But although they were treated well, he was apprehensive that torture would be used in the interrogation, and he doubted his ability to withstand it. Gradually he came to terms with prison life. He had never been so creative – drama, a novel and poems poured from him. Letters to his family mentioned his anxiety for his young fiancee, and she moved to Berlin so she could be near him, in the Tegel prison.

They met unexpectedly when the officer in charge of the interrogation thought to surprise him into an admission by her sudden appearance, but the duplicity he had acquired during his time as a double agent stood him in good stead; he gave nothing away, only indicating his emotion by a pressure on her hand. In a smuggled letter he spoke of its being God's will that he should bring her sorrow and suffering, so that their love for each other should achieve the right foundation and the right endurance. The same letter looked forward to their marriage as "a 'yes' to God's plan."

He hungered for the family festivals, the warmth of the sun, the sweet pain of Maria's visits, but he kept in touch with the services of the Church by listening to the sound of bells penetrating his prison walls. He became a good friend to the other prisoners, sustaining them by his calm during the air raids of the winter 1943-44. But deep within himself the man who directed the warders with courteous commands, like a country squire with his servants, was riddled with self-doubt; he even contemplated suicide, afraid he might not be able to keep silent under torture. His trial was postponed because of

Von Dohnanyi's illness and the tension mounted, but he never wavered in his faith and certainty that God was with him.

Gradually, as his time in prison lengthened, he treated it as a monastery, setting aside hours of the day for prayer and Bible study. He contemplated the lack of religion in the world and asked if it was right that the Church should only have the allegiance of those who were too demoralised to sustain life without God. He admitted that he felt more at home with those who were not religious, than the pious who regarded God as a *deus ex machina* who would somehow make everything right in the future; he saw God as always present, at the centre of the world. He spoke often in his letters of the need for 'selfless self-love'. He became the counsellor of his correspondents, and was especially close to his nephew by marriage, Eberhard Bethge, who was fighting on the Italian front. To him he formulated the thought that God should not be used as an explanation of what was a mystery to the science of the day, but to explain what it had discovered.

His brother Klaus was involved in the plan to kill Hitler, which was to take place in July 1944, and he tried to shield Bonhoeffer by failing to contact him. Since he did not know the reason, he felt slighted; but the life of the prison had taught him that the way of Christ was the way of the cross. He believed that man was summoned to share in God's suffering in the world, as exemplified by Jesus's request to the disciples at Gethsemane to watch with him for one hour.

Then the coded messages got through. The attempt on Hitler's life was to be made in the 'Wolf's Lair', in East Prussia. All those who were in the secret were listening to their radios on 20 July, and they were devastated when they heard the intended victim broadcast his intention to take vengeance upon his enemies. It had been a narrow escape; the briefcase in which a bomb had been planted was moved, killing four of the officers present at the conference and severely injuring two others. The plan to take over the capital was abandoned, and hundreds of people were arrested and condemned to death. Hans von Dohnanyi was sent to a concentration camp, and Klaus Bonhoeffer, his brother-in-law Rudiger Schleicher, and Eberhard Bethge were imprisoned at the Reich Security Office in Berlin. On 8 October he himself was taken from Tegel to the cellar of a Gestapo prison.

Here there was no amelioration of his sufferings, but he wrote brave letters to his mother and Maria for Christmas. By great good fortune he was placed in a cell next to a cousin of his fiancee, and they took advantage of frequent air raids, and meetings in the washroom, to hearten one another. Hans von Dohnanyi, who was very ill, with both legs paralysed, was also an inmate. They were questioned, and Bonhoeffer did his best not to incriminate anyone. Beyond his brief description of it as 'disgusting', he was silent about his interrogation. Those who survived testified to his calmness and self-control.

By Easter 1945 the Russian guns were heard in the East, and the prisoners knew their fate would be sealed one way or another. Some, including Bonhoeffer, were packed into a closed lorry and driven off. They stopped at a school in Schonberg; Bonhoeffer unpacked his books and talked to a Russian fellow-prisoner, a nephew of the Soviet Foreign Minister, Molotov. The following Sunday he held an ecumenical service, which his new Russian friend joined, although he was an atheist.

When it was over, two civilians came and asked Bonhoeffer to follow them. He left his name and address in a copy of Plutarch he had with him, so that his passage could be traced. All through 9 April he travelled to Flossenburg Extermination Camp, and with the remaining conspirators he was sentenced to death. Through the half-open door of his cell, the camp doctor saw him kneeling in prayer. Then he and his four companions were taken out into the yard and hanged from long nails driven into the walls. The doctor was present, and noticed he remained brave and composed, and that his death took place in seconds. His farewell to the world was in a message to Bishop Bell: "For me it is the end, but also the beginning."

Gradually, during the years after the war, his writings became known.

At first they gave heart to his fellow-countrymen, humiliated by their defeat, and anxious to prove that there had been resistance to the Nazis. But his message was not always comfortable. He had wished to live, and share the guilt for his country's crimes against humanity. As his books were translated his theology was embraced by the world, and fanned the flame of faith that was kindled in those who had fought on either side. Many of those imprisoned had died without trace, and we are richer for having, in one of his last poems, a vision of their resurrection:

"Come now, thou greatest of feasts on the journey to freedom eternal; death, cast aside all the burdensome chains, and demolish the walls of our temporal body, the walls of our souls that are blinded, so that at last we may see that which here remains hidden.

Freedom, how long have we sought thee in discipline, action and suffering; dying, we now may behold thee revealed in the Lord."

POPE JOHN PAUL II

The history of Poland is one of the saddest in Europe. Torn between her giant neighbours Germany and Russia, she has fought to save her language and culture from extinction. Far from blurring her profile, it has become more marked; even recently when, before the break-up of the Soviet Empire, she was one of its satellites, slipping in and out of orbit as the grip at the centre tightened or loosened on the controls. One of the better provisions of the Versailles Treaty which imposed an uneasy peace at the end of the First World War was to restore her nationhood. In 1920 this was challenged by the new Bolshevik state, which was decisively defeated by the Poles in a battle at Warsaw when the future Pope was just three months old.

He was born in a small town called Wadowice, about an hour's journey from Cracow. Sentiment has called him a peasant but in fact Karol Wojtyla's family, though not well off, were of professional status. His father, a junior officer in the army, was employed in the local recruiting office, and his mother had trained as a school teacher. With parental support and hard work, his brother Edward, fifteen years his senior, later qualified as a doctor.

At seven Karol entered the local primary school, where we may be sure he did not let the family down academically, and also showed an interest in football and other outdoor pursuits. When he was nine his mother, now in her forties, became pregnant again and died giving birth to a stillborn daughter. Both suffering shock at her death, Karol and his father turned to one another. It was an intense relationship; Edward, who might have shared their burden of grief, had left Wadowice to work in a hospital at another town.

The neighbours noticed that his father's military background dictated the pattern of the boy's life. Every moment of his day was planned and accounted for – even the necessary recreation. Satan was effectively prevented from finding mischief for Karol to do; his hands were never idle. Now his father had retired on a small pension, poverty dictated their lifestyle. No mother figure emerged to soften the hard edges of this masculine household, and in 1932 a further tragedy struck. The brilliant elder son died of scarlet fever during an epidemic at the hospital where he worked. By this time Karol had moved on to the local High School, where he won golden opinions from teachers and fellow-pupils alike. The bereavements in the family seemed to make no difference to his progress; he continued to receive high marks in all subjects, especially languages and literature, and did so without stirring up envy or derision among his peers.

His prowess at sport probably helped to cement his relationships, and a grace of spirit that made him spend time with the less gifted. They were all equal on swimming expeditions to the nearby lakes, or climbing and skiing in the Tatras Mountains. There he made friends with the local inhabitants, learning their language, absorbing their wisdom and love of freedom. Of all his activities perhaps acting was closest to his heart. He had everything that could make an outstanding performer: a beautiful and expressive baritone voice; an athletic physique, of which he had full command in the energetic dances of his country – the mazurka, the polonaise and the Krakowiak; and the intelligence to understand a text and interpret it to an audience.

When the Metropolitan of Cracow, Bishop Prince Adam Saphieha, visited the school, Karol Wojtyla was chosen to deliver the vote of thanks to him. Impressed by his talents, the aristocratic prelate asked one of the masters if the boy had any intention of becoming a priest. When a negative answer was given, the Bishop remarked that it was a pity. A director of distinction predicted that he would be a great actor; the conflict between the two vocations was to continue for several years.

In 1938 Karol graduated, and this caused a great change in

the lives of his father and himself. They had set their sights on his studying at the prestigious Jagiellonian univeristy in the beautiful medieval city of Cracow, so they left the well-loved streets of Karol's birthplace and the friends he had known since childhood, and made their home in the big city. The presence of his father waiting at home may have somewhat curbed his extra-mural activities; unlike the young men with no parental supervision, he neither drank heavily nor chased girls, though he occasionally joined his friends in the cafes to discuss Life. He was studying Polish language and literature, and philosophy, and revelled in the latest fashions and theories in both.

Thanks to his father's pious example, he remained a practising Catholic. The Church had a favoured position in the scheme of things; it was rich and successful, running small industrial firms and handicraft workshops, as well as farms, hospitals and schools. But Karol, who had been head altarboy at home, was not attracted to join the eleven thousand priests who ministered to the people of Poland. Practically unaware of the Nazi menace, the Church looked eastward to Communist Russia; she stood to lose much if it were tempted by Poland's thriving industries and agriculture to move against her.

By 1939, Karol had started to study for a diploma in drama. He also began to write poetry, performing it in public with other young poets, and joining a group calling itself Dramatic Studio 39. He took part in a verse drama staged outdoors in the courtyard of the university, and in spite of a rather bizarre costume comprising various items of sporting gear and a mask representing Taurus the Bull – all the characters were signs of the Zodiac – he impressed the audience with his delivery. After a distinguished university career, he had every reason to believe that success in the professional theatre awaited him. But the writing was on the wall for the young Polish state. Almost without warning, Russia and Germany signed a treaty of friendship that enabled Hitler to carry out his plan to march into Poland unchallenged, to take over her assets and enslave her people.

On the 6th of September 1939 Cracow fell to the Germans.

Despite a ferocious defence, the war was over in a fortnight, during which Warsaw was devastated. Cracow was miraculously preserved, and was made capital of the remainder of Poland, after Russia and Germany had claimed territories they had usurped centuries before. The Governor-General of this rump was Hans Frank, whose declared policy was that Poles should become the slaves of the German Reich. In order to suppress higher education, the university was closed after five and a half centuries of continuous success in the teaching of science and the humanities. Many of the professors were arrested, along with most of the intelligentsia, and put to death. By February 1940 a concentration camp was set up a few miles from Cracow, to avoid having to transport detainees to the Germam camps. Its name – which was to strike a chill in the heart of generations yet unborn – was Auschwitz.

This only served to fuel the flame of Polish patriotism. Underground groups were formed for resistance to the Germans, and to keep Polish culture alive. Karol Wojtyla joined with actors, a director and a designer to form a group called Rhapsodic Theatre. They took their lives in their hands when they met for rehearsals, arriving singly or in pairs at private houses, and giving performances to tiny audiences of fifteen or twenty people. This was not the theatre of self-indulgent emotionalism: meticulous care was given to utter fidelity to the text, the expression of every point of punctuation, and the articulation of every syllable. This was a school of iron discipline, of exact repetition of every word after the truth had been arrived at.

The world outside was governed by the sinister forces of tyranny. At any moment Wojtyla could be stopped and a pass demanded. If it were not produced, an arrest would follow and disappearance into a concentration camp. Like the Jews, the Poles were classed as subhuman. Wojtyla did his best to save Jewish families by arranging their transfer to safe houses; his own survival was ensured by obtaining a work permit. The only occupation considered proper for Poles was manual labour, and he was taken on at a stone quarry. The men making up the normal workforce were kind to the ex-students and helped them to fill their production targets. Wojtyla's physique stood him in good stead, and he did not allow the heavy work to blunt his mind. He arrived at rehearsals covered in limestone dust, but he was always on time.

Later he became assistant to the engineer in charge of dynamiting the stone from the ground, and was able to study in between assignments. It was many years before he could absorb the experience, but when he did so he encapsulated it in a very moving poem called simply 'The Stone Quarry', in which he expressed his feeling for the actual material of the stone, his pain and anger as he worked on it, and his compassion for his fellow-workers. He never forgot seeing a man die, his temples split open – "like plaster cracking on a wall".

When his father died in 1941, he spent twelve hours by his corpse, speechless with grief, which he assuaged by throwing himself harder into his theatre work. He also made a friend, nearly twice his age: Jan Tyranowski, a tailor by trade. Meeting him at the psychologically right moment, when he was looking for someone to take the place of his father, he was open to the man's extraordinary piety. Tyranowski led a group of four or five young men who met secretly to study the sixteenth century mystic, St John of the Cross, and also took turns to lead meditation on the mysteries of the Rosary.

The two interests that occupied Karol Wojtyla's mind – his desire to become an actor, and the growing call to the priesthood – were not as opposite as they might appear on the surface. At the heart of the priestly vocation is the celebration of the Mass – the supreme drama; the enactment of the suffering, death and resurrection of Jesus Christ. Wojtyla's experience was with the theatre of truth, and he had learned the techniques of its perfect reproduction. For him, the constant repetition of the sacraments of the Church would never become routine. All this was still in the future, but the foundations were being laid during the bleak years of the war, when he walked the streets of Cracow, half starved and always in danger.

Crossing the road one day, he was run down by a tram and his skull was fractured. As he lay between life and death, God made his most urgent summons yet, but Wojtyla did his best to ignore it; he would not surrender his ambition. Some months later a second accident, this time at work, left him with a permanently hunched shoulder, and a vocation that he could no longer deny; he joined the illegal seminary of his old university. Like the high schools, the seminaries had been forced underground. There was no doubt in his mind of the penalties if he were discovered: beatings, torture, and death in the gas chambers of Auschwitz. At any moment he could be trapped at a road-block, and disappear into the German extermination system.

At the time of the Warsaw uprising in 1944, when the Russians held back from entering the city and the inhabitants were left to their fate, the measures against the population were stepped up. To increase the chances of survival for his seminarians, the Metropolitan of Cracow, Bishop Saphieha, hid them in his palace. He had gained the reluctant admiration of the occupying forces by his refusal to be intimidated, and did not hesitate to entertain Governor-General Frank, who insisted on visiting him, with the black bread and grain coffee that were the meagre rations of the Polish people.

He hid his young students during the difficult months before the arrival of the Russians in January 1945. It was probably out of gratitude to his mentor that Wojtyla surrendered a wish to become a Carmelite, born from his studies of the great Carmelite saints, and was ordained a secular priest on All Saints Day 1946.

In the course of his duties, while he was still a seminarian and serving as porter, he opened the door and found a young Russian soldier outside. Trained to be deeply suspicious of Russians, Wojtyla asked him what he wanted.

"I want to enter the seminary", was the guileless reply. Disarmed, Wojtyla asked him in. Although the young man did not in fact try his vocation, Wojtyla said afterwards that he himself learned a great deal from the encounter, which convinced him that God can penetrate the minds of men in the most unpromising situations, and in spite of systems and regimes which deny his existence.

But the Russians had not come as liberators. They came to support the Polish Communist party, which had gained prestige through its resistance groups. A bitterly fought civil war developed between those who remained loyal to the Polish government in London, and the Russian-backed Communists. It was an unequal struggle; the Russians were the men on the spot, and they took a hand in the elections held in 1947, when a Communist government was put in office.

The new government knew that the Polish people equated the Church with patriotism, so to avoid another civil war if they attempted to repress it openly, they set up a puppet Church called the Polish National Catholic Church, and a lay support organisation called Pax. These privileged bodies were intended to minister to the needs of the population, but by this time they were too politically sophisticated to be deceived by such efforts to win their allegiance.

Meanwhile Bishop Saphieha, watching over his prize pupil, decided to send him to Rome to complete his rather scrappy wartime studies. He boarded at the Belgian College, and studied under a French professor, Père Reginald Garrigou-Lagrange, who was a traditional Thomist and a great enthusiast for St John of the Cross. Wojtyla had been trained by traditionalists and shared his feeling for the Spanish poet-saint; he learned the language so he could study him in the original, and his doctoral thesis was entitled 'Problems of Faith in the Writings of St John of the Cross'. For this he received his doctorate '*summa cum laude probatus*'.

During the vacations he was encouraged to travel in Europe, meeting his countrymen stranded in isolated groups and foreign lands by the tides of war. He studied at first hand the French answers to the problem of a working-class alienated from religion in the big cities. Most publicised was the worker-priest experiment, in which young priests worked alongside the estranged laity on the shop floor. Although it was banned by the Vatican in 1953, the idea never quite died out, and Wojtyla, who had been a worker himself, welcomed it. Another movement that interested him was the 'Jeunesse Ouvrière Chretienne' – a lay organisation of young workers seeking to lead Christian lives in the work-place, and its equivalent among students in schools and universities.

He returned to Poland in 1948. In spite of Secretary-General Gomulka's attempts to form a less restrictive Communist state (for which he was soon deposed by the Russian overlords) the Church was under threat, its property confiscated and its schools and hospitals laicised. After a year as deacon in a rural parish, Wojtyla went to St Florian's in Cracow, where he endeared himself to the inhabitants by his very real concern for them, but scandalised them by his disregard for his own comfort. They insisted on replacing the patched cassock that was his sole protection from the winter snow and ice. The children and teenagers found it impossible to treat him with the reverence due to his priesthood and called him 'Wujek' ('little Uncle'). He was an acclaimed preacher, trained long ago in the theatre to use his voice and bearing in order to drive home his words to his listeners.

In his discussions with his peers he did not use his intellectual powers to browbeat opponents. His method was to listen to all the arguments and then make his own contribution quietly and firmly. He was fascinated by both existentialism and phenomenology, and he received a second doctorate for a thesis 'On the Possibility of Constructing Catholic Ethics on the Basis of the System of Max Scheler' – a renowned phenomenologist whose philosophy he sought to harmonise with the Thomism he had studied in his youth.

By 1952 Cardinal Prince Saphieha was dead; eight bishops and more than nine hundred priests were in prison. When the Primate, Cardinal Wyszynski, protested against the particularly revolting humiliation of one of his bishops in a 'show trial', he was prevented from performing his office and arrested. Wojtyla lectured in an underground seminary in Cracow and in 1954 received a post as Professor of Philosophy in the Catholic University of Lublin, the last bastion of Catholic education. He was popular with his students, taking them canoeing in summer and climbing and skiing in the winter. The evenings were spent in informal discussions during which he encouraged them all to take part. He had already published poetry under a pseudonym, but now a series of articles, poems and plays poured from his pen, and this was to continue as he made his way steadily up the hierarchy.

In 1958, during a relaxation of restrictions in the Church, Cardinal Wyszynski was released from custody and Wojtyla was appointed Auxiliary Bishop to the Apostolic Administrator of Cracow – the youngest bishop in Poland. He had a very full appreciation of the privilege of his office, later saying that a bishop "wherever he goes, sees the people sharing in the royal priesthood of Christ". He was popular, and did not confine his ministry to those whose allegiance to the Church was unquestioned, but sought out unbelievers and offered them his friendship. In *Love and Responsibility*, published in 1960, he made a special study of the relationship between men and women; it took the orthodox Catholic teaching on love and sought to give it a scientific basis.

But what liberated him from taking a narrow national viewpoint was his attendance at the Second Vatican Council in 1962. In the first session he contributed to more than one debate, making his mark through his youth and energy. During the second session a year later, he was a moving spirit in redefining the role of the laity – "to measure up to the times, to make sure that man is allowed to reach his full potential, while at the same time allowing for his weakness", as he said in a broadcast on Vatican Radio. His fellow bishops from all parts of the world were impressed by his simple life-style, unaffected by Western materialism, and the learning he wore so lightly.

He was eventually made a member of the Congregations for the Eastern Church, the Liturgy, the Clergy, Catholic Education, and Divine Service.

More honours awaited him. He was made Archbishop of Cracow in 1964, and two years later celebrated with the rest of the hierarchy one thousand years of Polish Christianity. The liturgical changes were in place for the event; unlike some of his elders, he took these in his stride, welcoming the opportunities for greater contact between priests and people during the Eucharist. One of his innovations was an Institute devoted to the problems of Marriage and the Family, presided over by a psychiatrist who had been a victim of medical experiments in a concentration camp. Together with his fellow bishops he made overtures to their opposite numbers in Germany, seeking reconciliation in the spirit of Vatican II. He gained permission to travel widely in Western Europe, North

America, the Middle East, Africa, Asia and Australia, and seemed to have reached the summit of his career when he received his Cardinal's hat at Rome in 1967.

The following year was marked by student unrest. In Poland this came to a head when a play dealing with the nineteenth century Russian occupation of the country became a smash hit with students and the intelligentsia. When the authorities forced it to close, fearing an adverse Russian reaction, the students came out on to the streets to protest and were beaten up by riot squads. Cardinal Wojtyla defended their rights, battling for the Jews amongst them as well as for his co-religionists. In 1970 there were more riots, this time of workers protesting about rises in the price of basic foods. They brought down the head of the government, Gomulka, and prices were reduced. It was the beginning of education in collective bargaining which the Polish people were to perfect in the years to come.

Cardinal Wojtyla rejoiced with his fellow-citizens when Father Kolbe was beatified in 1971. Father Maximilian Kolbe was a national hero; he had led an active and saintly life as head of a Franciscan monastery and went on to create others in Japan and Malabar. A sick man, he returned to his country in 1936, and was put into the concentration camp at Auschwitz early in the war. His life was exemplary, and his death an inspiration. When a prisoner was missing from roll-call, ten were selected at random to starve to death in a sealed bunker. One of them was the father of a large family, and Father Kolbe offered to take his place. The guard who accepted this substitution asked who he was, and received the reply: "I am a Catholic priest."

Cardinal Wojtyla was present at his beatification in Rome and drew this telling conclusion: "At a time when so many priests all over the world are fussing about their 'identity', Father Maximilian Kolbe gives the answer, not with theological argument, but with his own life and death."

Often in the future Cardinal Wojtyla was to judge by this high standard, and could be badly misunderstood.

A mark of Pope Paul VI's regard for him was an invitation to give a Lenten retreat in the Vatican in 1976. His years as a

Bishop in Cracow, when Church and people struggled for freedom, had given him a wisdom lacking in those whose episcopate had a less stormy passage. He had used all his powers of persuasion to extract concessions from a government hostile to religion, making him a considerable diplomat, and he had never hesitated to take a firm stand when one was needed. But he remained a pastor, visiting every parish and monastery in his diocese, greeting every priest and religious, and every category of the laity. He was always at home to old friends, and constantly made new ones, even among atheists. Such was his charisma that each one imagined he enjoyed the greatest intimacy with him; yet the more perceptive sensed that there was a space they could never traverse – they felt he was a man set apart.

The Pope who steered the Second Vatican Council to its conclusion died in August 1978, and his smiling successor, John Paul I, only reigned for thirty-three days. Cardinal Wojtyla retraced his steps to Rome where the Conclave sat to elect the third Pope within a single year. For four and a half centuries the Holy See had been an Italian monopoly, but thanks to Paul VI's judicious creation of Cardinals outside the country, now only twenty-seven of them were Italians – and the question arose of the election of a Bishop of Rome from a wider field. After two days and seven or eight ballots, Cardinal Wojtyla was offered the papacy: the final vote was reported to be almost unanimous.

Had he any idea of the result? Before entering the Conclave he had asked a friend to book him a return flight to Poland. On the other hand he had provided himself with Paul VI's 'Constitution on the Election of a Pope', and read out the words: "We ask him who is elected not to refuse the office to which he has been elected for fear of its weight, but to submit himself humbly to the Divine Will" – and the following passage, about the strength that God would give as he shouldered the burden. He also referred to the suffering Church from which he came, saying that the office of Supreme Pontiff would provide even greater suffering. Then he made it known that out of his devotion to his two predecessors he would take the name of John Paul.

In his first hour of becoming Pope he made an innovation. He not only showed himself to the thousands gathered in the piazza outside St Peter's, but spoke to them in Italian, thus winning the hearts of those who had feared that a foreigner would not cherish the people of Rome. Within a few days he proved that he did not intend to become a fixture within the Vatican. The man who had enjoyed the freedom of the great outdoors – the rivers and mountains of his native land – thought nothing of going out and visiting a sick colleague in a Roman clinic. He also made it clear that he was going to be more open with the Press than any previous Pope, and go further in the direction of ecumenism. Like his immediate predecessors, he would consult with his bishops frequently, and not merely to check that they were following the party line.

He made clear in his first encyclical, published in March 1979, that, "the common good, that authority in the state serves, is brought to full realisation only when all citizens are sure of their rights" – and that, "Every man and woman has the duty to respect in others the rights claimed for oneself." He carried the Good News on a series of pilgrimages to every quarter of the globe, and lost no time in visiting Latin America, where he trod a tightrope between the believers in Liberation Theology, whose Catholicism was tinged with Marxism, and the traditionalists who thought the Church should uphold the status quo. While moved by the poverty of the faithful who greeted him, he made no commitment to either party, holding communism and capitalism equally guilty in the face of such misery.

For he had inherited a host of problems from previous pontificates. The heady freedom given by Vatican II had seriously affected a whole generation of priests and religious, who left their presbyteries and monasteries in droves.

The arrival of the contraceptive pill and its promise of sexual gratification without reproduction had changed the whole concept of the relationship between men and women. Abortion was legalised in spite of all the Church could do to campaign against it, and euthanasia began to be considered as an option for the terminally ill.

John Paul II, reiterating the sanctity of human life, was

practically a lone voice. As the cargo shifted in the Barque of St Peter, it needed a steersman of skill and iron nerve to keep it on an even keel. One was found in the man from the only country where there was a surplus of seminarians, and an overwhelming percentage of Catholics were practising. He used all the resources of the mass media to disseminate his message; his white-clad figure was a familiar sight on the world's television screens, blessing vast crowds, hugging babies, comforting the sick, visiting prisons.

In May 1981 an attempt on his life was was made by a young Turk in St Peter's Square. When the indignation over the shooting had died down, the Pope went to see his assassin, and on Christmas Day 1983 heard his confession and gave him absolution. After his brush with death, his attempts to interact with the multitudes that gathered wherever he went had to be curtailed. Bulletproof glass protected him as he drove among his people, and he became as security-conscious as any other Head of State. He met them all, surviving many who were prominent when he first came to the papacy, and living to see the break-up of Russia's eastern empire.

His championship of ecumenism has never been in doubt. At Assisi in 1986 he called together representatives of all the world religions, and shared with them the prayer of St Francis, that they should be instruments of peace. In particular he asked for restrictions on armaments, and was encouraged by God's answer in the treaties between the two great nuclear powers. Taking heart from this, he arranged for another meeting in January 1993 to ask for a miracle to conclude a cease-fire in Bosnia, where fighting between Christian Serbs, Moslems and Croats was threatening stability in Europe.

John Paul II has the actor's natural talent for the right gesture, and the ability to repeat it over and over again with every appearance of spontaneity. But in him art and life meet and become one. He is the true Renaissance man: poet, philosopher, athlete and pastor; his manner simple and kindly, his mind rich and complex. Whatever the future holds, for him and for the Church, his mark upon it will hold significance for generations yet unborn; some of whom would perhaps not have been born but for his protection of their right to life.

PADRE PIO

In the year 1210 AD, Pope Innocent III had a dream. He saw a small man in a ragged grey tunic propping up the Church of St John Lateran, which was tottering under immense pressure. He interpreted this in the light of a visit he had received the day before: eleven ragamuffins had approached him, and through their leader – equally dishevelled, but with remarkably penetrating eyes – had explained that they wanted to travel about the world, observing the strictest rule of poverty anyone had ever envisaged, and preaching the Good News to the poor. He was well aware that the Church had lost touch with the people; the crusades to recapture the Holy Places had displaced thousands of the fittest young men, and their want was felt in the fields and the cloister.

But he had hesitated before giving the gallant twelve permission to do what they asked. The place for holy men was in a monastery; no-one could possibly keep track of mendicants wandering about the world – and surely human beings were ill-equipped to endure the deprivation they proposed? Then came the dream, and he realised that here was the new blood the Church needed, to save her anaemic Orders from expiring. He sent for Francis Bernadone and his companions, and informed them that they could preach the Gospel in any diocese where the Bishop would allow them. The question of their Rule was left in abeyance for the moment, but they were given minor orders; Francis was made a deacon, and never progressed higher in the Order of priesthood.

It was the beginning of a whole movement in the Church toward a truer holiness. The Friars Minor increased in numbers and influence, though their leader turned increasingly to contemplation of the sufferings of Christ who had called him, leaving others to make plans and rules for the Order. He ate little, underwent heroic penances on behalf of sinners, and in 1224, while in retreat on Mount Verna at the very edge of Tuscany, received as a final mark of his union with God's redemption the stigmata on his hands, feet and side. He suffered the pain of this favour, yet very few people knew of it, as he kept silent on the subject.

This man, now known to the world as Francis of Assisi, was the saint after whom Padre Pio was named. He was baptised Francesco the day after he was born, the 25th of May 1887, to Grazio and Giuseppa Forgione. They already had one surviving son, Michael, who was six years old; and Francesco was followed by three younger sisters. Their home town, Pietrelcina, was in the Benevento district in the high mountains of Southern Italy, not far from the place where the *autostrada* now runs between Naples and Bari.

In the Eighteen-Eighties it was a collection of subsistence farmers, growing corn, maize, olives and grapes in the rocky soil. The small houses were grouped on a steep hillside, and the men were hard put to it to find a flat space to play bowls, their only recreation. It seemed as remote in time as it was in distance from the sophistication of the industrial society in the north.

When Francesco was still very young, his father was tempted by letters containing fabulous stories of the fortunes to be made in the New World, and he decided to try his luck in Argentina. He left his wife at home to manage as best she could; the children were certainly not neglected, but they had a larger part to play in their own upbringing. Francesco was an unusual child, but perhaps not quite so unusual when judged by the standards prevailing in a primitive society, close to fundamental piety. He recorded afterwards that he saw visions from the age of five, preceded by demonical visitations. He never discussed these happenings with anyone, as he believed that they were common experiences. With the intense ardour of the very young, he beat himself with chains in imitation of the Passion of Jesus, and when his mother discovered this and begged him to desist, he merely continued in secret.

Disappointed in his hopes of growing rich in Argentina, his father became ill and returned home, resuming his attempts to win a living from the poor soil of Pietrelcina. Francesco, in addition to his task of shepherding a couple of sheep owned by the family, picked up a little education through private lessons in town. Grazio Forgione was illiterate, but he meant his sons to have better opportunities than he had, and when Francesco asked if he could go to school, he decided to risk another attempt at emigration, this time to North America.

Once there, he managed to save enough money to buy another piece of land in a district called Pieria Romana, where farming was a little easier. Francesco joined the other boys in helping their elders, and fell in with the rough-and-tumble of games enjoyed by all small boys, but was sensitive about the loose talk used by some of them. When he was ten years old he had a severe bout of fever which left him more thoughtful than his contemporaries. His mother – for his father was still away – begged the local elementary schoolteacher to give him more formal lessons than he had hitherto received, and he brought Francesco to the standard required for entrance to a secondary School.

During his childhood, Pietrelcina was visited frequently by a member of the Order of Friars Minor known as the Capuchins. At that time they still solicited for alms, and Francesco was very taken by the cheerfulness and piety of this particular brother, Fra Camillo da Sant'Elia, and admired his splendid black beard. At the age of fourteen he expressed a desire to join him; his friends and relatives suggested less arduous alternatives in the religious life, but he insisted that he wanted to be a bearded friar. What seemed like a whim was in fact a vocation, and it is difficult to imagine him belonging to any other Order.

An impediment to his entry into the novitiate – in the form of a letter accusing him of dalliance with the daughter of the stationmaster – was overcome when the author confessed that he had slandered Francesco out of envy. He celebrated his last Christmas with his family, saying later:"It is not to be thought that this soul did not suffer on a human level from the abandonment of his family, to whom he felt strongly tied."

He felt his very bones crushed; as the day of his departure drew near, the torment intensified. On the Feast of the Epiphany 1903, he bade farewell to his mother, doubly dear to him in the absence of his father, and her natural nobility is apparent in her parting words:"My dear child, my heart is bleeding, but St Francis has called you, and you must go."

He received the novice's habit on 22 January, taking the name in religion of Fra Pio da Pietrelcina; it was the custom in the Capuchin Order that each friar should bear the name of his home town in his title.

The spartan life of the novitiate came as no surprise to the new aspirant; in his secular life he had practised austerities. The Rule was almost unchanged since St Francis had initiated the Order, and Fra Pio not only observed it as perfectly as he could, but outdid all his fellows. However, he was still adolescent, and it was at the expense of his health. When his father returned to Italy nine months later and went to visit him, he was shocked at his appearance. The Father Guardian, as the superior was known in Capuchin monasteries, reassured him that Fra Pio was suffering an excess of zeal that would become more moderate as he grew wiser in religion.

The next year he went to Sant'Elia in Pianisi where he embarked on a study of philosophy that would lead to his receiving the sacrament of Holy Orders, but he was moved constantly between different houses; contrary to the opinion of his superior, he would not moderate his austerities. He wrote afterwards to his director Father Benedetto da San Marco in Lamis, and his confessor Father Agostino who came from the same place, that he was subject to both diabolic visitations and divine consolation from his physical and mental torments. The accounts of these supernatural happenings mirrored those of other mystics in the history of the Church. His health was always affected whenever he lived in the plains, and his studies were frequently interrupted. He received minor orders in 1908, and on 10 August two years later, he was ordained priest, and celebrated Mass at Pietrelcina.

Soon after his ordination, he noticed a reddening of the palms of his hands, a circular patch that came and went, accompanied by acute pain; there were also pains in the soles of his feet. He endured this for a year without informing Padre Benedetto, but in answer to a question told him in a letter dated 8 September 1911. Padre Agostino also learned of this, in spite of Padre Pio's reluctance to speak about it. Fearful that his undiagnosed ailment might be some form of tuberculosis, and could be contagious, his superiors suggested that he should remain at Pietrelcina for the time being.

He sought the peace of the family farm, where he lived in a single room with the barest of furniture, contemplating the Passion of his Lord, and growing in grace. Constantly in touch with his director, he asked: "Tell me what Jesus wants of this ungrateful creature", deriding his own efforts.

Padre Benedetto replied: "Jesus wants to stir you up, thresh and sift you like grain, so that your spirit may reach that cleanliness and purity he desires" – but also assured him: "Your trials are no punishment, but a means which the Lord offers you to acquire merit."

Reading the advice of his superiors was his only respite from the pains of his illness, the origin of which remained a mystery. Years later, he spoke of appalling headaches and temperatures so high, they could not be read on a normal thermometer. This in itself might have produced hallucinations, which he regarded as manifestations of the devil. Eventually Padre Benedetto decided that as the illness did not abate at home, he might as well be in a friary. After a check-up by a Neapolitan specialist, Padre Pio was conducted to Venefro, where he remained from October 1911 to the December of the same year. Witnessing his agony and ecstasy was very different from merely reading about it; Padre Agostino, who remained with him, was shocked and brought in a doctor. He diagnosed catalepsy, as Padre Pio stared at something no-one else could see, and failed to notice a match lit before his eyes. The same doctor, after noting that his heart and pulse were normal, and that he began to laugh and joke when the ecstasy was over, later changed his mind and testified that a supernatural force was the only possible cause.

But the physical deterioration continued every time he left his native town, and it was decided that he should be given permission to reside there, while keeping his Capuchin habit; he had appealed to St Francis to defend him when it was projected that he should become a secular priest. He was allowed to say Mass, but – and in view of later events, this seems extraordinary – he was not authorised to hear confessions, on the grounds of lack of maturity in moral science. When Italy entered the First World War he was called up, but no sooner reported for duty than he was sent to convalesce for varying periods. His directors were delighted, since young priests were frequently lost to religion after military service.

In 1916 he went to the Capuchin friary in Foggia, where he visited a correspondent of his – a pious noblewoman called Raffaelina Cerase, who was terminally ill. She recommended him to his superiors as a confessor; when word got about in the town, he was nearly overwhelmed by penitents. He did not eat supper – it was always his practice to take a midday meal only, and that under obedience – and remained in his cell. His confreres heard loud noises coming from the cell, and upon investigation discovered Padre Pio bathed in sweat, pale and trembling. A visiting bishop who insisted it was medieval nonsense to believe that he encountered the devil, was convinced by the nightly cacophony, and cut short his visit in terror.

Padre Pio was emaciated, and suffering from chronic bronchial infection, but the Order had been so depleted by the call-up of the younger members that his presence within it was considered essential. A friar came to Foggia from San Giovanni Rotondo on the western slope of Mount Gargano, part of the 'spur' on the boot of Italy. When Padre Pio went with him to visit the desolate friary, the mountain air acted as a tonic. On 28 July, 1916, he took up residence there, where he was to remain for fifty years.

He was already directing people by correspondence, and now he was put in charge of hearing the confessions of the boys in the seminary. Every Thursday and Sunday he gave clear, simple and traditional instruction in the Faith to the villagers who made their way up the rough track to the friary. He accepted everyone, taking endless trouble to tailor his advice to their needs.

His method was to recommend meditation on the truths of religion – particularly the life, passion, death and resurrection of Jesus – at regular times, twice a day, for at least half an hour; preferably in Church before the tabernacle, but if that was not possible, at any place away from distractions. One invalid was assured that he could profitably meditate in bed. Frequent confession and Communion received his endorsement, and spiritual reading; he emphasised the Gospels as the source of the knowledge of Christ, and recommended his favourite author, St Paul – "The guide and master of my doctrine". There was no doubt that the purity and simplicity of his teaching reached everyone in a way that extensive references to philosophical treatises could never have done; his appeal was universal.

In September 1917 his military service again impinged on this useful work, and he donned his uniform in Naples. Even the smallest size that could be found hung on his emaciated frame, and he was employed on a series of menial tasks, unable to find the facilities to say Mass. Though he hated the whole experience, he admitted that it had done more good than many sessions of spiritual exercises. It gave him an insight into the temptations of ordinary men, teaching him to deal with them and share their trials. He endured this ordeal for two months, before the incongruity of his situation struck someone in authority, and he received another leave of absence until his final discharge in March 1918.

Life went on much as before in San Giovanni Rotondo, until the night of 5 August. Padre Pio was confessing one of his young seminarians when he had an interior vision of a heavenly being, holding a steel sword with flames coming from its point, thrusting it into his soul for the space of a second, and causing him such distress that he was almost unable to cry out in pain. He managed to tell the boy to leave, since he was too ill to complete his task. For two days he was wracked by exquisite agony. He was under obedience to report such things to Padre Benedetto and Padro Agostino, and they assured him he was not undergoing punishment, but receiving the mark of God's favour to a privileged soul.

This was merely a preliminary to the consummation of his

love. In his own words: "On the morning of the 20th of last month (September) in the Choir, after I had celebrated Mass, I yielded to a drowsiness similar to a sweet sleep. All the internal and external senses and even the very faculties of my soul were immersed in indescribable stillness... While this was taking place I saw before me a mysterious person, similar to the one I had seen on the evening of 5th of August. The only difference was that his hands and feet and side were dripping blood... The vision disappeared and I became aware that my hands, feet and side were dripping blood too. Imagine the agony I experienced, and continue to experience almost every day."

He was not a willing sufferer, but prayed to be delivered – not from the pain, as he had long ago made an offering of himself to suffer for sinners, and souls in purgatory – but from the continual embarrassment of the outward signs.

It was impossible to hide his wounds, which bled profusely when he was in the company of his brothers. In a short time, the people of the village who attended his Mass in the Church of Our Lady of Grace became aware that their Father-in-Christ had received the marks of his crucifixion, and they endured many hardships in order to be present. The news spread like wildfire in spite of the primitive methods of communication. Though Padre Pio's superiors considered it the rarest of privileges, they were afraid of scandal and decided that sceptical medical men should examine the stigmata and put their conclusions in writing. These gentlemen described the wounds as "holes with a delicate transparent membrane, which bled copiously from time to time." They ruled out any form of disease that could produce such phenomena, and dismissed any suggestion that they were self-inflicted. This was not one man's opinion, or based on one examination, but the conclusion of many.

Although the pain he suffered was continuous, he seemed to function normally in spite of the loss of blood, which stained many bandages in the course of each day. For fifty years he wore mittens on his bleeding hands; he received no medication after the early months, when he had treated the wounds with iodine. The surrounding areas always remained healthy and uninfected, which was an additional miracle. Many times in the next fifty years he was subjected to scrutiny, which caused him great distress. Left to himself, it is impossible to believe that he would not have kept it secret, as St Francis had tried to do.

The Catholic press remained silent, in response to an official request, until November 1919, when they were forced into a declaration by exaggerated reports in the popular press. There was no shortage of sceptics to pour cold water on the general enthusiasm; some of these were converted by a visit to San Giovanni Rotondo, where they saw hardened sinners returning to the practice of their faith. Many more were moved to write of their spiritual and temporal difficulties, asking for Padre Pio's prayers, following up with grateful thanks for favours they believed they had received as a result.

The Pope himself, Benedict XV, gave it as his opinion that Padre Pio was "a truly extraordinary man, of the kind God sends on earth now and then to save sinners."

Padre Pio was not so fortunate in his successor, Pius XI, who was elected in 1922; during that year the Holy Office ordered a series of measures which severely restricted his activities. He was not to celebrate Mass at a fixed time, and then preferably to do so in private, in order to discourage those who wished to attend. There was an absolute ban on his blessing people, talking about the stigmata, or allowing the wounds to be kissed – in other words, an attempt to prevent a popular cult springing up around him. This he could happily comply with – but then came the body-blow. He was forbidden to communicate with Padre Benedetto, even by letter, and in fact they never met again. It was a heavy deprivation for both men, who had formed a close bond over the years, but they had taken a vow of obedience and remained faithful to it in mind and spirit.

But he wrote of his feelings at that time to others, saying: "I am devoured by love for God and my neighbour." He told of being "immersed in extreme grief, in the most hopeless desolation, in the most agonising affliction, not because I fail to find my God but because I am not winning over all my brothers to God." He asked pathetically for direction, but found that the men he approached were anxious that he should direct them. There is no doubt that, like many of the great mystics, the best director he had was God himself.

The faithful penitents who queued for up to a fortnight to meet him through the confessional were warned that nothing supernatural had been proved about Padre Pio, and they were not to treat him as an object of devotion. By 1926 the ban was expressed more explicitly; possibly because unauthorised pamphlets about him had started to appear. When it seemed that official policy was to move him from San Giovanni Rotondo, a flood of protest arose from the local population, who threatened to keep him there by force. One man pulled out a revolver at the end of Mass and declared that Padre Pio should remain – dead or alive. The Mayor, who had marched on the friary at the head of a crowd of three thousand, accompanied by brass bands, posted two guards to report any unusual activities that might herald a move. The central figure in the drama remained calm, bowing his head in obedience and awaiting the orders of his superiors. Eventually, since it seemed that no transfer could be made without bloodshed, the idea was quietly dropped.

But investigations by a series of Apostolic Visitors continued. Every few years they came to meet Padre Pio at San Gioivanni Rotondo, anticipating fraud, and for the most part were converted by his obvious sincerity and rugged peasant commonsense. His days were arduous – he rose in the early hours to prepare himself to say Mass; when it was over he went straight to the confessional and was fully occupied there until his frugal meal at noon. After a short rest he went back for another long session. His day led him between the altar, the confessional, and the meditation that gave him strength to perform his sacramental duties as a priest.

In 1925 he had to undergo an operation for a hernia. Arrangements were made in the friary, and Padre Pio insisted on undergoing it without an anaesthetic, since he was afraid that the doctor would examine his wounds while he was unconscious. The operation was successful, and the patient bore it heroically, only to collapse from shock when it was over. The doctor took this opportunity to make an examination of the stigmata, and found them very little changed since the last time he had seen them, five years earlier.

Padre Pio's parents came to visit him as often as they could, staying at the house of Mary Pyle, one of the first 'spiritual children' of the director of souls. She was a wealthy American who had travelled as an interpreter with Doctor Montessori, the pioneer in child education, and in San Giovanni she found the end of her journey and the beginning of a new life, as a member of the Third Order of St Francis. She trained a choir to sing sacred music, and organised the cultural life of the town as it grew. It was in her house, during the Christmas of 1928, that Padre Pio's mother died, having developed pneumonia during her son's celebration of the feast. He gave her the last rites, and was present at the end, weeping bitterly for several hours afterwards. His lack of stoicism under these circumstances endeared him to all who knew him.

Rumours still abounded, and when a strange friar arrived in the village in April 1931, the always-explosive situation erupted. A group of people pulled up a lamp-post and used it as a battering-ram to break into the friary and overrun the living-quarters. Padre Pio was awakened and managed to calm them, but serious measures had to be taken. Obviously the friary could not be governed by the volatile whims of the mob.

On the 9th of June the Father Guardian received a letter from Rome, outlining its policy in the case of Padre Pio of Pietrelcina. He was to refrain from exercising his priestly office, and could only celebrate Mass privately, apart from the rest of the community. This was his greatest trial yet, and he submitted to it with the humility that characterised him. Freed from the obligation to restrict the Mass to its normal length, he prayed each part of it with such fervour that it took up to three hours, and the thanksgiving added another hour at least.

The ban on communicating by letter with his penitents and well-wishers was probably less of a burden, for he had almost given up trying to cope with the volume of correspondence he received; but we are deprived of the intimate thoughts he used to send to his spiritual directors, that give such poignancy to his descriptions of the dark night of the soul, and its converse – his joy in the goodness of God. His obedience was absolute; his acceptance of what had happened to him was total.

He was heard to say: "The hand of the Church is gentle even when it strikes us, for it is always our mother's hand."

A mother's chastisement often comes from an exaggerated care for the reputation of the family, and the case of Padre Pio aroused the wrath of the ungodly. The stories of his deep knowledge of people he had only just met – the reported sightings of him far from San Giovanni Rotondo, when it was known that he never left the friary – his ecstasies – all these were foreign to the arid materialism of twentieth-century philosophy, and his detractors were virulent.

But he was not to remain exiled from his beloved penitents for long. In 1933 Pius XI ordered an enquiry into the background of the case that had been made against him, and in the light of further evidence decided to dismiss it. The news of Padre Pio's reinstatement was swiftly conveyed to the community, and received with joy. He returned immediately to the celebration of Mass in the Church of Our Lady of Grace, and heard the confessions of his confreres, and of the public at large.

A close friend who visited the community frequently during the Thirties, and was evidently the kind of friend who prides himself on loving the total man, tried to detail his faults. If the worst that could be said of Padre Pio was that he was occasionally seen to yawn during Vespers, that he drummed his fingers during meditation, that he took snuff or that he lost his temper with hypocrisy and sensation-seeking, then he was in a better state of grace than most people. It is easy for those who suffer no pain to criticise a man who suffered continually.

The news that Padre Pio was back in the confessional spread far and wide. People from all parts of Italy and further afield were anxious to have access to his unique method. He usually confined himself to Italian speakers, but he had been known to understand foreign languages that he did not speak. He gave advice to talented and learned people from all walks of life, and dealt with them in the space of minutes. He had a gift of reading souls; some of them he dismissed out of hand, but many returned, admitting a lack of sincerity the first time they approached him, and genuine conversions were commonplace.

Gradually – and embarrassingly, for a follower of St Francis – large and small gifts began to mount up into a substantial sum. Many sick pilgrims flocked into San Giovanni Rotondo in the hope of receiving a blessing and perhaps gaining a cure, and it had always troubled Padre Pio that there was nowhere they could be treated; there were already too few beds in the local hospital for the people in the district. In 1940 Padre Pio was talking in his cell with a doctor, a vet and a chemist, when he first conceived the idea of building a hospital.

The war put an end to this plan for the duration, but in 1946 the work of gathering contributions was accelerated, and the foundation stone of the 'House for the Relief of Suffering' was laid in 1948. The enterprise had been begun in hope rather than certainty that funds would prove adequate, but a visit by the English economist Barbara Ward, later to marry Lord Jackson (whose conversion was foreseen by Padre Pio) ensured the couple's interest. They used their influence to obtain a substantial grant from the United Nations Relief Agency. During the ten years before the hospital was opened to receive patients, the financial arrangements were in the hands of a limited liability company, and Padre Pio was absolved from his vow of poverty so that he could play a part in collecting funds.

The official opening was on his feast day, 5 May 1956. In time it was enlarged to a thousand beds, and has kept abreast of the very latest technology. Two farms owned by the Institution provide for its agricultural needs, and there is a training school for nurses and an Institute for the care of spastic children, many of whom are treated in a day centre at San Giovanni or three further centres in the surrounding area.

Over the years, Padre Pio set up Prayer Groups: little knots of devotees who became known to one another and met regularly to pray and study. Their patron insisted that they should be under the care of a chaplain, as he did not want them to stray without direction. They were officially approved by the Holy See in July 1968, and by September of that year they were holding their fourth international convention in San Giovanni.

They were also celebrating the fiftieth anniversary of the appearance of the stigmata on Padre Pio's suffering flesh – though in fact the wounds had been slowly healing in the past two or three years. On 22 September Padre Pio said Mass, standing on a platform in the town square as the crowd was much too large for the Church. It was his usual time of five-thirty in the morning and he was so frail that he had to be supported by another friar, and sat down to celebrate. During the morning he blessed his spiritual children from a window in the old Church; and the first stone of the Stations of the Cross which still lead pilgrims up the mountain.

He stayed in his cell for most of the day, except for a visit to the new Church in the afternoon, where he blessed the crowd again from the gallery overlooking the high altar. In the evening the prayer groups met by torchlight in a field in front of his cell, awaiting a last wave of his handkerchief, but they were disappointed.

A friar called Padre Pellegrino was standing by in a neighbouring cell to assist him during the night, and Padre Pio called him six or seven times before midnight, asking him the time. At midnight he asked, through childlike tears, if Padre Pellegrino would stay with him, and squeezed his hand as if in need of human contact. But he remained awake, and insisted on making his confession – this was unusual, and put Padre Pellegrino on his guard. He asked for blessings on his fellow friars, his spiritual children, and for the sick, and he renewed his vows.

About one in the morning his breathing became laboured, and to relieve it he left his bed and walked about, without Padre Pellegrino's assistance. Then the temporary respite was over, and he used his wheelchair to get back to his cell. Although his fellow friar was now anxious to call a doctor, for his face was deathly pale, he tried to dissuade him, but Padre Pellegrino insisted on alerting everyone from the Head of the Hospital to the Father Guardian, and the little cell was soon crowded. In spite of all that the medical men could do, Padre

Pio's life was ebbing away. He was anointed, and his confreres began the prayers for the dying. When he could no longer speak, his lips formed the words, "Jesus, Mary" – over and over again. His last breath was imperceptible, and for several minutes they supposed he was sleeping. At about two-thirty a.m. his head dropped gently to one side. His life was over – and just beginning.

The media spread the news throughout the world, and a hundred thousand people gathered to pay him homage. Pope John Paul II – who as Archbishop of Cracow had already visited him (and it is popularly supposed that Padre Pio had foreseen his election to the papacy) – gave permission for a judicial enquiry into his life and virtues, which opened in March 1983. His devotees speak of innumerable favours received through his intercession, and of the perfume he sends to remind them that he who was never confined to one place by the weight of the flesh is now totally free in heaven.

The Easter people who rejoice in the Resurrection of their Lord learn much from Padre Pio about the suffering and death that made redemption possible. The emphasis of the twenty-first century may be different, but the message is the same as in the past two thousand years, and Padre Pio carries it from his remote friary to the ends of the earth.

ALBERT SCHWEITZER

Alsace should have produced a larger number of schizophrenics than anywhere in Europe, lying as it does at the border of France and Germany, and governed by whichever country held temporary power over the other. Instead, the inhabitants gave their allegiance to neither, and farmed their rich land with the devotion and tenacity of the guard-dogs that take their name from the province.

Albert Schweitzer was born in the pleasant town of Kaysersberg on 14 January 1875, just five years after the triumph of Prussia over France had ensured that he would be a German citizen. His father, the Lutheran pastor, not normally demonstrative, was so pleased by the birth of his elder son that he took a mighty leap that cleared the crib. He was something of a scholar and historian, reading the classics of French and German literature, and collecting local stories which were published in a slim volume.

He left his wife to set the tone of the family. She was a daughter of the manse; rather humourless, seeking the respect of her neighbours, well-informed and ambitious for her children. Among the qualities that her famous son inherited were kindness that drew no boundaries of class, and a love of nature. When Albert was only months old, the family moved a few miles to Gunsbach, where a damp, dark house did nothing to improve the serious fever he was suffering. The new congregation noticed that he was an unhealthy colour, lying apathetically in his cradle, and his mother was so ashamed of his appearance, she removed him from the company, shedding tears of humiliation. They were the first of many; the young Albert often thwarted her plans for him. A younger brother and three sisters made up the family, devoted to one another in a way that was always understated, sharing rather earthy jokes and making a great deal of noise.

Albert later recalled one of his earliest memories, watching his father collect honey from the beehive. One of the disturbed inhabitants crawled over his hand, and he watched it, fascinated – until it stung him sharply. His father and the maid in charge tried to stem his cries; his mother blamed them for the mishap. The centre of all this unaccustomed attention, Albert deliberately prolonged his tears to retain it; then became remorseful over his self-indulgence and spent a miserable day. It would seem a complicated reaction for a very small child, and showed both his sense of fairness and unusual thoughtfulness.

At the age of three or four he was taken to Church, which was presented as a privilege due to his advanced years. Owing to an edict by a former King of France, Protestant churches were compelled to house the Catholic minority and give them provision for the celebration of Mass. Instead of causing friction, this promoted ecumenism. Catholic statues and a gilded altar met Albert's wondering gaze, but it was also arrested by the sight of an ugly face peering down at the congregation from the organ loft. It was the reflection in a mirror of the organist, looking for his cue to play, but Albert was firmly convinced that it was the devil, because it seemed to disappear when his father prayed.

The family had by now inherited his maternal grandfather's piano, and his father would improvise on it by the hour. Albert was an avid listener, observing him to such good effect that he taught himself to play, supplying harmonies to familiar tunes. This talent for music came from both sides of the family, which boasted some fine instrumentalists, principally organists. When he was eventually dragged unwillingly to school, it proved to be his sole accomplishment. He took no pleasure in surpassing his singing teacher, who had to produce accompaniments with one finger, and he was loath to parade his achievement, feeling he was belittling her. Many children are more sensitive than the adults who try to educate them, but Albert retained his childlike qualities all his life.

However, at this time his dreaminess in the classroom caused him to lag behind the others in every department of learning.

He obstinately refused to be better dressed than his peers, in spite of his mother's entreaties and beatings by his father. His fellow-pupils remained unconvinced; he could not submerge the difference in background by dressing like them. Once, on the way home from school, he indulged in one of those wrestling matches by which small boys decide the pecking order for their games. He was the victor over a bigger boy, who from his defeated position on the ground taunted him with:"Yes, if I got broth to eat twice a week like you do, I'd be as strong as you are!"

Forty years later he remembered the name of the boy who had effectively pricked the bubble of his success – George Nitschelm. He had a great deal to answer for; perhaps a lifetime spent in expiation of the sin of being privileged.

On visiting nearby Colmar, the image which struck his imagination indelibly was a statue of a black man, in a series representing the principal races of the world – no doubt the romantic European idea of the noble savage. The little Teuton never failed to ponder it; the unruly hair reconciled him to his own, which was the despair of all who tried to subdue it.

By the time he was nine he was able to play the Church organ. It was also the age at which he discovered the pleasures of learning to read. His father satisfied his request for a Bible, which he searched for answers to such knotty religious problems as why the Holy Family still suffered poverty after receiving the Wise Men's gifts, and the nature of the Great Flood.

When he was ten it was decided to send him to the secondary school in Mulhouse, whose grim industrial districts reflected his own depression. He lodged with his childless uncle and aunt, who were determined to mould him in their own crabbed image. Every hour of the day was planned; he had to fight for time to read newspapers – which was surely a harmless occupation in those days – but not in the eyes of Aunt Sophie, who demanded an examination of what he retained from them before permission was granted. He became very aware of the misery around him, and accepted it, writing that:

"it seemed to me a matter of course that we should all take our share of the burden of pain which lies upon the world."

This depression lasted for three years; then two things happened almost simultaneously. The first was that he acquired a teacher whom he could respect, and the second that his music teacher gave him one of Mendelssohn's 'Songs Without Words' to play, with the despairing remark, "I suppose you'll spoil this, like everything else. If a boy has no feeling, I certainly can't give him any."

Stung, Albert's underlying emotion, dammed by years of criticism, burst forth. After he had heard him play, his teacher (the organist Eugene Munch) performed another of the 'Songs' as an introduction to the brotherhood of musicians. At fifteen Albert was given organ lessons, and at sixteen accompanied at a performance of Brahms's Requiem. He also paid his first visit to the theatre – a performance of Wagner's Tannhauser that left him reeling with its romantic grandeur.

He approached his Confirmation with great solemnity – "So moved by the holiness of the time that I felt almost ill", as he explained. He combined this with a terrier-like tenacity that sought answers to religious problems based on reason. It was not only religion that he subjected to this scrutiny; history and science were presented at that time as explaining every question that arose, but they seemed to Albert mere catalogues of experience, capable of being manipulated and needing rigorous examination. At last he rose to the challenge even of subjects that did not interest him, like mathematics and languages, and passed his final examinations with a special mention.

Before entering the university at Strasbourg, he spent time with relatives in Paris. They knew the organist at St Sulpice, who also taught at the Conservatoire, Charles-Marie Widor, who had taken over this post from the great Cesar Franck. Albert was diffident about playing for him, but Widor saw his potential, and confided to him: "Organ-playing is the manifestation of a will filled with the vision of eternity", and gave him lessons to improve his technique.

For the young Albert Schweitzer, Strasbourg – a comparatively new university, free from traditional stuffiness – was the right place at the right time. There he met Ernest Munch, the brother of his Mulhousean music teacher, and spent nights at his house arguing over the right way to interpret Bach. He read theology and philosophy, but his lecturer Holtzmann – whose picture of Jesus, culled from exhaustive study of St Mark's Gospel, was of an enlightened liberal like himself – failed to satisfy the young Schweitzer. He sought Jesus as a historical figure, set against the background of his time. Gradually he emerged – a Messiah, whose kingdom had not materialised, who died in expiation of the world's sins, but probably did not rise again. Schweitzer was ready to rock orthodoxy; but he had learned tact and caution, and he left Holtzmann in peace for the time being. But it was probably in the music of Bach that he came nearest to finding Jesus.

The introverted dreamer of his schooldays was left far behind. He could not get enough contact with his fellow human beings of all classes and degrees of awaremess. So determined was he to communicate with the poor, he travelled fourth-class on his way between Strasbourg and his home, listening to the conversations in the railway carriage. With German thoroughness he made notes of the stories that were told, telling his own when there was a suitable pause. If it is not a contradiction in terms, he made the most determined and conscious effort to react spontaneously.

In the hot summer of 1895 he found himself at an ill-attended lecture on the history of the mission. The lecturer, a Professor Lucius, was enlarging on the exploitation of the colonies by their white overlords, and spoke of the missions as a way of paying the debt incurred. Schweitzer's carefully-cultivated spontaneity made itself felt – he was impelled to answer the call to missionary work – though it was not until the following Pentecost that he discovered the path he would take.

We have seen how he travelled as if by flashes of lightning – pausing only to absorb the shock, then moving on with certainty. Now he took his decision: until he was thirty, the age at which his master Jesus had begun his ministry, he would live for his studies in science and art – after that he would devote himself to the service of humanity. He counted himself outwardly happy with his great gifts, his united family and his talent for friendship. Now he was to experience inward happiness in repaying his debt to those less fortunate.

He renewed his relationship with Widor, exchanging new insights on the playing of Bach's choral preludes, and they gradually became colleagues, rather than teacher and pupil.

The last year of the century found him in Berlin, preparing for the viva examination for his doctorate. The universities were full of discussion about Nietzsche's latest books, with their emphasis on self-realisation. Schweitzer discussed them as eagerly as anyone else, and contemplated writing a book on philosophy himself; with these distractions he made only an average impression on the examiners, but received his degree in the summer of 1899.

He had set his sights on a professorship, and determined to take a licentiate in theology, to qualify himself. In addition to playing the organ, he found a pulpit for himself at the Church of St Nicholas, where he acted as deacon. His sermons were not tinged with the controversial nature of his thesis, an examination of the meaning of the Gospels centred on the Last Supper; as a preacher he was simple and direct – an indicator of how he was to develop.

He received his licentiate and within six days passed his examination to become a curate; characteristically finding the lesser qualification more difficult, through underrating the sensitivity of his examiners.

He was able to use his talent as a teacher when taking Confirmation classes, and his insatiable curiosity about people's trades and professions led him to discover much about his parishioners. When he could find someone to stand in for him, he would make flying visits to Paris, to officiate as organist for the Johann Sebastian Bach Society; he took the opportunity of studying French organs, which he found more congenial than the more technically advanced German instruments.

During these visits to Paris at the height of its fin-de-siecle extravagance of fashion and ideas, he became a social lion and something of a dandy. He enjoyed women's company, especially if they were of an age and experience to contribute

236

something to the relationship; he also had the charming habit of seeking out the wallflowers at dances.

Some voices were raised against his appointment as deputy principal of Strasbourg Theological College. His recently-published book *The Mystery of the Kingdom of God* was a summary of all his views on the historical Jesus, and although it only claimed to deal with the human side of his personality, it left very little room for a divine side. Schweitzer measured Jesus, whom he loved and revered, by the yardstick of modern historical and scientific thought; putting, in fact, his divinity on trial, whether that was his intention or not. A further book, *The Quest for the Historical Jesus*, was no more orthodox. Yet in spite of this, he depicted a heroic teacher, of tremendous power yet touching humility, worthy of reverence – and he followed him with no ordinary devotion.

Several of the younger people at the university volunteered for a project announced by Central Government, calling on social workers, professionals and amateurs alike, to help with the problem of poverty and distress. The amateurs saw to the distribution of food and fuel, and undertook the delousing of deprived children. Among the volunteers was Schweitzer – and a young woman, four years his junior, called Helene Bresslau. She was the daughter of a Christian convert from Judaism; she had helped to run a state orphanage – co-founded a home for unmarried mothers; she was a pioneer in women's skiing, and an accomplished organist. Still more amazingly, she had resolved to dedicate her life totally to the service of humanity on her twenty-fifth birthday, which lay just three years ahead. She even dared to criticise Schweitzer's mode of preaching in a down-to-earth Alsatian dialect, and helped to adapt his literary style into 'good' German.

During 1902 and the two years following, he undertook to write a book in French about Bach, claiming his favourite composer as a true romantic. Even this was bound to appear unorthodox, as Bach was considered the most cerebral and mathematical of composers. He allowed Widor to read each chapter as he wrote it, and when it was published Widor provided a preface. The German version, which was not a translation but a complete re-writing, gained him the friendship of Wagner's widow, Cosima. He also found time, though the deadline he had imposed upon himself was fast approaching, to write a seminal work on organ-building, based on his practical work as an instrumentalist.

Four months before his thirtieth birthday, when he still had to decide what form his service should take, he came upon a magazine article that outlined the needs of the Paris Missionary Society for workers in the Gambon, in the north of Congo Colony. It concluded a simple appeal to those who had heard Jesus's call, to answer, "Lord, I am coming." All Schweitzer's generosity rose to it; the die was cast – he had found the location of his future life.

On Friday, 13 October, 1905, he circulated letters to his friends stating that he would enrol as a medical student in order to go to Equatorial Africa as a doctor. The friends, who had no idea that such a decision was likely, set up a storm of protest, which was echoed by his family – his mother in particular. To them it seemed he was throwing God's gifts back in his face. If he had to persist in such a Quixotic notion, why did he have to choose a territory that was known to be the White Man's Grave? There was pathos in his attempts to justify his gesture, and explain the way he was misunderstood. For him, the exploitation of native peoples was a crime that had to be expiated, as Jesus had shown by his life and teaching. "I want to be a simple human being," he wrote, "doing something small in the spirit of Jesus."

He contacted the Paris Missionary Society, only to find that his unorthodox reputation made them wary of him, until he explained that he wanted to go to Africa merely as a doctor. It was necessary for him to make money for living expenses (his colleagues arranged that the fees for his medical training should be waived) so he seized every opportunity to give organ recitals, travelling through France and Spain. He was still writing the German version of his book on Bach, and already marshalling his ideas for another, using the historical technique on the life of Jesus's great missionary apostle, St Paul. In the course of writing these books he fell in love with his subjects as an artist does, showing the depth of his creative talent.

His first examinations in medicine were successfully passed, in spite of being a mature student. Helene Bresslau was a regular visitor at the family home in Gunsbach – where the children called her 'Aunt Prim-and-Proper' – and when he enrolled for his medical degree, she began to train as a nurse. He always observed scrupulous discretion about his own and others' private life, but he did mention to a friend that he had one confidante about his plans; since she was included in them, it must have been Fraulein Bresslau.

His thesis for the finals of his medical degree was a psychiatric study of Jesus, and he dealt with the subject of paranoia in depth. This essay into the expression of religion in terms of science led him to believe in the absolute sanity of his Master, whose behaviour never deviated from the norm.

It gave him a great deal of satisfaction to make this contribution to his twin interests, and the books were influential in making other scholars examine doctrine by the light of reason.

Now he had to study tropical medicine, and the only place that seemed right to him was Paris. He contacted the Paris Missionary Society, assuring them that he would seek finance from well-disposed friends to defray the cost of his missions. Naturally they leaped at his offer, and his unorthodox writings seemed less of an impediment to his going to Africa under their auspices. Helene helped in the acquisition of equipment for his life there, and it became clear to both their families that she intended to accompany him. Judged in the light of future events, their marriage may have been one of convenience. At that time young women did not accompany young men to the back of beyond unless they were closely related. They were married in June 1912, and spent what would have been their honeymoon in anticipating every contingency that might occur in setting up a hospital in practically virgin jungle; laying in equipment to deal with them, packing it all up in seventy cases, and sending it to Bordeaux for shipment. On Easter Monday 1913, the young couple set out for Africa in the steamship 'Europe'.

It took them three weeks to reach Libreville, the capital of the Gambon, where they transferred to a paddle-steamer that would take them up the Ogowe to their goal. Nothing they had heard or read had prepared them for the appearance of the river and the forest, which seemed to merge into one another in a tangle of tree-roots and creepers. The vegetation only approximated to species they recognised, being on a giant scale, luxuriant in the steamy heat. Strange birds flew over the water, and sometimes they caught glimpses of monkeys.

The last lap to the village of Lambarene, where Schweitzer was to make his home for the rest of his life, was covered in dug-out canoes brought by white missionaries who came to meet them, and they travelled for an hour beyond the village to the bungalow allotted them. They were not prepared for the sudden darkness at six o'clock in the evening; daylight appeared with equal inevitability at six in the morning, and with it the procession of the sick began. The jungle telegraph had signalled the doctor's coming, and the newly-qualified Schweitzer was presented with every known human disease. The climate caused wounds to suppurate – there was malaria, sleeping-sickness, leprosy and elephantisis, among many other conditions. All were aggravated by poor diet, and the superstition that could convince a man that he had been cursed.

Doctor Schweitzer treated them in the open air, until offered the only unoccupied building on the mission station – a hen-house, which he gave a coat of whitewash and used as both surgery and operating theatre. Helene was his assistant in every task, and supervised the running of the house. They discovered that the native African, who would work all the hours possible to care for his own village or bring his relatives to the hospital, had no sense of the social structure outside his home territory. He had to be bribed or coerced into the service of the white man, and the traders in hardwood, the only export, did most of their bribing with alcohol.

Schweitzer gained an African assistant, a man called Joseph Azowani, who came to him as a patient and stayed on after he was cured. He was an invaluable source of information about the life and customs of the region, and acted as cook, medical orderly and interpreter, making the doctor's simple rules for the regulation of treatment clear to the patients.

The hen-house was soon outgrown, and Schweitzer made

plans to build a hospital. He consulted the missionaries and, observing the way African villages were constructed, he contrived to blend all their ideas into a practical shape. The finished building served him all his days in Africa, and was to shock a number of visiting Europeans, but it was cool and free from harmful insects.

Some patients were able and willing to build their own beds, but it was difficult to spur the labour force into action. Schweitzer did so by throwing himself into the work, and where he led the Africans followed. He had to retain their respect, and such was the moral force of his personality, he always did so – in spite of a temper with a very short fuse, aggravated by the excessive heat.

Soon his stores arrived, including the specially designed piano with organ pedals, given him by the Paris Bach Society. It was built to withstand predatory insects, and the donors hoped he would practise on it, so that he would not lose his musical skills. At first he could not bear to be reminded of his former passion, but as he spent the tropical nights completing his edition of Bach's work, he also found peace in playing again. Later, whenever money for the hospital ran short, he gave concerts to replenish the coffers during his visits home.

Having treated over two thousand patients in the first nine months, both he and Helene were very tired, but they did not propose to take home leave until 1915. It was the outbreak of war that interrupted their activities; as Germans in a French territory, they were placed under arrest, but the absurdity of imprisoning such benevolent aliens eventually percolated French officialdom, and they were allowed to continue until they were finally deported to France in 1917.

All this time, Schweizer continued to work on his major book: *The Decay and Restoration of Civilisation*. In it he outlined the causes of the malaise in European thinking – the downgrading of labour, in which everything was judged by its market value – and the acceptance of the law of the jungle. He, who lived in a real jungle, sought some kind of philosophy that he and others could live by. He found it in September 1915, three days up-river on his way to treat a French missionary's ailing wife. The steamer on which he travelled was passing through a herd of hippopotamuses when the phrase 'Reverence for life' came into his mind, and the search that had led him through the night hours, scribbling ideas on pieces of scrap-paper, was over.

It meant reverence for every form of life – animal, vegetable and human. The instinct that made him allow all kinds of animals to roam through his hospital was expressed in it: antelopes, and a pet pelican, followed him about. The man who battled against malaria would preserve the life of a mosquito invading his room, carefully putting it outside – it was not consistent, but somehow it was inconsistency on a grand scale. Yet he always put his human patients before animal ones, and would not prolong the life, even of his own pets, if they were in pain.

The following year tragedy struck. Schweizer's mother, out for a walk with her husband and friends, was knocked down by a soldier's horse, galloping out of control. They were in a war zone, and aid was hard to come by. Her son heard the news a month later, and mourned her, draping her photograph in jungle blossoms. He was not able to visit her grave until he was repatriated in August 1917. A legacy of his time in the tropics was an abscess of the rectum which was operated on in Strasbourg. Previously he had shown no diminution of his immense physical strength, but now he realised that even he could join 'the Fellowship of those who bear the mark of pain'. In the clinic of the same hospital, his daughter Rhena was born on his forty-fourth birthday. Both he and Helene suffered at this time: Helene's health was so badly broken, she could not return to Africa until after World War II.

As his books were published, Schweizer became in demand both as lecturer and organ recitalist, and recovered his energy after a second operation. He went back to Lambarene in April 1924, to find that the jungle had moved in on the neglected hospital, and he had to rebuild it almost from the beginning. He called upon patients' relatives as labourers – and the patients themselves when they were convalescent – and worked tirelessly himself, since the only way to encourage them was to set an example. For twelve years the pattern of his life in Africa became hard physical labour, with the simplest of life-styles, broken by visits to Europe and America, fund-raising and receiving an increasing number of honorary degrees and international awards.

Foreseeing the outbreak of war, he cut short one of his visits and spent ten more years in Africa, and Helene managed to join him after a hair-raising wartime journey from France. When the war ended, he allied himself with those who felt that the dropping of the atom bomb imperilled civilisation. He also campaigned for the adoption of vegetarianism. On his journeys he met nearly everyone of note, and they were proud to shake his hand. He always wore an old coat that had been made for him in 1905, though on formal occasions he added a made-up bow tie to his threadbare shirt. Now there was no-one left to tell him to brush his unruly hair, as Helene had died in Switzerland in 1957, and he buried her in Lambarene, so that he could feel her presence close to him. Theirs was an unconventional marriage; they had lived more apart than together, but she and his daughter completely respected the demands of his work, and Helene took Rhena on lecture tours to raise funds for the hospital. She was, not unsurprisingly, sometimes jealous of the women who followed her husband to Africa and assisted him in his labours, but no breath of scandal was ever aroused.

Schweizer was awarded the Nobel Peace Prize in 1953, enabling him to add a three-hundred bed leprosy unit to the hospital, and received the Order of Merit in 1955 from the British sovereign. He coped with fame by strenuously ignoring it; journalists and lion-hunters were given short shrift.

When the Gambon was made independent of France in 1960, he was asked if he would speak for it at the United Nations, but he felt that the young country should have a native representative. He returned to it in 1959, never to leave again. He no longer played Bach on the old piano with the pedals; it was crated up to be sent to Gunsbach, where he had spent his childhood and his most restful home leaves, climbing above the village and regarding it from a rocky outcrop.

Some people strove to find fault with the famous doctor's methods; his hospital was judged to be hopelessly old-fashioned and unhygienic. He was accused of paternalism – a favourite charge by the new anti-racialists – but even when he treated his African helpers and patients like irresponsible children, they loved him. By the time of his ninetieth birthday they had grown together in a community that was his nearest and dearest family; the hospital had an airport, and Rhena had come to work there as a laboratory assistant.

On 23 August 1965, he announced after the communal evening meal that when he died she should take over the whole complex, and his death took place quietly and with dignity, in the midst of his people, on 4 September. The dynamic physical machine that had served him so long had worn out. He was buried beside Helene, their graves marked by simple white crosses. His monument, a splendid new hospital – which he would probably not have cared for – was opened in 1981.

Although his birth took place in the nineteenth century, he was a spokesman for the children of the twentieth. He shared their hopes and fears for the future of civilisation, the disintegration of which he foresaw, and the current hunger for moral certainty. Christianity was his driving force; he had given his love to Jesus early in his career, and never wavered. If he accepted only what he could test by reason, and never concerned himself with the mysteries of religion, he fulfilled the two greatest commandments – to love God and his neighbour as himself.

CHARLES DE FOUCAULD

A rather run-down and shabby housing estate in South London – not the worst, but far from being a desirable residence. A maze of walkways, each with its row of blank front doors, which seek anonymity as if trying to avoid unwelcome attention. There are no bells or knockers; you gain access by rattling the letter-box, or thumping the door. The man who opens it is unremarkable until you look into his eyes. They are dark brown – humorous yet grave – wise and innocent. You cannot look away, nor do you want to.

The kitchen is a meeting-place; you feel there is always a kettle on the boil, and conversation generated by the consumption of tea and biscuits. The working tops are bare and tidy; someone has cut photographs out of magazines to decorate the walls. But it is the chapel that causes an intake of breath – a lightness of heart. It is of modest size, and the furnishings do not distract from the altar, which has a woven mat behind the tabernacle, and another of the cheapest Indian variety beneath it. The resting-place of the Host is like a large white pebble with a heart carved into it, surmounted by a cross. Beyond the open window is the faint sound of a transistor tuned to Radio 1; nothing of the world is excluded, but nothing disturbs this radiant peace.

The silent prayer over, conversation is resumed. In answer to the query: "What attracted you to the Little Brothers of Jesus?" the reply comes: "I read about Charles de Foucauld..." There is no need to hear more. It is as if a third person were present in the room.

Charles Eugene de Foucauld was born in Strasbourg on 15 September 1858 in the house where, just over sixty years earlier, Rouget de l'Isle had composed the marching song which became known as the Marseillaise. Charles's family came from the old French aristocracy, originating in Perigord, and producing an ancestor who had been killed in the Crusades, as well as a priest who had been murdered at the dawn of the Revolution. In 1861 his little sister Marie-Ines was born, known to him as Mimi. His mother was pious, but not forbiddingly so; she taught him to ask God's blessing on his family, and set up a little altar in his room, decorated with the flowers they gathered when they went for walks, accompanying his father who was Chief Inspector of Waters and Forests in the region. At Christmas, since they lived among those who kept German customs, there was a tree as well as a crib.

This idyllic life was ended by tragedy. When Charles was five his father was diagnosed as suffering from tuberculosis, and left the family so that he should not infect them. His young wife was pregnant, and no doubt undermined by anxiety for her husband, she had a miscarriage and died as a result. A few months later the death of their father made orphans of the two young children. Taken to see his mother at the last, Charles always remembered that she had said: "Thy will, not mine, be done." She also seems to have had a premonition that her son was destined for a special saintliness.

The crushing double bereavement was somewhat mitigated by their not having to leave Strasbourg, merely moving to the house of their maternal grandparents, Colonel de Morlet and his wife, who did their best to provide a stable background for the six-year-old Vicomte and his sister. Like many an army man, the Colonel had a pacific hobby – in his case, archaeology – to which he introduced his grandson. He took him out on digs, and taught him to make accurate drawings of his finds. Charles was evidently an attractive child, with dark eyes and hair. As he grew up his health gave some concern, because of his parents' early demise; far from imposing military discipline on his daughter's son, Colonel de Morlet perhaps made too many allowances for his childish fits of temper. It was in the summer of 1866 that he first met his cousin Marie Moitessier, who was eight years his senior, and had helped to nurse his father during his exile from the family.

This bond was transferred to Charles, and three years later he was old enough to share Italian lessons with her, and accompany her to Church.

She was beautiful and sensitive, and when in 1874 she married Olivier, Vicomte de Bondy, the fourteen-year-old boy seems to have suffered from jealousy; like some other adolescents, he tried to compensate for his misery by over-eating.

However he passed into the military academy of Saint-Cyr – a respectable eighty-second out of over four hundred candidates – and remained there from 1876 to 1878. They were vintage years, and many of Charles's contemporaries had distinguished careers. Although his own stay was fairly disastrous – he passed out low on the list, and lost his first-class stripes because of general slovenliness – he made an indelible impression. He read widely, and his gastronomic feats were legendary. The story of his eating foie-gras with a silver spoon in the dormitory went the rounds.

His excesses may have been influenced by the death of his grandfather in the February of his final year. Colonel de Morlet, whose sympathy and encouragement had bolstered up his belief in his own powers, left his grandson a substantial fortune, but that, compounded with a very genuine grief, was to be his undoing. At the Cavalry School at Saumur, he was often confined to barracks with his room-mate, another sprig of the nobility. They held court to their friends, providing the most expensive dinners and presiding over card-parties that went on into the small hours. To evade the authorities, Charles passed himself off once as a beggar and on another occasion as a tradesman. Perhaps what he really wanted to escape from was himself.

The one person in whom he could confide was his cousin, Marie de Bondy. To her, the young sub-lieutenant, who was supposed to be cold, withdrawn and self-indulgent, revealed a heart that she alone could touch. He saw to it that his posting should be near home at Nancy, but in spite of a captivating mistress he kept in luxury in Paris, he became easily bored, and welcomed a move when his regiment was posted to Algeria. There he occupied himself with learning Arabic and making expeditions amongst the native tribes. He had also taken his mistress along with him, which might have been overlooked in the permissive climate of the time, but he insisted on giving her the title of Vicomtesse de Foucauld, which could not. He was dismissed from active service for serious misconduct in March 1881.

Charles was living in Switzerland when he read that his regiment, the Fourth Chasseurs d'Afrique, had gone into action to quell a rising by a holy man defying the colonial powers. What military discipline could not do, his country's need accomplished; he gave up his mistress and offered to enlist as a trooper. Such evident ardour convinced his superiors, and he returned to North Africa as an exemplary officer, held in high regard by his men and his colleagues, who included several lifelong friends.

When the insurrection was put down, he sought more excitement, and eventually resigned his commission to make an expedition to Morocco. In Algiers he acquired the map-making skills he needed to undertake a useful exploration. He had two alternatives: either to travel as an Arab or as a Jew, and he studied both Arabic and Hebrew. He found a Rabbi called Mardochee who agreed, at a price, to accompany him. An experienced traveller, the Rabbi seemed as reliable as Charles could hope, given the instability of the region, and he collected all the meteorological instruments needed to accomplish his task, and adopted a Jewish costume.

Living in the Rabbi's one-room dwelling in Algiers, Charles Vicomte de Foucauld took on the persona of Rabbi Joseph Aliman, born in Russia, but having completed his Rabbinical studies in Jerusalem. By all accounts he delighted in the deception; the young man who had passed himself off in his youth as a beggar gained freedom by abandoning his wealth and class. Despite his unfamiliarity with Jewish rituals, he was protected from discovery by the fact that Jews were universally despised and ignored.

They travelled mostly in company, which made the observations Charles was engaged upon very difficult. He evaded suspicion by travelling only in the vanguard or in the rear, writing with a stub of pencil in a notebook barely two inches

248

square. While his fellow-travellers slept, he would copy his notes into a larger book. The sextant was too cumbersome to be hidden in the folds of his robes like his compass and barometer, so he busied himself, putting clothes out to dry on the flat roof of each night's lodging-house, and under cover of these he was able to use it.

He fell in love with Morocco, its flowing rivers and high mountains and stretches of barren desert, but on 23 May 1884 he returned to French territory in Algeria, and the adventure was over.

The following year, when he returned to Algeria to write his book, *Reconnaissance au Maroc*, his cousin Marie's husband received the gold medal of the Geographical Society of Paris on his behalf. It took Charles four years to complete his manuscript, which was published in 1888 to universal acclaim. An English geographer praised it as "the most important and remarkable journey in Morocco which a European has accomplished for a century or more." He had included birds-eye views, sketches and maps, and showed a real talent for descriptive writing.

When he went back to spend six months with his family, they realised that he had undergone a radical change. Even physically, it was remarkable, for he had shed his excess weight and had become very good-looking. When he returned to Algeria, while consulting Commandant Titre, a geographer who had some maps he wished to see, he was introduced to the Commandant's daughter: she was twenty-three years old and attractive with a determined and unusual character. Her family was Protestant, and when she converted to the Catholic faith her grandmother, from whom she had expectations of a considerable fortune, disinherited her. It may have been this that put the more worldly members of Charles's family against her; in any case they certainly opposed the match; they considered her insufficiently aristocratic – and she did not have a dowry.

Perhaps his cousin Viscomtesse de Bondy had a deeper reason for using her influence against the marriage. She was still hoping for spiritual riches for Charles, and her intervention was successful. After a scant six months, most of which he spent with his family in France, the engagement was ended.

Charles took an apartment in Paris, and came to a gradual realisation that it was not only a physical change he had undergone in Morocco. He had lived alongside the faithful of two great religions, Judaism and Islam; he admired their observance of regular prayer, and the ethics of the Torah and the Koran – but the spiritual life of Mademoiselle Titre and his cousin impressed him still more. They were intelligent, attractive women, not swayed by superstition, and they challenged his scepticism. He took to haunting churches, offering up the prayer, "My God, if you exist, make your existence known to me."

A decisive step was taken when Marie de Bondy introduced him to her confessor, the Abbé Huvelin. He was a remarkable man who had given up the idea of a career as a historian to become the unpaid curate of a Church, St Augustin, near Charles's apartment. His health was always precarious, but he spent hours each day counselling all who came with wisdom and humour. Charles was so impressed, he decided to ask for instruction in the faith he had lost twelve years earlier, and sought him out in the confessional. When he made his request, the Abbé hurried the business along by telling him to make his confession and receive Communion without waiting for any further instruction.

So it was in the Church named for the saint whose life in some ways resembled his own that Charles de Foucauld came back into the fold.

In 1887, when he was staying with his de Bondy relations, his cousin suggested they should visit the Trappist monastery at Fontgombault. He was deeply impressed by the poverty of the brothers, and was often to remind Marie that it was at her instigation he made the visit. But it was the Abbé Huvelin who persuaded him to go to the Holy Land the following year. He was overcome by the sight of the places where Jesus had lived, worked, died and risen again. Christmas found him in the grotto of the Church of the Nativity, assisting at the Mass of the feast. It gave him a real feeling of the presence of the Holy Family, and he followed it with a visit to Nazareth. All through his life there would be references to the place where Jesus had grown up and pursued his hidden life of manual work and poverty; the word 'Nazareth' came to mean his ideal of the way to follow him. His travels in Morocco had brought him close to those whose lives were lived in obscurity, and he was no stranger to deprivation. The difference was that then he knew he was only being poor for a limited period; now he was proposing to dedicate his whole life to taking the lowest place.

Having discussed his future as a religious with Abbé Huvelin, his generous heart responded to the call of the most austere order of monastic foundations. After making over his material fortune to his sister, he entered the Trappist monastery of Notre-Dame-des-Neiges in the Ardeche on 15 January 1890, dividing his time between prayer, reading and manual work. He received the habit on the feast of Candlemas, and took the name of Brother Alberic. In search of greater austerity, he asked to be removed to the most remote monastery, Notre-Dame-du-Sacre-Coeur, at Cheikhle in Syria.

There among the mountains, the monks grew corn, potatoes and vines, and he described the work as "harder than you imagine if you have not done it. It moves you to compassion for the poor, for workmen and labourers. You understand the cost of a piece of bread when you see the effort that goes to produce it."

He imposed stricter austerities on himself, refusing to augment a bread-and-water diet even on the greatest feasts. His superiors were impressed by his zeal, but tried to discourage him from writing his own version of the Rule. When he became professed in February 1892, great things were hoped from him. He was urged to take up theology with a view to becoming a priest, but he felt no vocation; for him, the 'lowest place' did not include the great honour of celebrating the Eucharist.

Once he had complied with the directive to take up theological studies he found them congenial, but he did not relish the idea of having more security than the agricultural labourers who surrounded them. Spending a night in one of their homes, watching over a deathbed, he came to realise that what he really felt called to do was share their lives. If the Trappists could not satisfy his craving for austerity, where could he feel at home? It was in 1893 that he had the idea of founding his own Order, to meet his exacting requirements. He laid it before Abbé Huvelin, inviting him to decide if it were feasible or desirable.

The Abbé realised that Brother Alberic would always be restless if he were forced by obedience to stay at La Trappe, and he advocated a change. As to the Rule he had drawn up, it was even more impractical than that of St Francis in the thirteenth century; no modern man could live by it. With this limited approval, Brother Alberic applied to his Abbot for permission to leave La Trappe, and after a short stay in Rome during the winter of 1896/7, trying to resign himself to study there for the priesthood, he received the news he wanted. The Father General of the Cistercian Order released him from his vows, and the Abbé Huvelin suggested that he should live the life of poverty he longed for in the vicinity of a Franciscan house, but apart from it. "But do not try to attract companions", was his final directive. He also made the suggestion that Charles should take up residence in Capharnaum – or Nazareth.

Again the significance of Nazareth flooded his mind, and he began his journey in February 1897, arriving there a month later. He attached himself to a community of Poor Clares, working in the garden, running errands, drawing pictures for them to sell, and acting as server and sacristan. Gradually he began to warm to the idea of becoming a priest; perhaps after all he could help people by bringing them the sacraments.

He was ordained at Viviers on 9 June 1901, and said his first Mass at the monastery where he had entered the Cistercian Order, in the presence of his sister, Mimi. Then came the problem: where should he practise his priestly vocation? He was convinced that the hidden life of Nazareth could be pursued anywhere, and he envisaged a small group of five or six brothers, living a life of great austerity, eating only what they grew themselves, and spending the time which Trappists gave to singing the Offices in choir, to praying long hours before the Blessed Sacrament. They would be committed to welcoming strangers and offering them hospitality, but they would be hermits rather than evangelists.

The question of a suitable location was solved when he remembered his sojourn in North Africa, where French soldiers died without the sacraments for want of a priest to administer them, and the people of the country lived close to starvation. He consulted one of his fellow-cadets from Saint-Cyr – Henri, Comte de Castries – who was an expert on the region, and eventually settled on the oasis of Beni Abbes, near the Moroccan border, where there was a small French garrison. The soldiers helped him to build his hermitage, a chapel and sacristy; three cells for the companions he hoped to attract, and a guestroom. The little group of mud and palm-trunk huts became a meeting-place for travellers, and was known as the Fraternity. He assured his cousin that, "I want to accustom everyone here – Christian, Moslem, Jew and pagan – to look on me as a brother to every one of them."

He was ashamed of the French Government, who turned a blind eye to the slave trade which had been carried on for two thousand years, and begged money from his family to buy and free as many slaves as he could. These he baptised and tried to see that they received a Christian education. One, an old blind woman named Mary, remained true to the faith she barely understood; another – Paul – left it, but was to come back later in time to witness Brother Charles's death.

His restless spirit prompted him to try and build other hermitages, and he responded to a request by Henri Laperrine, another Saint-Cyr friend who was now Commander-in-Chief of the Saharan Oases, to go to the Hoggar and work among the Tuareg. He received the neccessary endorsement of this plan from Abbé Huvelin, and prepared to leave for the south in January 1904.

When he had acquired a knowledge of the Tuareg language, he embarked on his literary life-work, the translation of the Gospels and a French-Tuareg and Tuareg-French dictionary, a grammar of the language, and collected verse, prose-texts and proverbs. He ministered to the people, giving them medicine and alms, and gaining their trust; it was a great joy to think that their native tongue had been spoken in the time of St Augustine. He had never slept in a bed since his first exploration of Morocco, and seemed impervious to heat and cold; illness never made him reduce his prodigious work-load. For a while he shared the officers' mess without embarrassing his hosts, while managing to remain deaf to any unseemly conversation, but eventually he reverted to his own company.

After considering several alternatives, he decided to settle at Tamanrasset, a village of about twenty families. There he proposed to live the hidden life he had chosen, his only contact with civilisation a monthly courier passing through on his way between two garrisons.

A reed hut was replaced by one of stone; his ex-slave Paul had his own dwelling nearby. Brother Charles's life centred round the chapel, part of which was curtained off to form his living quarters. The resulting long, thin building was nicknamed 'The Frigate' by some officers who visited it; within its narrow confines Brother Charles lived in isolation from his own kind. Gradually the Tuareg approached him, requesting the needles and medicines he gave them to ameliorate their poverty. When the nomads arrived, starving, he shared what food he had.

In his letters home he explained his strategy for gaining the trust of the people: "I... do them small services, give them useful advice, tactfully encourage them to follow natural religion, show that we Christians love them."

By 1906 he was visiting them in their camps and villages, reaching a wider circle. He met the Tuareg women, who carried on the cultural life of the people, composing songs and accompanying themselves on an instrument shaped rather like a violin with a single string. He made a particular friend of an influential poetess, Dessine; she was the counsellor to Moussa, the head of a tribal group, who listened to Brother Charles's plea for him to educate his followers, encourage them to improve their farming techniques, and strengthen their family life.

He was always critical of the French authorities for missing the opportunity to study their colonial subjects, complaining that they knew nothing of the way their people lived; having no contact with them, regarding them as strangers and – usually – as enemies. On the other hand, he wrote: "They have for us the same feeling of scorn that the French have for the cannibals of Central Africa. They regard us as pagans or savages." It was to break down these barriers that he passed to and fro between them; gaining respect and making friends.

He made three trips to France in 1908, 1911 and 1913, hoping that beside seeing his beloved family he might be able to induce companions to join him in Africa. Each time, he returned alone.

In August 1914 Germany and France were at war. In his isolation, Brother Charles heard stories of priests serving with the armed forces, and was anxious to do the same, but he was considered too valuable in keeping an eye on the nomads who were being used by the Germans and Turks to stir up trouble. Spending so much time in travelling between the four hermitages he had built, he was in a unique position to provide information.

He continued to divide his day between eleven hours of work, seven and a half hours of sleep and five of prayer; eating received scant attention, and there was no provision for recreation, though he was sometimes entertained in the mess by visiting officers. Ahead of his time, he saw possibilities for the laity to become spiritualised, and had drawn up a Rule for an association whose members would live by the Gospel, showing by their friendship and warmth their vocation to love and respect members of other faiths.

In 1916 as the news worsened, he moved from his 'Frigate' at Tamanrasset into a substantial fort built to his own specification. It was like a medieval castle, with room to accommodate all the villagers as well as any visiting nomads, and had food and medical supplies, and an armoury furnished by the local French commander. As darkness fell on 1 December 1916, he was in the fort, writing letters; Paul cooked his evening meal and left. A note in his diary shows his summing-up of the situation: "I do not think there is any danger to us from Tripolitania and the Senoussites;" – (a tribe that was under the influence of the Turks) – "there have been no alarms since September; the country is very quiet."

So when a familiar voice called him outside, telling him the courier had arrived for his letters, he answered the door without suspicion. He was immediately seized by a mob of some forty Senoussites, who had enlisted a local man Brother Charles had helped in the past, in order to deceive him. Paul was dragged from his house, and forced to crouch in front of the fort, which the marauders lost no time in pillaging, leaving Brother Charles guarded by a lad with a rifle.

Two troopers on camels approached, and when Brother Charles made a movement to warn them of their danger, the boy in charge of him panicked and shot him in the head. The bullet passed through him and lodged in the wall, where the hole can still be seen. According to Paul's account, he had remained silent, like Christ, under questioning by his captors.

It was Paul who put his body in a temporary resting-place in a ditch; it was eventually moved to a place called El Golea, to the north, at the edge of the desert. His Moslem friend Moussa wrote to his sister: "When I heard of the death of our friend, your brother Charles, my eyes closed. There was darkness all about me. I wept and shed tears... Charles has died, not only for all of you, he has died for us too. May God have mercy on him, and may we meet him in Paradise."

His story, made known by his spiritual writings, and a biography by René Bazin published in 1921, fired some young men to follow him. The first Fraternity of the Little Brothers of Jesus was set up in 1933 on the edge of the Sahara, but it was not until the wave of devotion that surged after the Second World War that the movement was really established. The Little Brothers of Jesus, always numbering around two hundred and eighty, work alongside the poorest in the world, 'taking the lowest place' like Charles de Foucauld himself. Living in groups of two or three, Jesus in the Blessed Sacrament is the centre of their lives. There are some fifteen hundred Little Sisters of Jesus, and two congregations, more monastic in spirit, dedicated to the Sacred Heart. Two more branches of the family – Brothers and Sisters of the Gospel – are evangelistic; the Association for the Laity he longed to found is represented by a number of groups within the Church.

To those living at the end of the twentieth century, with material goods amassed at any cost, global communication, and a vandalised earth, Charles de Foucauld may seem to be a frail bulwark against its self-destruction. He chose poverty and isolation, and failed to attract converts and fellow-workers, so his life appears to be one of failure. His death was far from glorious, gunned down in a moment without any resonant last message. But his life shines like a light in darkness, a perfect mirror of Our Lord's life in Nazareth – and in the chapels of the Order, with their sparse furnishings, the worker priests and sisters renew their strength before the Blessed Sacrament, to save us from ourselves.

MALCOLM MUGGERIDGE

At first, after the death of Queen Victoria as the twentieth century dawned, it must have seemed that nothing had changed after all. Quite a relief for most of her subjects, who could not remember a time when she had not represented, even at long range as the Widow of Windsor, ordered government. Prosperity reigned with her, at least for the middle and upper classes; an empire that gave little England a sizeable stake in what went on in the rest of the world. Disraeli, master of the magnificent gesture, had made her an Empress, and some of her numerous children had intermarried with the crowned heads of other states, still firmly in place on their thrones.

But even as she lived, the forces of reaction against what we have come to know loosely as 'Victorian values' were stirring. Darwin had launched his theory of evolution, which seemed to have abolished God as the author of Creation. Freud had stripped the innocence from childhood, and set man's gaze inward, at his darker self. Marx and Engels had exposed the ugly face of capitalism, and taken a hefty sideswipe at the throne. In England, the land of mists and fogs, the sharp edges of these new ideas were blurred into a more comfortable liberalism. Thinking men and women joined the new Labour Party, with its intellectual outriders, the Fabian Society; and Malcolm Muggeridge's father was a thinking man.

In 1903, when Malcolm was born into a family of boys, by day Henry Muggeridge was a pen-pusher in the City – a soul-destroying job, if ever there was one – adding up the total of other men's wealth. His nonconformist conscience ensured that he would do it scrupulously, but this was practically all that was left in him of formal religion. Jesus Christ, as far as he was the champion of the poor and oppressed, was acknowledged to be a Good Thing, but rather inferior in performance to Marx and Lenin.

Muggeridge Senior carried over from his noncomformist past a gift for speaking in public. Malcolm remembered heady Saturday nights in Croydon, the suburb in which they lived. His father preached in the street about the coming of the perfect society, when the common people would be the equal of the monarch, and he had a fascinated listener in his small son, bursting with love and pride.

Another recollection, apparently his earliest, was of walking down a street of suburban semi-detached houses, wearing his brother's hat. He was often to come back to it; it may well have left such an impression because it was the first time he could recall being alone. He said that it left him with the feeling of being a stranger in the world. When he was very old, he elaborated the memory by saying that he pictured his fatther and mother being rushed by the police to a hospital, where he had been taken, following a street accident. His imagination added all the drama of a death scene, before returning to life and reality; he thought in the stuff of headlines, human interest, life and death – there was already an actor and journalist in him, waiting for a suitable opportunity to emerge.

His school career was not distinguished; he was inclined to relieve the boredom of lessons by asking questions designed to mock the teachers. This puckish quality was an enduring trait. His reading, like that of his father, was wide and mostly outside the school curriculum. It also included the Bible, which he read surreptitiously, making a brown paper cover for it – presumably to escape the ridicule that religion provoked in his father. Malcolm seems to have been sensitive to ridicule, protecting himself from it by attacking first. He came to love the language of the Authorised Version, the thrilling stories and the poetry, the epistles of St Paul, and the gradual unfolding of the life of Jesus. An insomniac, he took it to bed with him as comfort against the horrors of the night. He suffered from nightmares; a recurrent dream was of being imprisoned in a dark cell. Once he awoke to find himself breaking the window of his bedroom, his hand covered in blood.

His adolescent years were spent amid the casualty lists and clarion calls to arms of the 1914-1918 war. Taking the Fabian stance, his father deplored it, but Malcolm was secretly excited by the fervour it generated.

When he was seventeen, he fulfilled his father's wish that he should go to Cambridge. It was the logical step upward from his place in the lower-lower-middle class; in Croydon the fine grades of class distinction were always apparent, even to a thorough-going Socialist like his father. He went to Selwyn to read physics, chemistry and zoology, subjects in which he took very little interest. There for the first time he met the products of the public school system, with their ease of manner and exclusive camaraderie, and felt himself strange and alien, with his South London accent and background.

But in religion all persons are equal, and he had the good luck to meet with a real Christian, some three years older than himself and within a year of ordination – Alec Vidler, who became a lifelong friend. An ex-serviceman, who had done well at his public school as a scholar and an athlete, he corresponded in Malcolm's eyes to the elite he had only read about in the pages of schoolboy comics. He was flattered to be noticed by such a being, and put in abeyance his natural tendency to deride what he did not understand.

The ex-servicemen had come back full of hope that the levelling of human beings in the face of the tragedy of war would continue in the peace. Along with this went a devotion to the Anglo-Catholic wing of the Church of England; the ceremonies, for which the English have a natural talent, were scrupulously enacted. Malcolm joined in, quelling a certain feeling of distance that overcame him at such times. He seems always to have been unaware that his real calling – to be an observer and communicator – involved this distancing, the penalty of such a vocation.

Yet the pull of the world was strong enough to call him into the post-war permissive society. He drank and smoked to excess, and embarked upon amorous adventures that lost nothing in the telling when he recounted them afterwards. He even tried to make a splash by playing games for which he had no aptitude. In other words, he was a young man struggling to find himself.

Finally he met the sister of a fellow-undergraduate, an attractive young woman called Kitty Dobbs. She was not only pretty, her background was impeccable; she was the niece of the formidable Beatrice Webb, a fellow Fabian, so he could be assured that his father would welcome her – and that was important. He was convinced this was the love of all loves; that it had existed from the beginning, was now, and ever would be. There was just the little matter of economics; in order to get married, he needed money.

The pass degree he achieved did not qualify him for anything exalted in the job market. Then, thanks to his connections with the churchmen, a post was offered him at the new Union Christian College in the Indian state of Travancre (Kerala) to teach English Literature. He went native, wearing Indian dress, and identifying with Indian aspirations to independence. When Ghandi visited the college, to recruit the incipient intellectuals for his movement of non-violent resistance to the British Raj, Malcolm was enchanted by him.

When his contract ended, he returned to England. His friend Alec Vidler was now working in a Birmingham parish, and he lodged with him in the clergy house while acting as a supply teacher. Although he enjoyed the ecclesiastical regime, attending services and praying with the Church, when he married Kitty Dobbs it was in a registry office; he decided to make nothing but the legal commitment.

Teaching in the Midlands could not compare with the excitement of teaching abroad, and anyway Malcolm had itchy feet. Kitty found herself setting up the first of what would become a total of twenty-two homes in different countries. It was in Cairo that their eldest son was born, while Malcolm was acting as lecturer in English Literature at the university. Recording the event over sixty years later, the joy and pride of that moment shine out undimmed. It bound them together, in sickness and in health, for richer, for poorer, as if they had taken those tiresome vows. They were later to thank God for it – but emphatically not yet.

261

He had an ability to catch the exact tone that the owner and editor of the *Manchester Guardian*, C.P. Scott, wanted in a leader-writer; when he sent in an article on the Egyptian political situation, an offer came back to go to Manchester, Malcolm and his young family upped and left Egypt. He discovered that he could use his gift for words to present any point of view; when the nightly assignments were given out, he knew, or he could enquire from older hands, the acceptable line to take, turning out a vivid and readable piece.

He enjoyed the praise he received, and his family needed the money.

He was too honest not to suffer at times for compromising his talent. Going home in the early hours, he was haunted by the feeling that the prizes of this world were not worth fighting for. He accompanied his steps with a recital of the Lord's Prayer – the only one he knew by heart – in an attempt to get in touch with the God to whom he had paid lip-service in the past, challenging him to become real.

He angled for the post of Moscow correspondent, and got it. The night before he left for Russia he was received in audience by Kitty's aunt, Beatrice Webb, and her husband. They were immensely flattered that their books were highly thought of in the Soviets, and had been told they were icons of the new socialist state. This enabled them to reconcile themselves to the fact that opponents of the ruling party sometimes disappeared mysteriously, never to be seen again.

Any hint that all was not well with the politics and economics of communism had to be kept out of the foreign newspapers, as it was kept out of the Russian press. The official briefings were a tissue of optimistic lies, and immmense ingenuity was needed to comb the columns of *Izvestia* and *Pravda*, the permitted papers, reading between the lines for some kind of truth. This news Malcolm would then filter again – writing between the lines as it were – to satisfy the censors.

Kitty, expecting another child, fell ill with typhus, and Malcolm was distraught. On a brief absence from nursing her in their dacha outside Moscow, he took a walk for a breath of fresh air. There amongst the grey buildings was a Church front that someone had dared to paint in glowing colours. The great cathedrals in Moscow had been turned into anti-God museums, but this little edifice had escaped desecration, and someone still cared for it. Moved and heartened, he returned to Kitty's bedside, to find her so much improved in health that she would be able to return to England to have the baby. These incidents seemed to him to be connected.

He stayed on for a while, making a trip to Kiev in the Ukraine, when the forced deportation of the peasants was at its height. There he attended the cathedral where the Easter Mass was being celebrated. It was crammed to the doors, and the deprived faces took on light from the guttering candles, and the chants swelled round them with a grandeur not of this world. Malcolm saw in them the soul of Russia; still alive, still deeply spiritual.

This visit was the inspiration for three articles, telling the truth about the Ukrainian disaster and the suffering it had caused. He had the manuscripts smuggled out in the diplomatic bag; knowing that on their publication he would be persona non grata in the U.S.S.R. he made his preparations to leave Moscow.

On one last walk round Red Square, he took stock of his life. He felt that only the Christian religion taught that the kingdom of God was elsewhere. He was filled with a desire to change his life from the daily indulgence of the appetites for money and sensual pleasure. Dramatically, he pictured himself as a priest – or better still, as a Franciscan monk.

The mood passed. When the train that took him back to Kitty and the children reached the frontier, as if moved by a single impulse the previously silent passengers crowded into the corridors. As they looked back at the grim guards on the Russian side, they felt liberated and burst into excited chatter. The sight of the then free Republic of Latvia, full of people who were comfortable and unafraid, was like a glimpse of paradise.

But war was darkening the horizon. Malcolm, like many other men of his age who had observed the rise of the dictators, was anxious to join the army. He was thirty-six, and journalism was a reserved occupation, but he managed to talk his way into the Intelligence Corps.

He was posted to serve in MI6. Later he was to get a great deal of quiet fun out of the motley collection of oddities who were his colleagues, and the atmosphere of secrecy that was built up around the most commonplace activities. He reached the lowest point in his service career in Mozambique, then a dependency of neutral Portugal. His job was to pose as a British Vice-Consul, keeping an eye on his opposite numbers in the Consulates of Germany and Italy, and doing his best to frustrate their attempts to prosecute the war. It felt like a backwater, far from the centres of action, and his duties led him to patronise the seedy night-life of Lourenco Marques. This disgusted and bored him, and he always made his worst decisions when he was bored. He took refuge in the consumption of too much alcohol, which compounded his mood of depression.

He walked out into the night, determined on self-destruction, drove along the coast, and undressed on a remote beach. When he waded into the sea, the tide was out, but he was too tipsy to find it absurd, and persisted in his gesture until there was enough water to swim in. Out of his depth at last, his arms flailing the water, he swam on doggedly; the cold got to him, and he shivered uncontrollably. Glancing back, he saw the lights of a little cafe far away. A sort of languor crept over him; he felt that he should lie upon the water, and yield to a desire for sleep.

Suddenly he turned back to the shore, fighting against great weariness, the cafe lights a guiding beacon. In panic he shouted cries for help to the empty air, until he found he was extricating himself from deep mud in a river estuary, a long way from his starting-point; some instinct enabled him to find his car.

At first he was uncertain what had called him back; it seemed to have happened in spite of himself. The goal seemed so tawdry – a sleazy seaside cafe – yet he reflected that God had chosen ordinary things and ordinary people to show the world how to live. He was not yet able to look upon the sea in which he had tried to drown himself as a symbol of the water of baptism, or his return to life as a rebirth; but he did regard it as a turning-point – an acceptance that God had supreme power over him, and that he must journey on until God released him from his pilgrimage.

At least he was released from Laurenco Marques, being sent as a liaison officer to the French Securit Militaire. After a spell in North Africa, he reached Paris at the moment of its liberation. The frenzied atmosphere embraced him, as it did all members of the Allied forces; they were received everywhere with cheers and flowers.

The call to action, that had drawn him to join the army, vanished with the cessation of hostilities, and he lost no time in returning to civilian life, resuming his trade as a journalist. Ensconced as a leader-writer on the *Daily Telegraph*, he strove to fit into the mould demanded of him, and did it with characteristic verve, but it went against the grain. He deplored the city's shabbiness, the untouched bomb-sites, the war-weariness London had settled into after the first fine flush of victory. The young and inexperienced looked forward to creating a new world. Malcolm was now in his forties; he had seen new worlds, and watched them crumble. In an effort to avoid this sorry spectacle, he applied for the post of Washington correspondent.

The American lifestyle, with its emphasis on prolonging youth as far as possible, and its insatiable consumer appetite, appalled him, but he always wrote best when a subject lent itself to satire. His writing was highly thought of, and in 1953 he was invited to become the editor of *Punch*. He claimed never to have read the magazine, and a perusal of some old bound copies left him no wiser about what was required of him – beyond a preference for the early years when it was politically active in criticism of the Establishment. But all forms of pretentiousness were grist to his mill; at the beginning of an article he would declare a great fondness for his subject, before proceeding to assassinate it with a polished stiletto.

This caused great distress to old readers during his five-year tenure of the editorial chair. Gone were the gentle jokes, the backward glances at the old England of rural quiet and great houses; Malcolm was blazing a trail for the young satirists of the sixties, creating a climate in which they would thrive.

At the same time, he was becoming known as a broadcaster, his resonant voice edged with a sharp wit was distinctive in his contributions to the panel of 'The Critics' and 'Any Questions'. It brought him a wider public than his writing had ever done. Then came the expansion of television, and he developed, in middle age, into a unique performer. His technique was in part his old one of leader-writing journalist, part interviewer, and part actor. The millions of words he had written meant that he had a great stock of telling phrases stored in his head; his targets were those in the public eye, yet he was never cruel. He disliked people in the mass, but face to face they fascinated him. He was not tempted into the sly thrust that hurts – he was too naturally courteous for that. He drew out his subjects, and presented an accurate and sensitive picture. As for the actor – he had always been that. His mobile face, like a wrinkled Puck, transmitted his every thought.

He started, as a self-confessed sinner with an interest in religion, by interviewing the American evangelist, Billy Graham, and became a frequent contributor to the documentary programme 'Panorama'. He continued to write, and an article about the British Royal Family, which appeared in an American magazine, made him notorious, and caused him to be banished from the screen for a time. He had thought of it as a comic piece about a rather over-revered set of harmless anachronisms, and was totally unprepared for the torrent of abuse that was hurled at him from all sides.

A great deal of it was libellous, and a letter addressed to Kitty said that the writer was glad their youngest son had been killed in a ski-ing accident... Sometimes, perhaps, his low estimate of human nature was justified. But he had underrated the love that the un-televised millions projected on to the royal family. In some ways, their love was for the longest-running soap-opera in the world; for the lonely and bereaved, they occupied the place of the family they did not have, and became the focus of their emotional life. Secure in the love of his own family, Muggeridge was insensitive to these hidden depths.

In 1965 he undertook a visit to Lourdes, to make a television programme. Initially he could not generate much enthusiasm for the idea. He was convinced that he hated shrines of any kind, with their attendant commercial enterprises, and scope for unintelligent credulity. When he got to know the sick and their helpers, he was blind to the tawdry shops that disfigure Lourdes for the casual observer. He concentrated on the life of the Grotto, the healing water that cleansed body and soul, the silence that fell as the Holy Food was held on high. He even came to like the constant repetition of the Lourdes hymn to Our Lady, though he knew it was not musically distinguished.

He recorded a miracle meant for him alone. A woman came to him, saying that her sister was dying, and that she wanted to meet him. Out of courtesy, he went, apprehensive that he would not know the right things to say – he who had conducted a host of interviews in front of the cameras. He approached the dying woman, and she looked at him. Suddenly he felt the stirring of love: "What marvellous eyes!" he burst out. There was something in those eyes – perhaps the perfect serenity that is Lourdes' greatest gift to pilgrims – which moved him deeply, and the memory was to return to him every time Lourdes was mentioned.

In an article for the *New Statesman* – 'Is there a God?' – he confessed that he had felt God in pursuit of him all his life: when he had explored the attempted establishment of an ideal state, and seen it wither away; in churches that tried to make a compromise with the world and popularise themselves by adopting the prevailing pursuit of happiness here and now; in escape befuddled by alcohol or in the indulgence of carnal appetite.

Finally, he said, he could no longer avoid confrontation with this being who cared for the very hairs of his head, and robbed him of the words which were the tools of his trade. He felt he should go into training like an athlete, to make himself worthy of such love, murdering vanity and pride and lust in order to rise to eternal life. At this point he spent three weeks in a Cistercian abbey at Nunraw in Scotland, and began to lead a life nearer to that of the monks.

He defended them against the accusation that they were fleeing from the world – although he found that the younger monks were (as he thought) dangerously near to the new humanism. But Muggeridge found it easier to love God than his neighbour, especially if his neighbour happened to disagree with him, or admire his pet aversions in literature or politics.

In 1968 he visited the Holy Land, seeking the Christ of the Gospels in the places where he had been born, lived, died and rose again. It is possible to detect in his account of the journey a growing knowledge and love; what began as a job of work – to communicate the story to television viewers of the twentieth century – became a labour of that love.

Then he met for the first time the little Yugoslavian nun from India whom he was to make known to the world as Mother Teresa. She had come to England in late 1968, where news of her work with the derelicts dying in the streets of Calcutta had percolated by word of mouth. Her story was made known to the BBC by Oliver Hankin, for whose influence Muggeridge was always grateful, and an interview was hastily set up. Muggeridge admitted that his preparation was of the sketchiest on the train to London from his home in Sussex, at Robertsbridge.

It is quite a common occurrence with artists that they are unconscious of having done their best work. They are so absorbed in their technique from moment to moment – too busy to realise when they have achieved something of special excellence. Muggeridge, like other artists, was at his most creative when he was in love with his subject. Yet just as it is possible to be in love and not know it, he did not feel that the interview was a very satisfactory one. It had begun badly; Mother Teresa was late in arriving, and his professionalism demanded that he should not keep the camera-crew waiting. There were no preliminaries to break the ice; he merely said: "Come on, Mother Teresa", and led the way to the makeshift studio in the convent where she was staying.

Muggeridge wanted to go to Calcutta and make a film in the Home for the Dying where her work had started, so that everyone might see the faces in which she saw the image of Christ. He wanted the affluent West to pause in the headlong rush to gratify its whims, to observe the extent of Mother

Teresa's mission. He hoped that the sight of her passion for life would overcome the death-wish apparent to him in modern society, with its twin abominations, abortion and euthanasia.

Mother Teresa didn't convert England, but she did cause a sensation, and became an overnight star. But even the love of this radiant being, and her desire to see him at her side receiving Communion, did not result in Muggeridge's conversion. His deeply ingrained distrust of all institutions prevented him from making the final commitment.

Although he was deaf to the bell that called the faithful to Mass, he still heard the feet of God pursuing him. He went on pilgrimage again, this time in the steps of the Apostle of the Gentiles, St Paul. He took with him his friend of fifty years and near-neighbour, Alec Vidler, and it was a very happy journey. The two elderly gentlemen, both in their late sixties, travelled on donkeys for the benefit of the cameras, as they approached the task of revealing St Paul to modern viewers.

Alec Vidler provided the scholarship of a man who had studied St Paul all his life. Malcolm Muggeridge, though he admired the saint for his opinions about the Christian stance on politics and his condemnation of the pursuit of pleasure, at first gave the impression that he championed him simply because he was unpopular with modern churchmen; it was the old inclination to swim against the tide.

By the time the programme was completed, he loved everything about St Paul: his energy and endurance, his zeal and impetuosity. The letters Paul dictated, containing everything from practical advice to great poetry, came to life for him. When they stood in the remote waste that had once been the splendid harbour of Miletus, they recalled Paul's farewell to the elders of the Ephesian Church, who knew they could not hope to see him again – for he was old and ill, and his journey to Rome might well end in martyrdom.

As Malcolm Muggeridge heard his friend read the account of the scene in Acts, he felt he had himself been present at it. His concentration was so perfect, he could make such a meditation while still working at his job as a communicator. What makes his conversion unique – though of course every conversion is unique – was that it took place while he was actually talking, or writing, or taking part in television programmes. It is probably why St Paul and St Augustine had such an appeal for him; they were communicators who thought on their feet.

From the time he declared himself as a Christian, though still outside the Church, he had a strong reaction from his critics. He had always been sensitive to ridicule and the labels 'St. Mug' and 'The Sage of Robertsbridge' were not always affectionately applied. He was accused of condemning the pleasures of this world at a time when age had rendered their temptations negligible. He denied this strongly, pointing to Bunyan's Pilgrim, who had to shut his eyes and ears to the call of this world while within sight of the Heavenly City. He had his full share of actor's vanity – the reverse side of those feelings of inadequacy with which he wrestled to the very end.

As Kitty and Malcolm grew older together, the tide of active work receded. Inevitably their contemporaries died, or drifted away. For the first time Malcolm communed more with his maker than with human audiences. He gradually came to accept the doctrines of the Church, still seeing them more as an imaginative and artistic truth than a historical one – but the prayers of Mother Teresa and Father Paul Bidone, an Italian priest with an apostolate to mentally-handicapped children, were finally answered.

On a late November day in 1982, Malcolm and Kitty were received into the Catholic Church at the Chapel of Our Lady, Help of Christians, in Hurst Green, near their home in Sussex. Their sponsors were Lord Longford and his wife Elizabeth. Some of Father Bidone's Downes' Syndrome children were spectators; it was Malcolm's stand upon abortion that had led him to enter the Catholic Church, and he found it fitting that children who might have been eliminated as genetic failures should share his reception.

Many correspondents, known and unknown, welcomed him. Malcolm wrote in his last full-length book *Conversion, A Spiritual Journey*, that he felt he had at last come home. His life, never luxurious, became even more simple.

He found the infirmities and isolation of age irksome, and looked on death joyfully as the only experience left to him. Daily he said farewell to the country round his home, which he loved so much, finding even greater beauty in the sight. Eight years after his reception he had a stroke and was taken to a nursing-home in Hastings. Every evening, as his life ebbed, Kitty read to him from a large-print version of his favourite Bunyan, until he reached the culmination of his own Pilgrim's Progress, and surely 'the trumpets all sounded for him on the other side.'

MOTHER TERESA

Margaret was the last person you would expect to be a Co-Worker with the Missionaries of Charity. An object of charity, perhaps? – a member of the Sick and Suffering Co-Workers, possibly? How could a blind woman of eighty-eight with arthritic hands, living alone, be of any practical use to the Order? But Mother Teresa never wastes anyone or anything; and she has found a way.

In her shabby, cluttered house, Margaret knits about ten brightly-coloured blankets a year to send to the M.C. warehouse in India. She can't knit for very long, but she does it regularly, buying the wool out of her pension. It amounts to five pounds a month, which as a proportion of her tiny income is very high. Mother Teresa does not want what people can give out of their abundance. What God wants – what she wants – are gifts that hurt. Margaret is one of thousands of people all round the world who supply the needs of her poor, from the child presenting the sugar he has given up, to the donation of the purchase money for a house.

Mother Teresa was born Agnes Gonxha Bojaxhiu, on 26 August, 1910; the youngest of three children. Her father was a well-to-do merchant dealing in food imports and pharmaceuticals, who also turned his hand to other ways of making money, fulfilling a contract to build a theatre in Skopje, where the family lived. He was a fervent Albanian nationalist, but that did not prevent him from being proficient in the several European languages he needed to carry on his business. His prosperity was not hindered by the chaos in the Balkans, which resulted first in Civil War in 1912, and then the conflict between nations in the First World War. Following the Treaty of Versailles in 1919, Skopje became part of Yugoslavia, but Albanians still had national aspirations, and it was to promote these that Nikola Bojaxhiu left his family and went to Belgrade to discuss the future of his country. There he was taken ill – with such suddenness that there were rumours he had been poisoned. He was hurried home, but died after an unsuccessful operation.

His widow, usually known as Drana, was devastated by grief, even handing over the housekeeping keys for a time to Agnes's elder sister Aga who was fifteen; but she soon cut short her period of mourning and prepared to make a living for herself and her children. The district was known for its skilled needlewomen, and she produced wedding dresses and the embroidered garments worn on feast days. There was a deep vein of piety in her nature which she shared with her children, who were also involved in her charitable work. The house was open to the poor, but the sharing was unobtrusive. They did not differentiate between relatives and guests who were in need. In spite of the tragedy of her father's death – Agnes was only eight years old at the time – she remembered her family as "full of joy and love; and we children were happy and contented."

The Roman Catholics of Skopje were a minority amongst their Orthodox and Muslim neighbours, but although rather isolated, they were faithful. Once a year the Bojaxhiu family joined the parish on pilgrimage to the Shrine of Our Lady of Letnice, a black Madonna, her son standing on her lap with a ball in his hand. Agnes had poor health at that time, and the visit was always combined with a recuperative holiday. She was small for her age, and subject to malaria, as well as the illnesses of childhood. When she was fourteen a new priest came to the Church of the Sacred Heart and set about providing outlets for the youth of the parish. Agnes joined in the social events with gusto; she was a talented musician, and a stalwart of the Church choir. The same priest also publicised the missions; from the magazines he introduced, she learned of her countrymen who worked in India, and listened, rapt, while those who were on leave described their work.

273

Her brother left home to join the army in 1924, and it was not long before Agnes felt a vocation to the religious life which she confided to her mother and to her confessor. Still very young, she obviously had to finish her secondary education. She was not only a good student at her state school, but was prepared to coach others, so her talent for teaching manifested itself early. Eventually it was decided that she should apply to join the Order of Loreto nuns, a missionary Order who taught in India. This meant travelling to the Mother House at Rathfarnham in Ireland, to begin her novitiate.

Over a hundred people saw her off from the station at Skopje in 1928; she was never to see her mother and elder sister again. Her mother had said: "Well, daughter, go with my blessing. But strive only to live all for God and for Jesus Christ." Tthese heroic words would echo whenever her mother came to mind. Once at Rathfarnham she took a strenuous course in English; not because it was the language of the Raj, but as the only alternative to a plethora of Indian dialects amongst her prospective pupils. In Ireland she took the name in religion: Sister Mary Teresa of the Child Jesus. The Little Flower had been canonised recently in 1925 to the joy of the faithful worldwide. As a Carmelite, she had a special devotion to pray for the missions, and in claiming St Therese as her patron, her choice was a very happy one.

On the Feast of the Epiphany 1929, she was on a ship sailing up the Ganges through Bengal, astounded by the beauty of the country. Her destination was Darjeeling, where she and another sister from Yugoslavia gave each other the comfort of fellow-exiles during their novitiate. As they progressed toward taking their vows, they taught the privileged amongst the inhabitants of the city, at that time the Government's summer headquarters. Sister Teresa also worked in a hospital, assisting the nurses in their never-ending task of treating the poor. In 1931 she wrote a moving account of her experiences for the magazine that circulated in her home town, explaining how the verandah was crowded with the sick who had walked long distances to seek help. "What a state they are in!" she wrote. "Their ears and feet are covered with sores; on their backs are lumps and lesions, among the numerous ulcers." It was her first acquaintance with the poverty of the Third World, and made an indelible impression.

In the same year she had taken her temporary vows; these were to be renewed annually until she made her final commitment six years later. When she was proficient in English, she was sent to a convent known as Loreto Entally, in the eastern part of Calcutta. It was a large complex, containing two schools: one for some five hundred privileged girls, mostly boarders.

Here Sister Teresa taught geography and history. She also taught at the other school, St Mary's, where the girls came from different backgrounds, though they were taught with no discrimination, in Bengali.

During the Thirties, while Ghandi was conducting the Indian people in their non-violent marches for independence, Sister Teresa was deepening her religious life behind the walls of the compound, and she was made headmistress of St Mary's. The girls she taught joined the same Sodality of Mary that she had belonged to in Skopje; she encouraged them to go out into the slum hospitals that surrounded them, though she herself was prevented by the rule of enclosure. When the war came, the pupils dispersed and Sister Teresa taught the few who were left, while Calcutta became a centre for refugees. In 1943 there was a famine in which millions starved to death.

After the war came partitition and independence. On 16 August, 1946, just a year before the Union Jacks came down for the last time, the Muslims of the city declared a Day of Direct Action against partition. A Mass rally exploded in an orgy of killing that went on for four days. Sister Teresa was marooned in the convent with three hundred hungry girls, as supplies broke down completely. She went out in the streets of the city, which were literally running with blood, and some soldiers in a lorry shouted a warning that she must take shelter. When she explained her predicament, they offered her a lift back to the convent, and gave her some bags of rice.

Barely a month later she was travelling to Darjeeling to make her annual retreat. On 10 September, 1946, as the train made its way through the foothills of the Himalayas, she felt a "call within a call", as she described it, to "give up all and

275

follow him into the slums – to serve him in the poorest of the poor."

All through the retreat she pondered what seemed to be the inspiration of the Holy Spirit, and it became clear to her that she must leave the comfort and fulfilment of her teaching life to work for the poor while living among them. She consulted one of the Jesuit Fathers in Calcutta, in whom she had great faith, Father Van Exem. He had good contacts among the Muslims and was widely travelled. He promised to approach the Archbishop of Calcutta who was wary of giving her permission to leave the convent; there was no direct refusal, but he counselled a year of waiting.

As soon as she could, in January 1948, she applied for permission again, and after a tortuous passage through the hierarchy, she received the necessary authorisation. Her farewells were kept to a minimum, but even so pupils and staff alike shed tears, mingled with her own. It was on an early August day that she asked Father Van Exem if he would bless something for her: a sari, of the kind that could be bought in the bazaars for a few rupees – white, with a blue border – along with a cheap metal crucifix and a rosary. It was to become known all over the world. Wearing it, she travelled to Patna to learn basic nursing skills from the Medical Mission Sisters who had a house there.

She stayed with them until December, packing a great deal of experience into the few short months. As soon as a call came, for whatever task – delivering a baby or conducting an operation – she answered the summons at the same time as the doctor or nurse. At first she merely observed, but she gradually became adept at lending a hand when needed. She discussed her plans with the other nuns; her original idea was to live on the same diet as the poor, but they persuaded her that she needed adequate calories to support her while carrying out the hard work she wished to do; rest was also important – no excesses in fasting and penance could be indulged in – they also stressed the importance of daily laundering for the habit, and she saw instantly the practicality of their advice. Although often described as from a peasant background, which in fact she was not, she had a great deal of the pragmatic common-sense associated with those living close to the land.

All alone, with just five rupees, she walked the streets of Calcutta, obeying her call. Not surprisingly her first instinct was to start a school. She gathered a few children around her and sat on the ground with them, teaching in the open air. Word got about that this odd European in the poor cotton sari welcomed children, and more and more of them gathered. She began to receive gifts to enable her to carry on her work, and had an offer of a room to work in from a Bengali school-teacher called Michael Gomes, a married man whose family also tried to help. Her days were spent washing the children and fighting the illiteracy that kept them prisoners in the filthy alleyways of the slums.

As St Francis started his mission by kissing a leper, Mother Teresa took the step from which there was no return when she rescued a woman from the street, eaten by rats and ants, and persuaded a taxi-driver to take them to a hospital. This der-elict, barely recognisable as a human being, was denied treat-ment – but Mother Teresa refused to leave until it was given. She accepted food and medicine in order to carry on her work, and such was the power of the diminutive figure, whose brown eyes brimmed over with compassion, that she could always have something to offer her poor. In the first instance, her permission to leave the convent was valid for one year. When she was tired after a day's work, surrounded by dirt and disease, Loreto Entally must have seemed like a lost paradise, but she wrote later: "My true community is the poor – their security is my security, their health my health. My home is amongst the poor, and not only the poor, but the poorest of them; the people no-one will go near."

She did not go back to Loreto; Loreto came to her in the form of a wealthy Bengali girl, a former pupil called Shubashini. She offered herself as an assistant, and she had all the attributes Mother Teresa required, being a level-headed young woman, in good health, intelligent, and joyful in her giving. Other girls who had been taught by Mother Teresa followed her, adopting the cotton sari and taking names in religion. They lived as nuns but without a Rule, quite certain that they would be recognised as an Order when the time was ripe. Mother Teresa insisted that they should have time to complete their academic courses if they had left before taking their final examinations; she did not want uninformed obedience, but intelligent acceptance.

Mother Teresa finally identified herself with the new India by becoming a citizen of the country. It was yet another manifestation that there was no turning back from the course she had chosen. In April 1950, when her little community numbered ten, Father Van Exem helped her to draft a Constitution for the congregation which would have to be approved by the Archbishop of the diocese, and forwarded by him to Rome. Mother Teresa was anxious to add a fourth vow to the usual ones of poverty, chastity and obedience: her innovation was "To give whole-hearted and free service to the poorest of the poor." She was anxious that no payment should ever be given to her Missionaries of Charity, in contrast to those who believed that the poor would only respect charity to which they themselves had made a contribution, however small. It was her way to point to the free gifts of God, and follow his unlimited generosity.

Recognition was given on 7 October, 1950, the Feast of the Holy Rosary, and celebrated by a Mass in the room they shared in the Gomes household. It was their great joy that they could now have their own chapel. The Archbishop was the celebrant, and Father Van Exem read out the Decree of recognition. Already it promised that the Sisters would go to the poorest of the pooor throughout the world, though at present they were only a small band, confined to the Calcutta diocese. They resolved to seek out "The poorest, the abandoned, the sick, the infirm, the leprosy patients, the dying, the desperate, the lost, the outcasts, taking care of them; Rendering help to them; Visiting them assiduously; Living Christ's love for them, and Awakening their response to his great love."

As their numbers rose, another house was needed and eventually a Muslim who had decided to leave Calcutta, owing to the religious tensions, agreed to sell his house for a nominal sum, declaring: "I got that house from God – I give it back to him." The money was paid by the archdiocese, in order to respect the Sisters' vow of poverty. Here, in 54A Lower Circular Road, Calcutta, began the movement that was to spread throughout the world. Over and over again in speeches and writing, Mother Tesesa was to repeat Jesus's words: "I was hungry, I was naked, I was sick and I was homeless." It was to Jesus in every one of the outcasts that they ministered; Jesus in the mishapen face of a leper, the faint cry of an abandoned baby snatched from a dustbin, the last radiant glance from a dying person, cared for as never before in life.

By 1955 Calcutta had become home to thousands of refugees, who were spewed forth from the trains coming across the border, and remained in the railway station where the Missionaries of Charity brought them the parboiled grains of wheat known as 'bulgar'. Those who had them set up mud stoves and cooked their own ration; for those without, the Sisters provided great vats of bulgar and soy that kept starvation at bay for a few more days. The abandoned children – some only a day old – were taken to Shishu Bhavan, where these pathetic scraps of humanity were transformed into healthy, mischievous children with the strength to play and respond to the loving care of the Sisters.

Kalighat, the home for the dying, received its daily caravan of carts and ambulances, bringing those for whom the hospitals could do nothing, and gave them the blessings of a good wash, a clean bed to die in, and the comforting smiles of dedicated women who saw the Lord of heaven and earth in them. The building had been a hostel for pilgrims, and was adjacent to the Temple of Kali. At first the Hindu priests were wary of the Sisters, until one of their number came into their care, when the prejudice disappeared. Each of the mortally ill was treated as an individual, with all the information that could be gathered about them written on a card by their beds.

Soon others wished to associate themselves with the work; men and women of all religions and none. They were designated Co-Workers, and took on the task of providing clothes for the children, raising funds for dowries for destitute girls, for maternity services, and particularly for the lepers who came from all walks of life, as anyone who developed the disease was automatically an outcast. Mother Teresa was anxious to provide a refuge and dispensary for them, and it was with the help of the Co-Workers that the centre at Titagarh was opened in March 1959.

The following year Mother Teresa was invited to America to speak about her work to groups of Co-Workers there, and to charitable foundations that had provided relief supplies. The diminutive figure, dwarfed by those who introduced her, spoke simply and directly, telling of her experiences and reaching the hearts of her listeners with her shining faith. On the way back to India she visited Rome for the first time, where she made an application for her congregation to be recognised as one of pontifical right. This was something not usually granted until much later in the history of an Order, but she was anxious to obtain it, as until she did so she could not answer calls outside India.

All through the early Sixties she was crisscrossing the country, assessing the next location of each house, to see what the Sisters had to do and the best way to do it. One thing they all had in common; their chapels were bare of furniture, and behind the altar was a large crucifix with the words 'I thirst' painted on the wall above it, so each of the Sisters at morning Mass was reminded of the One they would see in all those they met in the course of the day. They were under obedience to eat an adequate breakfast, then set out with their khaki holdalls containing a supply of drinking-water in a recycled bottle, and the appropriate equipment for their assigned tasks. They were forbidden to accept hospitality, either from the poor or the rich, for fear of complicating their relationships with others. They travelled by public transport whenever possible, which had the effect of making their poverty widely known and respected.

The steps by which they became professed began with six months as a postulant and then a novitiate of two years. Each novice received a sari and sandals, a change of clothing and a bucket. They did not spend the time in purely spiritual pursuits, but went out to work alongside the professed – dealing with worm infestations and cleaning maggots from open sores were not considered as tests of their devotion, though they

280

soon disclosed any mistaken vocations. They returned to the convent for lunch and a short rest; the afternoon session lasted until six and could be in a different branch of activity.

On return to the Mother House, their day was put before the Blessed Sacrament in an hour of adoration in the chapel. Supper, reading and recreation made up the evening, and they retired to bed in the communal dormitory at about ten o'clock, when after an examination of conscience and an act of contrition their strenuous day ended in sleep. As for Mother Teresa – she did not observe her own rules, but spent most of the night dealing with correspondence and doing administrative work. Thursdays were spent in the convent, doing routine maintenance and mending clothes, or taking part in small treats like picnics. It was no regime for those who were solitary by temperament; work and play, waking and sleeping, were all done in community. Because of the nature of the work, no day was so structured that it left no space for the workings of Divine Providence, which often manifested itself in small miracles.

The longed-for recognition as a congregation of pontifical right came on 1 February, 1965. Only a few months later they had established a house in response to a request from Venezuela, and more foundations followed in every part of the world. The Sisters were also used as shock troops in times of famine, earthquake and war, to look after the casualties of man-made and natural disasters until more permanent arrangements for their care could be made. In 1966 an Australian Jesuit, Father Ian Travers-Ball, was asked if he would become the first General of the Missionary of Charity Brothers, and he consented, taking the title of 'General Servant'.

Mother Teresa made it known that she would welcome offers from contemplative orders to twin themselves with Missionary of Charity foundations, so that they could become spiritual power-houses of prayer for them, and the Sick and Afflicted Co-Workers had a similar arrangement with individuals in the field.

In 1968 Malcolm Muggeridge, the English journalist whose astringent wit had attacked all manner of established shibboleths, met her for a television interview in London. He questioned her about her work, and ignoring the microphones and cameras as if they did not exist, she answered him simply and directly. The sense of occasion, of being the centre of attention, almost invariably makes people act up in such circumstances; she was utterly unmoved.

Muggeridge, whose hobby was religion, wanted to make a film about her in Calcutta. At first she refused, until the Archbishop of Westminster pointed out that she would be making the world aware of those it had rejected – and she could refuse nothing for her poor. She stipulated that the film must be made in the shortest possible time, to minimise interruptions to the work, and that the Sisters and Brothers must take part, since she claimed they were the ones who did it. Everyone on the film unit knew that the time taken to make a fifty-minute documentary would normally be two or three months; this one had to be compressed into five days. It should have set up unbearable tensions, but in fact they proceeded from location to location as if on oiled wheels.

One of Mother Teresa's miracles occurred when the cameras were taken into the House for the Dying, where the light came from small windows high up in the walls. Muggeridge was anxious that this part of the work should be seen, but the lighting cameraman gave it as his opinion that it needed special equipment which was unobtainable on the spot. He added that he would go ahead and film anyway – and when the sequence was shown, it was seen to be bathed in a beautiful, luminous glow.

The pious are sometimes given to speculation, asking what would happen if St Francis of Assisi could appear on television – would it herald mass conversions? Every viewer brings his or her own prejudices to television, and filters every programme through that lens – but everyone welcomed the sight of a woman who could look into the camera with the eye of faith as she appealed: "Let God use you without consulting you." It really seemed that God had created an incorruptible celebrity who would not behave like one. She made the cover of *Time* magazine under the headline 'Living Saint', and received every conceivable award and honorary degree. Muggeridge's book about her, *Something Beautiful for God* –

her own phrase – became a best-seller, amusing its author when he found it on airport bookshelves next to the soft porn. In 1979 came the final accolade – the Nobel Peace Prize.

The President of the World Bank, Robert S. McNamara, commented: "Mother Teresa deserves Nobel's Peace Prize because she promotes peace in the most fundamental manner, by her confirmation of the inviolability of human dignity." The chairman of the Nobel committee, Professor Sennes, pointed out that her work for the poor was performed without condescension, and as a witness to the dignity of every person, building bridges across the great gulfs that separate parts of the human family.

It would have been easy for her to reply in kind, flattering the assembled ranks of influential persons, uttering pious platitudes. Instead she took the occasion for an attack on abortion as a final solution to over-population. She said: "Many people are very, very concerned with the children of India, with the children of Africa, where quite a number die, maybe of malnutrition, of hunger and so on – but millions are dying deliberately by the will of the mother." She pointed out that if a mother could kill her own child, there was an end to peace because all killing became possible.

It must have been something of a shock when she said she found the poverty of the West more intransigent than that of the East, where she could give comfort with a plate of rice. In the West people were rejected by society, shut away like the lepers; healing that kind of poverty with love she found both difficult and hurtful. She concluded: "This is very important for us to realise that love, to be true, has to hurt. It hurt Jesus to love us – it hurt him." She told the press later: "I am myself unworthy of the prize; I do not want it personally. But by this award the Norwegian people have recognised the existence of the poor. It is on their behalf that I have come."

The celebration of her golden jubilee in May 1981, the fiftieth anniversary of her profession, took place at the Mother House in Calcutta with her community around her, and went on wherever she happened to be, making known the needs of the poor. She was proud that her adopted country, once a missionary province, was now sending out Indian Brothers and Sisters to bring care to the poor in all parts of the world, including the West.

By now she was stooped, and her face heavily lined, though the radiant smile still shone out on everyone she met. But ironically the great heart that had been beating so long and so lovingly was beginning to wear out, and eventually had to be assisted by a pacemaker.

Through the Eighties, while vocations were dwindling in all other congregations, hers received a steady stream of new enquirers. It was not only Catholics who joined the ranks; people of compassion from all religions, especially the young, offered their help. Their desire to attain simplicity of life was satisfied by the life she offered. Like her, they wanted a better world – to create a kinder and more compassionate society.

They prayed with her the prayer of the Co-Workers; the one she had taken from her fellow-founder of a revolutionary Order, St Francis of Assisi. She had called on the assembly that presented her with the Nobel Peace Prize to pray it with her, and there is probably no moment when it goes unsaid over the face of the globe.

"Make us worthy, Lord, to serve our fellow men throughout the world, who live and die in poverty and hunger.
Give them through our hands this day their daily bread; and by our understanding love, give peace and joy.

Lord, make me a channel of your peace, that where there is hatred, I may bring love; that where there is wrong, I may bring the spirit of forgiveness; that where there is discord, I may bring harmony; that where there is error, I may bring truth; that where there is doubt, I may bring faith; that where there is despair, I may bring hope; that where there are shadows, I may bring light; that where there is sadness, I may bring joy.

Lord, grant that I may seek rather to comfort than to be comforted; to understand, than to be understood; to love, than to be loved; for it is by forgetting self that one finds; it is by forgiving that one is forgiven; it is by dying that one awakens to eternal life. Amen."

BIBLIOGRAPHY

William D. Miller: *Dorothy Day - a biography*, Harper & Row, 1982.

Dorothy Day: *Loaves and Fishes*, Harper and Row, 1963.

Robert Coles: *Dorothy Day - A Radical Devotion*, Radcliffe Biography, 1987.

Dorothy Day: *The Long Loneliness*, Harper and Row, 1952.

June E. O'Connor: *The Moral Vision of Dorothy Day (A Feminist Perspective)*, Crossroad Publishing Co., 1991.

Robert Ellsberg & Tamar Hennessy: *Dorothy Day, By Little and By Little*, Alfred A. Knopf Inc., 1983.

Thomas Merton: *The Hidden Ground of Love*, Collins (Flame), 1990.

George Woodcock: *Thomas Merton, Monk and Poet*, Catholic Book Club, 1978.

Thomas Merton: *Elected Silence*, Hollis and Carter, 1949.

Monica Furlong: *Merton, a biography*, Collins (Fount), 1980.

Thomas Merton: *No Man is an Island*, Hollis and Carter, 1955.

Sue Ryder: *Child of My Love*, Collins Harvill, 1986.

Andrew Boyle: *No Passing Glory*, Collins, 1955.

Russell Braddon: *Cheshire V.C.*, Evans Brothers Ltd., 1954.

Leonard Cheshire, V.C.: *The Face of Victory*, Hutchinsons, 1961.

Alenka Lawrence: *Where is God in All This?*: Leonard Cheshire interviewed by Alenka Lawrence, St Paul Publications, 1991.

Sian Miles: *Simone Weil - an Anthology*, Virago, 1986.

Simone Weil: *Waiting on God*, Routledge & Kegan Paul, 1951.

Simone Petrement: *Simone Weil*, Mowbray, 1976.

David McLellan: *Simone Weil - Utopian Pessimist*, McMillan, 1989.

J.M. Perrin & G. Thibon: *Simone Weil as We Knew Her*, Routledge and Keegan Paul, 1955.

Anne Arnott: *The Secret Country of C.S. Lewis*, Hodder & Stoughton, 1974.

A.N. Wilson: *C.S. Lewis*, Collins, 1990.

Roger Lancelyn Green & Walter Hooper: *C.S. Lewis,* Souvenir Press, 1988.

C.S. Lewis: *A Grief Observed*, Faber and Faber, 1961.

C.S. Lewis: *Surprised by Joy*, Geoffrey Bless, 1955.

C.S. Lewis: *Merely Christianity*, Fontana Books, 1952.

C.S. Lewis: *Miracles*, Fontana Books, 1960.

C.S. Lewis: *The Screwtape Letters*, Geoffrey Bles, 1960.

C.S. Lewis: The Four Loves, Geoffrey Bles, 1960.

C.S. Lewis, Ed. Walter Hooper: *All My Road Before Me (Diary)*, Harper Collins, 1991.

C.S. Lewis: *Letters to Malcolm*, Geoffrey Bles, 1964.

G.K. Chesterton and C.S. Lewis - Ed. Michael H. McDonald, Andrew A. Tadie: *The Riddle of Joy*, Collins, 1989.

Shirley du Boulay: *Tutu - Voice of the Voiceless*, Hodder & Stoughton, 1988.

Alan Paton: *Cry the Beloved Country*, Jonathan Cape, 1948.

Alan Paton: *Apartheid and the Archbishop*, Jonathan Cape, 1974.

Paul Johnson: *Pope John XXIII*, Hutchinson & Co, 1975.

Peter Hebblethwaite: *John XXIII, Pope of the Council*, Geoffrey Chapman, 1985.

Ernesto Balducci: *The Transitional Pope*, Burns Oates, 1965.

Pope John XXIII: *Journal of a Soul*, Geoffrey Chapman, 1965.

Jon Sobrino: *Archbishop Romero - Memories and Recollections*, Orbis Books, Maryknoll N.Y., 1990.

James R. Brockman: *Romero - A Life*, Orbis Books, Maryknoll N.Y., 1989.

W. Herbstrith: *In Search of God*, New City Press, New York, 1977.

Edith Stein: *Life in a Jewish Family*, I.C.S. Publ. Washington D.C., 1986.

Hilda Graef: *The Scholar and the Cross*, Longmans Green & Co. Ltd., 1954.

Waltrand Herbstrith: *Edith Stein, a Biography*, Harper Rowe, S.F., 1985.

Josephine Koeppel O.C.D.: *Edith Stein, Philosopher and Mystic*, Michael Glazier Book Liturgical Press., Minnesota, 1990.

Monk Matthew: *Edith Stein*, C.T.S. pamphlet, 1979.

Sr. Anita Neyer: *Edith Stein - A Saint for Our Times*, Darlington Carmel.

Edith Stein: *Woman*, I.C.S. Publications, Washington D.C., 1988.

Charles Raven: *Teilhard de Chardin, Scientist and Seer*, Collins, 1962.

Helmut de Terra: *Memories of Teilhard de Chardin*, Scientific Book Club 1964.

Teilhard de Chardin: *Letters to Leontine Zanta*, Collins, 1969.

Claude Cuenot: *Teilhard de Chardin*, Burnes Oates, 1965.

Teilhard de Chardin: *The Heart of the Matter*, Collins, 1978.

Teilhard de Chardin: *Le Milieu Divin*, Collins, 1960.

Christopher Mooney: *Teilhard de Chardin and the Mystery of Christ*, Collins, 1966.

Ursula King: *Towards a New Mysticism'- Teilhard de Chardin and Eastern Religions'*, Collins, 1980.

Martin Luther King: *I Have a Dream*, Harper, San Francisco, 1946.

Stephen B. Oates: *Let the Trumpet Sound*, Mentor, 1982.

William Martin: *A Prophet With Honor*, William Morrow & Co, 1991.

Billy Graham; the Authorized Biography, John Pollock, McGraw Hill, N.Y.1966.

George Burnham: *Mission Accomplished*, Fleming H. Revell, 1955.

Billy Graham: *Peace With God*, Doubleday, 1953.

Jackie Pullinger and Andrew Quicke: *Chasing the Dragon*, Hodder & Stoughton, 1980.

Geoffrey Hanks: *City of Darkness*, Chansitor Publications, 1984.

Jackie Pullinger and Carolyn Armitage: *Crack in the Wall*, Hodder & Stoughton, 1987.

E.H. Robertson: *Dietrich Bonhoeffer*, Lutterworth Press, 1966.

Edwin Robertson: *The Shame and the Sacrifice*, Hodder & Stoughton, 1987.

Eberhard Bethge: *Dietrich Bonhoeffer*, Hodder & Stoughton, 1970.

Dietrich Bonhoeffer: *The Cost of Discipleship*, S.C.M. Press, 1959.

Dietrich Bonhoeffer: *No Rusty Swords*, Collins and Harper & Row, 1965.

Letters and Papers from Prison, S.C.M. Press and Macmillan, 1971.

Otto Dudzus: *Bonnhoeffer for a New Generation*, S.C.M. Press, 1986.

Mary Craig: *Man from a Far Country*, Hodder & Stoughton, 1979.

James Oram: *The People's Pope*, Bay Books, 1979.

M. Malinski: *Pope John Paul II*, Burns, Oates, 1979.

Norman St.John Stevas: *Pope John Paul II - His Travels and Mission*, Faber and Faber, 1982.

Paul Johnson: *Pope John Paul II and the Catholic Restoration*, Weidenfelfd and Nicolson, 1982.

Timothy Walch: *Pope John Paul II*, Chelsea House Publishers, 1989.

John McCaffery: *The Friar of San Giovanni*, Darton Longman & Todd, 1978.

Alessandro of Ripabottoni: *Padre Pio of Pietrelcina*, Our Lady of Grace Capuchin Friary, 1987.

Anthony Pandiscia,: *For God and Neighbour - the Life and Works of Padre Pio*, St. Paul Publications, 1991.

Mary Pyle: *Bonaventura Massa*, Our Lady of Grace Capuchin Friary, 1986.

Clarice Bruno: *Roads to Padre Pio*, National Centre for Padre Pio, U.S.A., 1981.

Cecil Humphrey Smith: *A Saint on My Back*, 1983.

Sebastian Holland - O.F.M. Cap,: *The Capuchins*, 1963, revised 1984.

Mary F. Ingoldsby: *Padre Pio, His Life and Mission*, Veritas Publications, 1978.

Fr. Alassio Parente, O.F.M. Cap: Send Me Your Guardian Angel, Our Lady of Grace Capuchin Friary, 1984.

Fr. Augustine McGregor, O.C.S.O.: *Padre Pio - His Early Years*, Our Lady of Grace Capuchin Friary, 1981.

James Brabazon: *Albert Schweitzer*, Gollancz, 1976.

James Bentley: *Albert Schweitzer*, Exlay Publications, 1988.

Magnus C. Ratter: *Albert Schweitzer*, Allenson and Co.

Albert Schweitzer: *On the Edge of the Primeval Forest*, A. & C. Black.

Albert Schweitzer: *The Philosophy of Civilization*, A. & C. Black.

Albert Schweitzer: *Memoirs of Childhood and Youth*, George Allen & Unwin Ltd.

Albert Schweitzer: *My Life and Thought*, George Allen & Unwin Ltd.

Nina Langley: *Dr. Schweitzer, O.M.*, George Harrap & Co, 1956.

Fr. George Gorree: *Memories of Charles de Foucauld*, Burns Oates & Washbourne, 1937.

Margaret Trouncer: *Charles de Foucauld*, George Harrap, 1922.

Rene Voillaume: *Seeds of the Desert*, Anthony Clarke Books, 1972.

ed. Jean Francois Six: *Spiritual Autobiography of Charles de Foucauld*, P.J. Kennedy & Sons, N.Y., 1964.

Philip Hillyer: *Charles de Foucauld*, Liturgical Press, Minnesota, 1990.

Elizabeth Hamilton: *The Desert My Dwelling Place*, Hodder & Stoughton, 1968.

Rene Bazin, trans. Peter Keeden: *Charles de Foucauld*, Burnes Oates and Washbourne, 1923.

Malcolm Muggeridge: *Jesus Rediscovered*, Collins, 1968.

Malcolm Muggeridge: *Tread Softly for You Tread on My Jokes*, Fontana, 1969.

Malcolm Muggeridge: *A Twentieth Century Testimony*, Collins, 1979.

Malcolm Muggeridge: *Like It Was*, Collins, 1981.

Muggeridge and Vidler: *Paul - Envoy Extraordinary*, Collins, 1972.

Malcolm Muggeridge: *Conversion - A Spiritual Journey*, Collins, 1988.

Malcolm Muggeridge: *Chronicles of Wasted Time (Vols I and II)*, Collins, 1988.

Malcolm Muggeridge: *Something Beautiful for God*, Fontana, 1972.

Eileen Egan: *Such a Vision of the Street - Mother Teresa, the Spirit and the Work*, Sedgwick & Jackson Ltd., 1985.

Mother Teresa: *One Heart Full of Love*, Collins, Fount Paperbacks, 1989.

Georges Gorree and Jean Barbier, trans. Paula Speakman: *For the Love of God - Mother Teresa of Calcutta*, T. Shandalba Publications, London, 1974.

Angelo Devananda: *Mother Teresa - Contemplative at the Heart of the World*, Fount Paperbacks, 1986.

David Porter: *Mother Teresa - the Early Years*, S.P.C.K., 1986.

Jose Luis Gonzalez-Balado: *Heart of Joy: Mother Teresa*, Fount Paperbacks, 1988.

Kathryn Spinto: *A Chain of Love - Mother Teresa and Her Suffering Disciples*, S.P.C.K., 1984.